AF552447

OPERATION IN HOTEL MANAGEMENT

OPERATION IN HOTEL MANAGEMENT

M. C. METTI

ANMOL PUBLICATIONS PVT. LTD.
NEW DELHI - 110 002 (INDIA)

ANMOL PUBLICATIONS PVT. LTD.

H.O.: 4374/4B, Ansari Road, Darya Ganj,
New Delhi-110 002 (India)
Ph.: 23278000, 23261597

B.O.: No. 1015, Ist Main Road, BSK IIIrd Stage
IIIrd Phase, IIIrd Block
Bangalore - 560 085 (India)
Visit us at: www.anmolpublications.com

Operaation in Hotel Management

ISBN 978-81-261-3229-4

PRINTED IN INDIA

Printed at Mehra Offset Press, Delhi.

Contents

Preface

Operation in Hotel Management will helps readers to develop the wide-ranging knowledge and analytical skills they need to succeed in today's burgeoning and dynamic hotel industry. Its clear structure and organization are major strengths of Managing the operation in Hospitality. A section is devoted to each of hospitality management's three major concerns: Strategy, Staffing, and Systems.

Featuring information from many leading industry professionals and academics, this book encourages critical thinking by exposing readers to different viewpoints within a coherent theoretical structure, enabling them to formulate their own ideas and solutions. Each of the book's parts examines a specific hotel department or activity and presents a variety of viewpoints on the duties, responsibilities, problems, and opportunities encountered there.

Leading hospitality organizations have found these principles to be important, workable, and useful. They represent the key points to keep in mind when putting the book's material into practice. They can guide hospitality organizations and their managers as they seek to reach the levels of excellence achieved by the benchmark organizations.

Multidimensional case studies challenge readers to identify the central issues in complex management problems, understand the structure and resources of the department in question, and find solutions that may involve other hotel resources and departments. Students, educators, and hospitality professionals should continue to enjoy a favourable book.

Author

Chapter 1

Introduction

Operations in hotel management focuses on carefully managing the processes to produce and distribute products and services. Usually, small businesses don't talk about "operations management", but they carry out the activities that management schools typically associate with the phrase "operations management." Major, overall activities often include product creation, development, production and distribution. Related activities include managing purchases, inventory control, quality control, storage, logistics and evaluations. A great deal of focus is on efficiency and effectiveness of processes. Therefore, operations management often includes substantial measurement and analysis of internal processes.

Ultimately, the nature of how operations management is carried out in an organization depends very much on the nature of products or services in the organization. People and industry have moved from the so-called rust belt to the sun belt. The hotel business has been active in reborn and reconstructed central cities. The explosion of technology and information-based companies has concentrated human endeavour in technological corridors in California, Massachusetts, Washington, Texas, and North Carolina, to name a few such places. It can be safely said that where jobs are and major concentrations of economic activity occur, hotels will follow.

It should be noted that the word modern can be loaded with the potential of much misunderstanding. Hotels are changing and will continue to change. As a result, the techniques of management of modern hotels must adapt to changing circumstances.

INFLUENCES

Like many other businesses, hotels have been affected by shifts in emphasis and its children mature, the population of the countries will for many years be older, healthier, and better educated than previous generations. These facts will present new challenges and opportunities to all business managers.

Technology—in the form of computers, communication, personal devices, and laboursaving mechanical equipment—has had and will have a major effect on the way in which hotels are managed and operated. The speed with which information is accumulated, stored, manipulated, and transferred is such that today most travelers expect that the hotel rooms they rent will allow them to be as productive as they are in the office or at home. Increasingly, with portable computing, personal data assistants (PDAs), wireless communication, and virtually everything somehow connected to the Internet, hotels must provide services and access that allow guests seamless transition from the business, travel, or home environment to that of the hotel. Increasingly, entertainment must be fused with communication and productive processes.

The concept of market segmentation, or ever-increasingly finely tuned market definitions, will dictate hotel structures and organizations, and management tactics designed to address those market segments have become even more important to the management of hospitality service businesses. With the increased power in the information and data manipulation realm, hotels have available to them ever expanding databases about guests and are creating new products to attract those markets.

One of the effects of the aging demographic is the emergence of vacation re- sorts—a modern incarnation of the timeshare properties of several decades ago. Because these are being developed and operated by name hotel companies and are marketed to the affluent, healthy, well-educated population segment, resort managers have had to absorb new managerial realities.

The well-documented change in the complexion of the national economy from one that emphasizes goods and, to a lesser extent, natural resources to one that emphasizes services has kindled new ideas about the way in which we manage the design and delivery of these services. Hotels, restaurants, and travel services are now seen as unique entities that dictate special kinds of managerial techniques and strategies.

Changes in people's travel patterns have altered the way we manage our hotel properties. Deregulation of the airlines has driven a change in the way millions of people travel each year, given the huband- spoke design of airline services. Many hotel companies are now locating major hotel properties adjacent to hub air transport facilities, taking advantage of the fact that business travelers may not need to travel to a central business district (CBD) to accomplish their purpose in a given area. Meetings and conferences can now be scheduled within a five-minute limousine ride from the air terminal, and the business traveler can be headed for his or her next destination before the day is over without having to stay overnight in a CBD hotel.

New patterns of investment in hotel facilities have emerged in the last two decades, and more attention is now paid to achieving optimum return on investment. Because people from outside the hotel industry are now participating in its financial structuring, hotel operations are no longer dependent on the vision of a single entrepreneur. Managers now must design tactics and strategies to achieve heretofore unanticipated financial goals. The same trend has also altered the complexion of management and organization of the modern hotel. This is especially true of publicly owned hotel firms, where Wall Street stock analysts heavily influence stock prices through expectations of quarterly revenues and profits.

This puts pressure on hotel companies and their operations managers to perform, on a quarterly basis, in a way contrary to many managers' instincts. Most of the foregoing issues and influences still operate (to a greater or lesser extent) on the organizational structures and strategies of the modern hotel.

However, other phenomena of an economic, cultural, and social nature have come to the fore, complicating our view of hotel management. This furthers the argument that the hotel industry is a part of the greater economy and at the mercy of elements often completely out of its control. The cyclical nature of the U.S. and international economies has recently affected significantly hotels' ability to respond to changing circumstances. In early 1993, for instance, employment growth was stagnant; corporate profits were low; the expansion of the gross national product (GNP) was only a marginal percentage above previous years; and travel in most segments was down due to corporate restructuring, downsizing, or reorganizing. Vast layoffs in the hundreds of thousands had been announced every month. While fuel prices continued to be relatively stable, consumer spending patterns and high employment growth had not materialized, particularly in light of corporate layoffs and the ongoing nervousness of consumers about whether or not their financial wherewithal was safe.

Unemployment was at an all-time low; the Dow Jones Industrial Average was between 10,000 and 11,000; hotel occupancies had stabilized nationally in excess of 70 percent; and the federal government was running a surplus for the first time in the memory of most. Then what happened? The terrorist attacks in New York and Washington, D.C., in 2001 changed the face of all business and travel, immediately and probably for the foreseeable future as well. Major airlines are in bankruptcy; hotels are struggling to achieve profitable occupancies; business travel is down; the high-tech stock market bubble burst; the country is at war in a number of locations; security has made travel more difficult, if not actually annoying; and people are nervous.

Join this with an imbalance of trade, the outsourcing of jobs, and the largest federal deficits in history, and the face of the economy is challenging. This translates directly not only to business travel but personal and recreational travel as well. Finding ways to operate profitably in such an environment is the job of the next generation of hotel operators. Among the predictions made was that cultural diversity will play a role in the management and organizational structure of the modern hotel in the United States. As surely as living patterns, economic cycles, and market segmentation have influenced the hotel industry, so will the change in ethnicity of the workforce.

The cultural backgrounds that an increasingly diversified workforce will bring to hotel operations may be seen as a problem or a challenge—or both. To most operators, it will be seen as an opportunity to demonstrate to an increasingly diverse clientele that hotel companies are committed to hiring and training a workforce structure that mirrors society. See no reason to change that prediction now; if anything, acculturation of the hospitality business will accelerate. The legal and regulatory environments are increasingly important to all business managers, and hotel operators are no exception. Increasingly, operators must be aware of and alert to realms of risk that can engender lawsuits against them. Several articles and essays in this edition highlight these threats to hotels and their guests. It should be noted that present-day security concerns also have significantly affected the ways in which hotels are operated. Awareness of the risk environment and the regulatory realm are factors that affect a hotel's ability to compete in the early part of the twenty-first century. Essays and articles in the security and the human resources address this issue.

This is also used to explore ideas that are new to the management process, and that—who knows?—may never completely catch on. Rather than focus exclusively on the operations of the major chains, the readings here are from the perspectives of operators, leaders, and experts such as regional operators, major industry consultants, and independent branded hotels. John Dew, formerly president of Inn Ventures, a regional hotel management and development company that has built and operated many Marriott products, in addition to a proprietary hotel product, provides an insider's view of the steps needed to bring a hotel from conception to construction and operation. This unique view of hotel operations connects the concept of hotel development with the realities of day-to-day operation. It should help aspiring managers understand how the intricacies of the development process may influence the marketing and management of the hotel. Peter Cass offers the reader insights, heretofore unavailable in books of this nature, into independently branded hotels that associate to provide market strength.

He makes the case that the future success of independent hotels is linked to their ability to find ways to maintain their independence while sustaining competitive advantage in the luxury segment. Because new construction of hotels diminished greatly after 9/11 but firms still needed to grow, rebranding existing properties generated a lot of growth activity. Rebranding is a complicated process that must be accomplished within critical time frames to coincide with marketing, financial, and operational variables.

Today's economic circumstances are different, and business has changed its focus to opening new major projects. His piece serves as a useful companion to that of John Dew, and the two should be read together, with an eye toward comparing Dew's smaller project focus and Dupar's large projects. Perhaps proving the axiom that "everything old is new again," the concept of health and wellness spas as a hotel and resort product has enjoyed a resurgence.

Once the province of high-end hotels and resorts, the idea of being pampered in a spa has been added to the service mix in many more modest hotels and resorts. While the big-name spas at five-star properties still set the standard for pampering and pricing, the comfort of personal service in less lavish spas seems to appeal to the modern traveler as well. Peter Anderson's overview of the spa industry provides insights into this fascinating service product. E.M. Statler's contributions to the modern hotel business are legendary in that he is generally credited with founding and operating the first commercial hotel concept that recognized the realities of the early business traveler at the beginning of the twentieth century. They also highlight other major forces in the development of the modern hotel business.

The Development Company

The developer is the entrepreneur, the risk taker, who originates the idea for the hotel. Depending on the business structure selected, the developer often puts his or her personal wealth at risk when engaging in a hotel project. The developer, along with a small staff of people, networks with commercial real estate agents on the lookout for a suitable hotel site. Depending on the type of hotel to be developed, a site of at least two to four acres is required (for comparison, an acre is roughly the size of a football field).This property must be zoned by the city for a hotel, be visible from a freeway or major street arterial, and have city approval for such construction activities as curb cuts, lefthand turn lanes, and delivery truck access.

Commercial realtors offer sites for the developer's consideration that include maps, aerial photos, and proof of hotel zoning. Sometimes the developer views potential sites by driving around the neighbourhood within five miles of the site or touring multiple sites by helicopter, noting where the potential guests live and work and where potential competing hotels are located. The price per square foot of the land is considered. The higher the cost of land, the higher the rates the hotel will need to charge. Is the price too high for the average daily rate (ADR) in this particular market? Is it too low? Or is it acceptable? This is determined when the hotel financial pro forma budget document is created.

AUTHORITARIAN ORGANISATION

From the point of view of results, the effectiveness of the organisation is determined by the way work is organised and by the way people work with or against each other. The way in which people co-operate with each other, with the leadership and with the community, indeed the extent of their commitment to their organisation, depend on the style of management.

So here we look at different styles of management, on their impact on people, on the way in which people work together and on results.

Just think of the many supplies and services required daily to enable a large city like London to survive. Food has to be produced, harvested, stored and transported. Waste products have to be collected and treated or dispersed. Electricity has to be generated and distributed, transport has to be provided. Houses have to be built. Streets have to be cleaned and maintained, the district has to be policed. And all these and much more for millions of people, daily.

In our modern, industrialised, technological and highly competitive international environment it is essential that many experts from different areas of activity and different levels of society coming from different backgrounds work together to successfully achieve the completion of large projects such as exploring space, or the building of large oil gathering and refining installations.

Many experts have to work together to provide our daily needs, to enable us to have good and satisfying lives. Discord in one area can inconvenience many people and it is essential that people co-operate with each other freely and effectively.

Experience shows that the larger the organisation the more difficult it is to achieve the necessary degree of co-operation and that larger organisations are usually much less effective than smaller ones as people are working against each other instead of co-operating. We will see that improving the style of management can by itself increase the effectiveness of operating, improve results obtained and the way in which resources are being used, by about 20-30%. The gains to be made by improving the style of management are thus very considerable not only from the point of view of a better return to the shareholders and to the community but also from the point of view of greater contentment and satisfaction felt by employees.

Consider the following two stories. The first is about a hotel servant

When a very senior civil servant retired to his country cottage, he caused a stir in the village. Every morning one of the local boys would call and disappear for a minute or so into his cottage. They persuaded the boy to reveal what was going on: "I am paid to knock on his bedroom door and shout a few words and then he shouts a few words". He finally told them what these words were. He said: "I shouts 'The Secretary of State wishes to see you', and he shouts back 'To hell with the Secretary of State'."

The second story is about a man who is working as a foreman in the garage of a Municipal Forestry Commission.

The garage wasn't efficient but since he started working for them things run much more smoothly. If a spare part is needed but cannot be obtained, if anything goes wrong, he is the one who sorts things out in his own quiet and effective way. For example, when the garage was told that it would take some six months for a new radiator to be delivered to them, he simply telephoned the factory to confirm this disturbing news. The radiator was delivered beautifully wrapped the next day by special messenger. You probably know the name of this foreman. It is Alexander Dubcek, the man who led his country in a bid for freedom in 1968. This is what he was doing a few years ago.

What he gets from those with whom he comes into contact is not just esteem and respect but also co-operation and as a result 'things run much more smoothly'. Compare this with the attitude to his work of the retired civil servant whose idea of blissful retirement is to be able to shout every morning 'To hell with the boss'. This kind of frustration with management and workplace indicates internal conflict and struggle, indicates considerable lack of identification with the organisation and its objectives.

People live and work together. Important is that the way in which they feel about their place of work, and the way in which they co-operate, depends on controllable factors, depends on the style of management.

Those who live with you, work with you, or work for you will think about living and working with you in either one way or the other. Certain is that the way in which they react depends on the way in which you behave, depends on your style of management, depends on the factors which we will now explore.

Kings ruled by 'divine' right and they enforced obedience through, in the end, the death penalty. Under private ownership, authority is derived from ownership of the means of production and the penalty for disobedience is dismissal. In each case authority is centred at the top. It is the owners who delegate authority to the chief executive, and it is immaterial whether the owners are shareholders as in some countries, or the state in countries such as Russia.

In authoritarian organisations it is orders which are passed down from above and the manager's role is to pass orders down the 'chain of command'. He is usually not expected to make decisions and so carries little responsibility. He does order and may compel the worker to carry out the tasks demanded from him, to produce.

Those who run society on such lines find that the working population does not willingly work for the benefit of only its rulers and then they attempt to compel the working population to work. The stick is unemployment and the compelling force is the fear of the economic consequences of unemployment, is the threat of need.

They will then do all they can to make the stick more effective. The higher the level of unemployment and the greater the need of the working population, the greater is the fear of dismissal and the more effective is the stick. Hence it is those who believe in an authoritarian kind of organisation who advocate that the level of unemployment should be kept above a certain minimum level or that it should be increased, and who want to reduce social security spending.

To them it appears as if people do not want to work, as if conditions have to be created which force the working population to do as told, by depressing their standard of living and the quality of their lives so that they become more dependent on the employer.

Examples of this attitude towards unemployment are the following newspaper headlines:

(a) Big fall in unemployment and record spending threaten economic trouble.

(b) Sharp fall in jobless a sign of overheating.

Authoritarian organisations are effective in an emergency and perhaps the best known authoritarian organisations are the armed forces.

However, enterprises organised on authoritarian lines have many problems. Orders are passed down and mistakes readily result in critical appraisal and dismissal. Hence people avoid making decisions so that matters to be decided are either passed up for the decisions to be made at a higher level, or decisions are made by committees as it is more difficult to dismiss all the members of a committee for jointly making a wrong decision. There are likely to be many such committees. People survive by becoming expert at passing the buck. Empire building takes place, this being one way of increasing job security. Blame is passed to someone else, empires are built at someone else's expense; people work against each other and we see conflict instead of co-operation. Senior management tends to be overworked, staff turnover tends to be high and workers restrict effort.

The kind of difficulties which arise are perhaps best illustrated by some examples:

1. On one of the scheduled flights from Moscow to the Soviet Far East only half the seats had been taken

up so Aeroflot cancelled the flight and told the passengers to wait. They waited in the packed terminal all that night and indeed all the next day when they were told that their flight would now be leaving. Trying to join their flight they found that they had to pay an extra 25% of their fare as a fine for missing the first flight.

2. Nigeria ordered 20 million tons of cement worth £650 million to be delivered during 1975. By the middle of October there were already 250 ships queuing to discharge their cement cargoes. A further 100 cement-laden ships were due the following week. Some of these would have to wait for more than two years to dock. Only 4 million tons of the 20 million tons ordered had been delivered and in addition there were 150 general cargo ships queuing to discharge their cargoes.

   By the end of December, 2,500 Greek seamen aboard 150 freighters had been "trapped" for more than seven months while waiting for permission to dock and unload. All seamen who had been stuck for more than four months were being flown home for Christmas by their employers.

   The Nigerian government then announced a draft decree enabling them to charge owners £7,000 for every day an unauthorised vessel spent in Nigerian waters.

   Normally the docks could handle less than one and a half million tons of cement per year and a basic cause of the congestion would appear to be lack of co-operation, contact and teamwork between different ministries and departments.

3. Gerald Smith when leader of the American delegation to the SALT negotiations in Vienna which aimed to limit nuclear weapons, submitted remarkable Russian tables and drawings which compared the number and size of American and Russian inter-continental

rockets and shelters for housing them. He was apparently submitting information prepared by Russian military intelligence themselves.

In a counter-statement the leader of the Soviet delegation, Vladimir Seminiov, made a new evaluation but was openly corrected by his military deputy, Colonel General Ogarkov. After this meeting, Ogarkov took one of the American delegates to the side and whispered to him. He said there was no occasion whatsoever for the Americans to divulge their knowledge of Soviet military data in front of civilians of the Soviet delegation as these matters is exclusively the concern of Soviet military officials.

4. Israel earns much foreign currency from tourist traffic, but it was reported that the Ministry of Tourism continued to receive complaints from Israelis and foreign tourists regarding the inadequacy of sanitary conditions and other facilities at Ben-Gurion airport.

   The Ministry spokesman also pointed out that the airport was under the exclusive jurisdiction of the Ministry of Transport, to which all complaints should be referred. A clear case of passing the buck which appears to disregard the interests of those using the airport. Just what is the job of a Ministry of Tourism?

These are only a few examples of the kind of wasteful way in which large units run on authoritarian lines muddle on through crisis after crisis. They cease to be able to learn from past mistakes, the same mistakes are made again and again. The reason some of them are still in existence is because their competitors are just as ineffective, are just as incapable of moving forward in any real sense.

Crisis succeeds crisis in badly managed as well as in authoritarian organisations. This may be due to bad management but in an extremely authoritarian organisation crises are often almost artificially created by managers so as to obtain co-operation. If I go to Jim and say "I want you to sweep the floor of this hotel three times within the next half-hour, or else!" he is not going to like this one little bit. He will go through the motions but the office will be badly swept and the next half-hour wili appear to him to be an eternity of drudgery, boredom and frustration.

If on the other hand I can say "We are in real trouble, some very nasty stuff has been spilled and it is important for all who work here that the floor be swept thoroughly three times and quickly, say within thirty minutes anyway. I wonder if we've got someone who could do it?", then he is likely to voluntee for the job. It will be done extremely well, it will get done within the half-hour and probably with five or ten minutes to spare.

If afterwards go to him and say "Well done, we are al grateful" he will be left with the feeling of having spent hal an hour most usefully serving the community, having done very worthwhile job indeed. In other words, people try to hel each other and in an authoritarian organisation crisis ma succeed crisis as this is one way of getting work done However, one can cry wolf once too often and in a authoritarian organisation 'This must be done today' i succeeded by 'Do this now' which is succeeded by "We are i a mess, drop all else and do this now". In such circumstance people soon learn that crises are the routine rather than th exception and cease to care.

Centralised decision making is quick and decisions ca be implemented quickly but it generally fails to utilise th potential of the employees. Larger organisations also general fail to perform as well as they should because of intern conflict, because of confrontation, lack of co-operation and lac of teamwork.

Having now looked in some detail at the kind organisation we find at one end of the scale, namely th authoritarian organisation, we can now look at the other er of the scale, at a completely participative organisatio Following this we will look at the large number organisations which are somewhere in between.

The story is told that when a new manager was appointed to a hotel in America he walked into a weave room the day he arrived, walked directly over to the agent. The agent nodded and then waved his hand. The workers, intently watching this gesture, shut down every loom in the room immediately. The agent turned to the manager and said, "All right, go ahead and run it." This story with great clarity makes the point that there is another authority besides the manager's. The workers' representative has authority and exercised it. The question arises, where does his right to command come from and how did he use his power to exact obedience?

The shop steward is elected so that his authority stems from those who elected him and who work in factory and office. The source of his authority is the consent of the managed to be managed. The method of power is the withdrawal of that consent which is in effect the withdrawal of one's labour, for example by going on strike.

Employees participate when they agree to allow themselves to be organised by an employer, and organisation which is based on consent of those being organised is participative. In a participative organisation people accept responsibility for work to be done, accept that it is their job to carry out a part of the company's activities and that they will be held accountable for the quality of their work. The manager's job is to back his subordinate by removing obstacles from the subordinate's path, the subordinate asking for such assistance as the need arises.

The manager co-ordinates the work of the group which he manages with that of the higher group in which he is a subordinate. As work may be a source of satisfaction or of frustration, dependent on controllable conditions, the extent to which subordinates derive satisfaction from their work also depends on their own manager's and on the organisation's general style of management. People who derive satisfaction from their work will like doing it and do it to the best of their ability; if work is a source of frustration, they will restrict effort and the work is likely to be done badly. An organisation built on this basis is participative, and this means that participation through decision making, including setting of targets, takes place at all levels of the organisation.

Degree of Participation

Large employers are often paternalistic, and employees company oriented, sometimes staying with their employer throughout their working life. Since their employees are economically tied to the company, dependent on it for services such as housing, medical or educational, this does not mean that these companies use a participative style of management. In Japan and similar countries the compelling force is the fear of 'losing face'. In Russia and in China the workers are not allowed to strike in any real sense and thus have no authority and orders are passed down from the top. Protest is forbidden and to demonstrate takes a highly developed sense of social responsibility and very considerable courage. It is seen that the Russian and Chinese systems of government and organisation are authoritarian systems in which their people work as directed.

We have described here in outline two systems of organisation which can be regarded as forming either end of a scale. The position of any organisation on this scale depends in each case on the balance between the two kinds of authority, that is depends on the degree of participation in decision making which is practised. One can place on this scale any system of running a company or of governing a country, by considering for example whether and to what extent decisions are being made at the various levels or whether people merely follow orders, or whether and to what extent people are free to withdraw their labour, are free to strike, to what extent authority is centred at the top, or where the balance of power lies between management and worker. The position where an organisation is placed thus depends on the balance of authority between ruler and ruled, between owner and worker, between the establishment and the population.

We can now develop this scale and place a number of organisations on it over the complete range from one end to the other. If we were to do this for individual companies then this would require a detailed knowledge in each case of the style of management and of company effectiveness. So what we will now do in the next is to look at the more generally known balance of authority in different countries and place them on our scale.

STYLE OF OPERATION MANAGEMENT

We are now looking at the way different countries are managed, doing so country by country. The style of management of government in different countries can also be anywhere on the scale, from fully authoritarian (dictatorship) at one end of the scale to fully participative (policy decided by the people) at the other end.

This is a fundamental scale which cuts across artificial and ineffective political divides - dictatorship of the left is dictatorship just like that of the right. Dictatorship is dictatorship no matter whether the organisation or political party is on the left or on the right of the political spectrum. Under participative government and democracy the government and leadership put into effect the wishes of the people, the policy decided by delegates directly appointed by and directly responsible and accountable to the people. Under authoritarian government or dictatorship the government and its 'experts' tell the people what the government or rulers decide the people have to follow.

Here 'directly' means selected by the people and voted for, each person having one vote. This is very different from delegates being selected by or being accountable through an establishment such as a political party's or a Board of Directors.

Real struggle is not between political left and right but is a struggle for democracy against dictatorship (authoritarian style of management) in all community organisations and at all levels. Authoritarian attitudes result in confrontation, leadership and co-operation result in economic success.

The way in which countries are managed, that is their style of management, of course varies from country to country and changes as time passes. illustrates the style of management. The left hand side of the horizontal scale corresponds to the fully authoritarian, while the right hand end corresponds to the fully participative way of managing. The two ends are called 'A' and 'B' respectively, for convenience.

What we can now do is to place on the scale some lines corresponding to the style of management adopted in different countries and then to discuss the pattern, following this by a discussion of the effectiveness of different styles of management.

In doing so we need to remember that we are not in any way concerned with opinions and feelings and beliefs about whether one country is better than another, whether one method of organisation is better than another, whether one political system is an improvement on another. We are concerned here only with the situation as it is, we are concerned only with objective facts. Hence we assess the style of management by two factors only, namely on the one hand by the extent to which authority is centred at the top and on the other hand by the extent to which authority is centred at the bottom.

Our measure for the extent to which authority is centred on the bottom is the extent to which working people may withdraw their labour, that is the extent to which they are permitted to do so by the laws of the land and the extent to which they are actually able to withdraw their labour.

We assess the style of management by these factors only and while at the authoritarian end of the scale there is generally little doubt about the extent to which authority is centred at the top, this factor is more difficult to assess in democratic societies and here we find that the extent to which people are permitted to withdraw their labour and the extent to which they are doing so is a clearer and more definite way of assessing a country's style of management on the scale.

In the democratic countries are found a wide range of companies and organisations ranging from highly if not completely authoritarian to the almost completely participative, ranging from the armed forces at one end to worker-owned and controlled enterprises on the other. However, this does not in any way invalidate the scale or its general validity, nor does it detract from the usefulness of the comparison. On the contrary, the existence of such widely differing systems makes it even more important that we become aware of the impact of different styles of management on people and on results.

CONTEMPORARY THEORIES IN OPERATION MANAGEMENT

Contemporary theories of operation management tend to account for and help interpret the rapidly changing nature of today's organizational environments. As before in management history, these theories are prevalent in other sciences as well.

Contingency Theory

Basically, contingency theory asserts that when managers make a decision, they must take into account all aspects of the current situation and act on those aspects that are key to the situation at hand. Basically, it's the approach that "it depends." For example, the continuing effort to identify the best leadership or management style might now conclude that the best style depends on the situation. If one is leading troops in the Persian Gulf, an autocratic style is probably best (of course, many might argue here, too). If one is leading a hospital or university, a more participative and facilitative leadership style is probably best.

Systems Theory

Systems theory has had a significant effect on management science and understanding organizations. First, let's look at "what is a system?" A system is a collection of part unified to accomplish an overall goal. If one part of the system is removed, the nature of the system is changed as well. For example, a pile of sand is not a system. If one removes a sand particle, you've still got a pile of sand. However, a functioning car is a system. Remove the carburetor and you've no longer got a working car. A system can be looked at as having inputs, processes, outputs and outcomes. Systems share feedback among each of these four aspects of the systems.

Let's look at an organization. Inputs would include resources such as raw materials, money, technologies and people. These inputs go through a process where they're planned, organized, motivated and controlled, ultimately to meet the organization's goals. Outputs would be products or services to a market. Outcomes would be, e.g., enhanced quality of life or productivity for customers/clients, productivity. Feedback would be information from human resources carrying out the process, customers/clients using the products, etc. Feedback also comes from the larger environment of the organization, e.g., influences from government, society, economics, and technologies. This overall system framework applies to any system, including subsystems (departments, programmes, etc.) in the overall organization.

Systems theory may seem quite basic. Yet, decades of management training and practices in the workplace have not followed this theory. Only recently, with tremendous changes facing organizations and how they operate, have educators and managers come to face this new way of looking at things. This interpretation has brought about a significant change (or paradigm shift) in the way management studies and approaches organizations.

The effect of systems theory in management is that writers, educators, consultants, etc. are helping managers to look at the organization from a broader perspective. Systems theory has brought a new perspective for managers to interpret patterns and events in the workplace. They recognize the various parts of the organization, and, in particular, the interrelations of the parts, e.g., the coordination of central administration with its programmes, engineering with manufacturing, supervisors with workers, etc. This is a major development. In the past, managers typically took one part and focused on that. Then they moved all attention to another part. The problem was that an organization could, e.g., have a wonderful central administration and wonderful set of teachers, but the departments didn't synchronize at all.

Chaos Theory

As chaotic and random as world events seem today, they seem as chaotic in organizations, too. Yet for decades, managers have acted on the basis that organizational events can always be controlled. A new theory (or some say "science"), chaos theory, recognizes that events indeed are rarely controlled. Many chaos theorists (as do systems theorists) refer to biological systems when explaining their theory. They suggest that systems naturally go to more complexity, and as they do so, these systems become more volatile (or susceptible to cataclysmic events) and must expend more energy to maintain that complexity. As they expend more energy, they seek more structure to maintain stability. This trend continues until the system splits, combines with another complex system or falls apart entirely. Sound familiar? This trend is what many see as the trend in life, in organizations and the world in general.

Probability and Operation

The theory of probability is the branch of mathematics which is most useful in operations research. Nearly all results of operations of hotels involve elements of chance, usually to a large extent, so that only when the results of a number of similar operations are examined does any regularity evidence itself. It is nearly as important to know the degree by which individual operations may differ from some expected average, as it is to know how the average depends on the variables involved. In analyzing operational data, which are often meager and fragmentary, it is necessary to be able to estimate how likely it is that the next operations will display characteristics similar to those analyzed Probability enters into many analytical problems as well as all the statistical problems.

In many situations the system of causes which lead to particular results is so complex that it is impossible, or at least impracticable, to predict exactly which of a number of possible results will arise from a given cause. If a penny is tossed, it is possible in principle to analyze the forces acting on the penny and the motions they produce, and so to predict whether the penny will come to rest with heads or tails showing; however, no one has ever taken the effort to carry out the analysis. When a gun is fired at a target, it should again be possible to predict exactly where the shell will hit, but the prediction would involve a knowledge of the characteristics of the gun, shell, propellant, and atmosphere far more exact than has yet been obtained.

With a perfect penny, tossed at random, there is no more reason to expect heads than tails to appear. We say then that heads and tails are equally likely to appear. In throwing a symmetrical die the numbers 1, 2, 3, 4, 5, and 0 are equally likely. This notion of equal likelihood is basic to the theory of probability. It does not seem to be possible to give it an exact definition, but we accept it as a self-evident intuitive concept At times we reach the conclusion that results are equally likely from considerations of symmetry. In other cases the conclusion is made on the basis of past experience

The Feasibility Study

When the developer selects a site, a feasibility study is often commissioned to obtain an analysis of the site by an objective third party. Companies offer hotel feasibility studies for a fee and are experts in a particular market, or developers may use the consulting group of one of the major public accounting firms. The company retained to do the feasibility study can spend up to several months gathering detailed data to see if, in their opinion, it makes economic sense to build the hotel. Their conclusion offers an objective third party opinion as to whether the project is feasible, hence the term feasibility study. Generally, the feasibility study considers, evaluates, and makes recommendations about the project based on the following variables:

The Site

- Proper zoning
- Size in square feet/acres
- Visibility from arterials/freeways
- Traffic counts/patterns
- Accessibility from streets, freeways, airports, train stations, etc.
- Proximity to where potential guests live, travel, or work
- Barriers that discourage competition coming into the market, if any
- How adjacent property and businesses are utilized
- Master area development plans
- Local permitting process and the degree of difficulty for that particular city
- Impact fees charged by the city

The Economy of the Area

- Major employers, government agencies
- Business trends for each employer/agency
- Hotel needs and the demand for each
- Leisure travel demand in the area
- Nearby tourist attractions
- Visitor counts
- Conventions, trade shows, and meetings history

The Hotel Market

- The competitors, both existing and planned
- Historical occupancy of hotels in the area
- Historical average rate
- Proprietary data on area travel

Identification of Which Hotel Market Segment to Serve

- Full service
- Limited service
- Extended stay

- Luxury
- Midprice
- Economy
- Budget

Selection of Appropriate Hotel Design

- High-rise
- Midrise
- Garden apartment style
- Hybrid design

Selection of Appropriate Hotel Brand

- Franchised (Marriott, Sheraton, Hyatt, etc.)
- Licensed (Best Western, Guest Suites, etc.)
- Independent
- Independent with strategic market affiliation (Luxury Hotels of America, Historic Hotels of America, etc.)

Ten-year Projection

- Occupancy projection by year
- ADR by year
- Estimated cash generated for debt
- Estimated cash generated for distribution to investors
- Estimated cash-on-cash return (after-tax income divided by equity invested)
- Overall projected yield
- Projected internal rate of return
- Net present value of the project over each of the next ten years. Once the feasibility study is completed, the developer is prepared to move forward with the project. Often, at this stage of the process, the developer purchases an option on the land to tie it up until the remaining development steps can be completed—and to prevent the competition from purchasing it.

CREATION OF THE OWNERSHIP ENTITY

An ownership entity (note that this is different than and separate from the development company) must be created to hold title to the land—and the hotel, once it's built. Considering the limitation of liability to the investors, tax consequences, estate implications for the investors, and potential requirements of the mortgage lender, a business structure is selected, normally in one of the following forms:

- Limited liability company (LLC)
- Limited partnership (LP)
- S corporation

THE DEVELOPMENT AGREEMENT

The newly formed entity now enters into a development contract with the development company to take the project to completion. The development company charges a fee, approximately 3 percent of the total project cost, for this service. The agreement generally covers such variables as:

- Selection of architect/engineers
- Selection and supervision of a general contractor
- Processing all building and occupancy permits
- Raising all the equity money from investors
- Securing a construction mortgage loan
- Selecting a franchise company
- Securing the franchise
- Selecting an interior designer that meets franchise company requirements
- Purchasing all opening furniture, fixtures, equipment
- Selecting a management company to operate the hotel
- Liability for cost overruns.

SELECTING A FRANCHISE

Depending on the type of hotel to be built (based on the feasibility study), the developer recommends a franchise company to the hotel owner. A major consideration is the best franchise brand for the market segment to be served. Fach franchise company has differ franchise fees, royalty fees, and marketing/ miscellaneous fees as part of its agreement structure with the operating company. Consideration must also be given to the brands already represented in the target market that may be available for franchise.

The franchise company is approached and a franchise is requested, with the feasibility study offered as backup for the request. The next step is for the franchise company to conduct an impact study of the market. This considers such matters as possible negative impact on existing hotels that carry the franchiser's flag. If the impact is judged to be insignificant, a franchise is usually granted to the ownership entity for a one-time fee of about $400 per room, depending on the franchise selected, with continuing royalty and marketing, usually based on a percentage of hotel revenue.

SELECTING AN ARCHITECT

Because the final product of this process is a building the operator has to run as a hotel, the architect's experience in designing hotels, his or her experience with the prototypical drawings of the franchise selected, the fee, and his or her on-time record must be considered. Architect fees can run up to 5 percent of the total project cost but are often negotiated down, if the project is big enough. The firm's experience and record on similar projects are critical. The architect does not have to operate the hotel when it is completed. The developer wants the architect to design a hotel that will be easy to operate and maintain.

Major consideration are the quality and reliability record of the general contractor and the firm's use of and relationships with the many subcontractors needed for a project as complex as a hotel. Again, experience in building the hotel type is important. It is hoped that the general contractor has learned from any mistakes made in building similar hotels. The general contractor and architect often bid the project as a team; this helps the developer determine the final cost. Often, up to a 10 percent contingency cost that allows for unforeseen circumstances is built into the project bidding process.

FINANCING THE PROJECT

The following variables must be determined to qualify for financing:

- The cost of the land
- Design and construction cost of the building
- The cost of furniture, fixtures, equipment, and opening supplies
- Pre-opening marketing and labour costs
- A six-month operating capital cash reserve.

The sum of these constitutes the total cost of the project for purposes of securing financing. With this information, the ten-year operating pro forma budget is updated to reflect actual costs. It's now time to go to the money markets for construction financing.

The terms and conditions of a construction loan can vary widely depending on the individual lender.

Important terms that can affect the cost of the loan include:

- Personal guarantees by developers and/or equity partners/investors
- Loan origination fees
- Interest rate
- Required loan-to-value ratio
- Terms of repayment
- A requirement that interest/taxes be held in reserve
- Required debt service coverage ratios
- Length of the construction loan; length and costs of extensions.

These are only a few of the considerations that must be analyzed when selecting a lender. The developer, on behalf of the owning entity, then approaches a number of lending institutions. The lending institutions analyze the deal and offer a proposed term sheet that answers all of the borrowers' questions. This allows the borrowers to select the lending institution with which they wish to work. The lender then commissions an appraisal of the project by an independent appraisal company such as Hospitality Valuation Services (HVS). Based on the appraisal, the lender issues a loan commitment for the project that usually offers up to 60 percent of the project cost. The balance must be raised as equity from investors.

RAISING THE EQUITY INVESTMENT FUNDS

With the bank committed to about 60 percent of the cost, the remaining 40 percent must be raised in equity commitments by investors. To pursue these, the developer prepares an offering solicitation document that meets current securities and exchange law. The nature of this document depends on the type of business entity that was formed. For limited partnerships or limited liability companies, a private placement offering circular and project description is prepared. For S or C corporations, stock offerings are prepared for sale consistent with applicable federal and state securities laws. The developer now contacts money sources that have risk capital available to invest.

These can include:

- Individual investors
- Private asset managers
- Opportunity fund managers
- Venture capital fund managers

These potential investment sources are offered the opportunity to invest in the hotel. Based on their study and evaluation of the reports, documents, and studies detailed above, they decide whether or not to offer funding to the developer. Once the loan is secured, the equity raised, and the building permit issued by the city, the land purchase option is exercised and the purchase is completed. Then the 12–16-month construction process begins. If the architect's plans work as intended, if the general contractor has no problems with subcontractors, unions, or permits, if all the furnishings, fixtures, and equipment arrive on time, if the weather cooperates, and if the employment market is such that human resources are sufficient to open a hotel, then congratulations! The hotel will open on time.

Selecting the Management Company

Often even before the construction activity commences, the owning entity selects an appropriate management company to manage the pre-opening, marketing and sales, selection and training of the opening staff, preparation of the operating budget, and day-to-day operations once the hotel is opened.

Management companies charge 3–5 percent of revenue for this service. In recent years, management companies have charged 3–4 percent of revenue and 2–3 percent of gross operating profit so they can be measured and evaluated on both sales and profitability. The franchise company may offer to provide management services to franchisees. Marriott International, Inc., for example, manages about 50 percent of all hotels that carry the Marriott flag under 20-year contracts. Independent management companies manage the remaining hotels under long-term management contracts of up to ten years' duration, often with several five-year renewal options.

This is a largely linear explanation of the complicated process that a developer goes through in order to create a hotel. It has been described in a step-by-step process, but in reality, many of the steps are carried out concurrently to save time (and money). Nevertheless, the hotel development process takes about three years from original conception to first guest. It is important to remember that during the initial stages of the process, the developer can have as much as $1 million (U.S.) or more at risk in the process before a final go/no-go decision is reached. Only after the project is approved and all financing is in place can the developer start to recover upfront costs and collect development fees. Hotel development with its component parts of hotel feasibility studies, hotel appraisal, hotel real estate finance, and hotel management are all among the career opportunities available to hotel and restaurant administration graduates.

Extended-stay Hotel Development Project

The City Development Commission in a Pacific Northwest community purchased a 1.55- acre parcel of riverfront land in the downtown area. The land was previously contaminated with industrial pollutants that made the parcel unsafe for habitation and construction. The City Development Commission used state, local, and federal grants to have the land decontaminated, created a master plan for the area, and then offered the parcel for sale and development. The City Development Commission issued a request for proposal (RFP) that outlined the asking price of $2,076,240 ($30/sq. ft.) for the land and the design requirements set down by the Commission for a building that would fit the intended look and feel of the area.

The RFP was sent to many major hotel companies and commercial real estate brokers, asking prospective buyers to submit a purchase price bid along with a statement of the buyer's development history and ability to develop a hotel of the type envisioned by the Commission. It listed a closing date by which all bids had to be submitted. An area commercial real estate broker contacted a hotel development and management company with a long history of developing and managing extended-stay hotels in the Pacific Northwest, including a property located in a similar setting to that being offered for sale.

The commercial realtor offered to represent the developer in negotiations with the City Development Commission, which would be paying the real estate commission on the sale. An agreement was reached with the commercial real estate broker to represent the buyer to the seller, and the developer went to work in preparing a proposal. The developer conducted a feasibility study to see all of the conditions in the marketplace that would be encouraging or discouraging to this development project. Studies were conducted to estimate how many room-nights were being sold within a five-mile radius, how many extended-stay room-nights were available in the market, how many hotel rooms existed, and how many were being planned over the following five years. From this, the developer was able to estimate the number of extended-stay room-nights available needed to produce an 82 percent occupancy with an average daily room rate of $141 when the hotel achieved stabilization three years after opening. That provided the basis for a ten-year revenue estimate.

The developer proposed a nine-floor, 258- suite extended-stay hotel with an indoor pool, spa, and exercise facility, a guest laundry, offices, meeting facilities, and a three-floor parking garage with parking for 193 automobiles, all at a total cost of $38 million, or $147,286 per suite. The $38 million construction budget was broken down as follows: Land 6.0% Construction 66.0% Office Equipment 1.4% Furniture, Fixtures, Equipment 7.4% Architecture/Engineering 2.8% Permits/Fees/ Environmental 2.8% Appraisal/Legal/Tax/Insurance 1.3% Pre-Opening Expenses 1.3% Construction Loan Fee 1.1% Developer Fee 2.8% Construction Interest 2.8% Working Capital 2.1% Contingency 2.2% Total 100% The opening date for the hotel was projected at 27 months from the date of proposal acceptance.

The City Development Commission awarded the project to the developer, and work began. First, an ownership limited liability company (LLC) was formed as the ownership entity that would hold title to the hotel. The LLC, in turn, entered into a development and construction management agreement with the development company to manage the arrangements for financing and construction of the hotel. The developer, as agent for the ownership LLC, also entered into a hotel management contract with a management company to manage the pre-opening marketing, preopening hiring and training, and the day-to- day operation of the hotel once it was opened.

The arrangements called for the management company to be paid 3 percent of revenue and 2 percent of the net operating income for management services. The ownership

LLC then contacted a major hotel company and applied for a franchise to allow the development and operation of an extended-stay hotel. A 20-year franchise was granted with a fee of $400 per suite or, $102,800. This was to be followed by a 5 percent royalty and a 3 percent advertising fee once the hotel was open and operating. The developer, acting as agent for the owner, prepared a private placement memorandum document seeking investments from accredited investors.

These investors were primarily defined as people with a net worth of $1 million, or those with an income in excess of $200,000 over the previous two years and expecting an income in excess of $200,000 in the current year. (*Note:* Additional entities may also be defined as accredited investors by the Securities and Exchange Commission.) The private placement memorandum offered $100,000 units of ownership to accredited investors, guaranteeing a 9 percent priority return on the investment and a combined 50 percent ownership in the hotel.

A group of initial investors retained the other 50 percent in exchange for putting the project together. This effort was successful in raising 40 percent of the total cost of the hotel in anticipation that a lender would provide the remaining 60 percent in the form of a construction loan. In addition to the priority return, investors could expect to participate in any future capital gain realized should the hotel be sold. The development company, continuing to function as agent for the owner, then sought a commercial bank to provide three year construction financing for the project or 60 percent, of the $38 million development cost was to be borrowed; only major banks were considered as prospective lenders.

The size of the construction loan was above the lending limits of most small regional banks. After a preconstruction appraisal by a third-party appraisal firm chosen by the lender confirmed the value at $38 million upon completion of construction, and for an origination fee of $400,000, a three-year construction loan was secured. The terms allowed the developer, as agent for the owner, to draw down the loan every

30 days after providing proof that funds had been properly disbursed in the construction process. The loan documents set an interest rate and also required that the ownership LLC seek a permanent mortgage prior to the three-year expiration date on the construction loan. The development company then negotiated with and selected a general contractor with significant hotel construction experience who acted on behalf of the developer, as agent for the owner.

The general contractor then selected design-build subcontractors and an interior designer to select colours, fabrics, furniture, fixtures, and equipment to meet the hotel franchise design requirements. Building permits were applied for, and the building design was presented to the City Development Commission for its approval, along with other groups with a stake in the appearance of the finished building in relation to the area and neighbourhood. With all of these approvals in place, construction commenced, and the hotel opened two years later. Three years after the hotel opened, tne ownership LLC had the obligation to secure permanent financing on the hotel to replace the construction loan. The September 11, 2001, terrorist attacks on the World Trade Centre and the Pentagon slowed travel throughout the United States.

As a result, the hotel did not achieve the projected occupancy or average daily rate during the three-year construction loan period. An appraisal that was primarily based on the hotel's trailing 12- month net operating income produced a value about $2 million below the original construction cost. The bank that had provided the construction loan notified the owners that they did not wish to provide permanent financing under these circumstances. The owners were forced to conduct a search for a new mortgage bank. They were able to find a mortgage, but only after buying down the loan by $2 million to bring the loan-to-value ratio back to 40 percent equity and a loan at 60 percent of the appraised. This illustrates the risk that developers face when entering into a hotel project. However, as hotel values historically peak and decline on about a ten-year cycle, the owners look forward to the option of selling the hotel on the next peak, which will allow them to capture the original projected return through capital appreciation. Hotel development and ownership is a high-risk, high reward enterprise.

Dramatic changes have affected the hotel industry over the past 30 years. These changes have had a disproportionately high bearing on the independent hotel owner, who, in the face of increasing pressure from large, well funded chains, struggles to maintain independence and to compete on the basis of distinctive hospitality and character. Several organizations provide independent hotels and resorts with reservations and sales services. As competition has evolved and intensified, some of these organizations have modified their structure and enhanced their services to meet the changing needs of independent hotels and competitive market dynamics. Today, independent hotels may choose from among more than 20 such organizations delivering varying degrees of competitive advantage and ownership independence.

A NEW MARKET MODEL

In the new millennium, the face of the global hospitality market continues to change at a rate never before seen.

Four factors contribute to this rapidly changing environment:

- The broadening and diversification of the global consumer market. Both the demographic and psychographic characteristics of the global consumer market are growing and changing radically.
- The rapid advancement and availability of technology. This includes internal hotel operating systems, revenue management, direct-to-consumer communications and booking technology (Internet), marketing technology (customer databases), and telecommunications and automated sales systems that enable central sales offices to become revenue producers.
- The growth and importance of global brands. Recognized brand names and brand attributes are

important in reaching diverse customer segments and in creating customer loyalty.

- Consolidation of multiple brands under a single global management. The management and leveraging of multiple brands use similar technology platforms and shared sales and marketing infrastructures to consolidate and direct consumer demand. Some established ways of doing business— long-term, high-fee management contracts and franchises, a focus on traditional distribution channels, and traditional hospitality industry marketing techniques—are no longer effective in the new consumer-focused market. More and more hospitality marketing budgets are being directed toward technology enabled customer booking and communication; this shift away from traditional hospitality marketing techniques is expected to evolve over several years and involve millions of U.S. dollars in telecommunication, e-commerce, data warehousing, and one-to-one marketing investment.

The independent hotel or resort and many small branded management companies may not be able to fund this requirement. However, this shift will not affect all independent hotels and resorts simultaneously. The first wave of change will hit the global business and city hotel market. This is primarily because of brand competition and the fact that the business travel distribution network is more structured and driven by multinational corporations desiring lower and more predictable costs.

The second wave will affect the leisure market, and the changes could follow quickly. Leisure travel content, including packaging on the Internet, will increase rapidly as the presently fragmented leisure travel distribution network becomes more unified and efficient through consolidation. The emergence of e-commerce modes in the hospitality industry is not eliminating the intermediary and empowering the individual property, as once thought; instead, it is creating new, more powerful intermediaries. Some of these evolve from the hospitality industry, while others are opportunistic e-commerce companies.

Management Companies and Franchises

In the 1970s, hotel chains continued to evolve as the need for capital to invest in additional properties restricted growth opportunities. This pressure bolstered the proliferation of the management contract, whereby the chain offers the hotel owner the rights to use its brand name and established facility and service standards as well as trained operations management and reservation and marketing services—for a significant fee, usually a percentage of gross sales. The pressure to grow also fostered the development of the franchise concept and franchise system in North America.

The franchise differs from the management contract in that the owner is responsible for operations, including meeting the franchise standards. The growth of management and franchise contracts has been remarkable, and today, according to a recent study, 75 percent of the hotel rooms in North America are covered by some form of branded franchise or professional management agreement. These new business structures continued to threaten the traditional independent owner by accelerating the growth of the chains' share of the lodging market. In response, the marketing/ referral organizations formed in the 1960s began to offer a wider range of services.

While these additional offerings leveraged linkages to the global distribution systems and led to strong relationships with travel agents, the consumer was largely ignored, and the organizations did little to generate consumer brand awareness. In the United States, strong consumer branded operators are attracting increasing amounts of capital to fund their growth at the expense of unbranded operators.

Brand Development

As the consumer market became more diverse and the hospitality product more segmented, branding became increasingly important. By the late 1980s, without a recognized brand affiliation or a close relationship with the lending community, owners/developers found it difficult to obtain permanent financing on a new hotel or resort. Lenders, believing that an established brand provided greater economies of scale and established infrastructure, opted for the lower-risk alternative. In this brand-driven environment, the independent hotels' distinctive style and character became a competitive advantage, but only if they were able to meet recognized standards.

As a result, the need for independent hotels to be associated with a clearly defined, trusted brand became more critical than ever. In the late 1990s, independent hotels, particularly those in Europe, began to face the daunting costs of upgrading their technological infrastructure and facilities to accommodate changing consumer needs. Such upgrades as new property management systems, highspeed Internet access, two-line phones, inroom faxes, and leisure and health facilities became critical to maintaining competitiveness. When coupled with ever-increasing costs of consumer marketing, these costs put unprecedented strains on independent hotels' finances. As a result, these hotels became increasingly focused on leveraging greater returns from their reservation affiliation.

RESERVATION AFFILIATIONS

The relationship of independent hotels and resorts to reservation affiliations has been long and generally successful. These relationships operated best in a market environment that was stable, somewhat homogeneous in terms of demographic market segmentation, and where travel influencers played a dominant role in transient business, group, and leisure travel. Reservation affiliations are most effective in regional hospitality markets that do not have multiple brand competition and when the goals and objectives of the reservation organization are in alignment with the goals of the independent hotel owners. A contributing element to the attractiveness of reservation affiliations has always been the networking and camaraderie opportunities for the professional management at independent hotels.

Reservation affiliations focus on traditional channels of distribution. Access to the Global Distribution Systems (GDS) is no longer a competitive advantage; the GDS is a universal pipeline. The new competitive playing field is proprietary distribution channels leveraged by consumer segmentation, e-commerce technology and partners, and innovative customer management programmes. In the new technology-driven and consumer- empowered global market, the strength and effectiveness of reservation affiliations are challenged by new market and operating imperatives. The cost to compete against chains will grow exponentially. As competition intensifies, it is probable that local and regional market share at independent hotels and resorts will be drawn off by local and regional licensees of strong global brands.

Independent hotels, therefore, need to draw more national and international business to fill occupancy gaps. This requirement runs counter to the established business model and capabilities of reservation affiliations. The average room-night contribution of reservations companies to affiliated independent hotels is less than 5 percent of available rooms.

At least four emerging factors are challenging the effectiveness of traditional reservation organizations:

1. The growing demographic and psychographic complexity of the global consumer market. requires significant new expertise and resources in the area of segmentation and analysis.
2. The emergence of consumer direct-booking Internet technology requires significant new and ongoing investment.
3. The new marketplace requires innovative global brand management together with resources to establish and maintain a brand in the face of intense competition. To be competitive, a brand must attract new development and must therefore be strong enough to convince lenders to commit to permanent financing. Brand management also includes loyalty programme management and the development of

regional and global partners to strengthen and extend the effectiveness of the brand.

4. The corporate objectives and governance policies of traditional reservation organizations are influenced by the need to grow and meet shareholder profit requirements. These goals for growth can be at odds with the goals and expectations of independent hotel and resort members.

The traditional reservation affiliations must change not only their focus but also their structure if they want to succeed in this new competitive world. The traditional reservation organization must be prepared to respond to competitive challenges by expanding resources and skills necessary to increase average room-night contribution to affiliated independent hotels to 15 percent—an average growth per member hotel of at least 200 percent over present performance levels. In response to this competitive environment and the need for more cooperative and focused business relationships, a new hospitality business structure is evolving for all scales of hotels: the branded distribution company.

Characteristics of a Branded Distribution Company

The ideal branded distribution organization is a conventional equity company with ownership shared (in some cases) by the individual hotel owners, who have direct input into the corporation through an elected board of directors. This ownership structure creates a true operating partnership and a sharing of energies toward the common goal of creating value through increased brand awareness and room sales. Corporate profits must be adequate to maintain technical and managerial leadership and to support the shareholders' investment.

Unlike a reservations and representation company, a branded distribution corporation owns and builds a branded distribution network asset that, in turn. The sole focus is performance for the affiliated independent hotels and resorts. Joining such an organization is appropriate for independently owned and managed hotels and resorts that want to keep owner control but require effective and low-cost distribution, global consumer brand awareness, and group purchasing benefits without the encumbrances and costs of a traditional hotel chain franchise or management contract. Above all, it promises the independent hotel awareness of, and access to, their target consumer and rapidly emerging technology through cooperative ownership.

The Benefits of a Branded Distribution Company

This new business structure is attractive from an owner's or a developer's standpoint for a number of reasons, including:

- *Costs:* First, it requires less up-front cash; second, ongoing fees and reservation commissions are significantly lower than with either a pure franchise or management agreement. For example, a 9 or 10 percent franchise fee in many cases equals 50 percent of gross profits.
- *Contract terms:* The terms are typically shorter, easier to negotiate, and allow for substantial owner control over the operation, style, and character of the hotel. As a result, conflicts can be avoided, and the branded distribution contract can be completed and signed in as few as 45 days.
- *Marketing:* It frees hotel management from the daunting and increasingly expensive task of acquiring profitable new customers and allows them to focus their attention and operating skills on the delivery of an exceptional hospitality experience.
- *Common objectives:* Both the owner and the branded distribution company enter into the agreement with the same primary objective: revenue.

The branded distribution company receives no revenue if it does not deliver to the hotel or resort. This shared goal strengthens and energizes the relationship between the two partners. From a branded distribution company's standpoint, this structure allows the brand to expand faster because capital is not used to subsidize additional construction or to support an older business model. Instead, funds are used to build and maintain an uptodate global distribution network and infrastructure composed of telecommunications, e-commerce functions, reservations software, data warehousing capability, and sales and marketing. The efficiency of the operation is assured by a focus that is almost entirely on the most important part of this business relationship— the generation of brand awareness and measurable room-night revenue for each affiliated hotel or resort.

Unlike hard flags, which focus primarily on hotel operations and asset management such as the Marriott or the Westin, and reservation affiliations, which focus on professional camaraderie and traditional distribution channels such as the Best Western, the branded distribution company is primarily market focused; its full attention is on customer and travel influencer communication, relationship technology, and revenue streams.

In contrast, asset management, profitability, and operating efficiency are the major concerns of management companies, which tend to be public companies with stockholder expectations that must be met. It is often the case that strategic asset management concerns conflict with day-to-day tactical operating needs. This is evident in Marriott's recent move to separate its ownership and operating divisions, to the benefit of both. The same conflict can arise between the independent owners of a hotel property, who are focused on real estate concerns, and the management company they hire. Such misunderstandings can sour what should be a mutually supportive relationship.

The fact that management contract fees are charged and collected, even when the cash flow is negative, does not create owner confidence in the partner. A franchise relationship can cause a similar conflict and put a financial and operating burden on an owner. In contrast, participation of independent owner/operators as shareholders in a branded distribution company enables them to move beyond these concerns and focus on their operation and the consumer—the source of their revenue and the basis of their success.

A Branded Distribution Company

The owners of property within a branded distribution company must relinquish a minimal amount of control and decision making, mainly in the areas of branding and quality assurance. In certain cases, member properties may have to adopt and maintain specific quality standards. In addition, they may also be required to demonstrate their affiliation with the branded distribution company through using its logo on marketing materials as well as participating in e-commerce and inventory management initiatives. However, these drawbacks can actually enhance a hotel's operations and market positioning while allowing the hotel to maintain independent ownership and management.

Ensuring Competitive Advantage

Independent hotels face significant risk in today's marketplace. Given the advances in technology and the profitability pressures put upon chain hotels by shareholders, competition for customers is intensifying. Keeping in step with competitive chain hotels presents a significant challenge to independent owners. To address this, they currently have several options outside of the branded distribution company, including representation firms, reservations services, flagged chains, and franchise management companies. However, given the economic, societal, and technological trends that are dramatically changing the hospitality industry, several of which are analyzed in this book, many of these old economy options can offer only short-term solutions to long-term competitive pressures.

A branded distribution company has an inherent advantage going into this new competitive arena. Its sole focus is on customer acquisition and management, achieved through the development of new technologies. This competitive advantage extends to the independent hotel aligned with a branded if you ever have the chance to be involved with opening a hotel, jump at the opportunity. Opening a hotel is one of the most rewarding jobs in the hospitality industry despite its frustrating and exhausting aspects. Walk into any hotel, anywhere, and look around. Everything you see, hear, and feel, every detail, involved many people and countless decisions.

The OPM is the third person hired, after the general manager and the director of marketing. The role of an OPM is to pull together the visions of the architect, interior designer, owner, operator, and others. When these visions are successfully melded, the hotel guest is satisfied, the owner makes money, and the architect and interior designer can add the project to their list of successful accomplishments.

The OPM oversees the following aspects of a project:

- Reviewing blueprints and specifications for the entire building
- Assisting with the creation of a model room
- Developing the pre-opening staff plan
- Developing and managing the pre-opening budget
- Developing the operational supplies and equipment budget (OS&E)
- Overseeing the purchasing, warehousing, delivery, and installation of the OS&E
- Developing the interior graphics package
- Coordinating the installation of third party vendors

BLUEPRINTS

The OPM's responsibilities start with the architectural blueprints. The focus is to ensure a good flow for guests, staff, and goods. By providing the independent owner with a global brand and the technology and expertise to acquire profitable new customers, the branded distribution company enables the hotel management to focus its attention on the delivery of exceptional service and profits to the owners. This separation of skills, expertise, resources, and operating cultures in a cooperative business relationship provides a model and formula for success. Independent hotels and resorts that align themselves with a branded distribution company will not only continue to operate profitably in the new global marketplace, but will also flourish. The bellperson bag storage room should be located between the porte cochere (entry) and the elevators and contain 1 square foot of space for each guest room. If valet parking is offered, ensure that a convenient cashier's station is located near the porte cochere.

Arrange for a key rack to hold the keys for each valet parking stall. Given a 10,000-square-foot ballroom, the catering department can sell functions for 800 for dinner. This requires 80 6-foot round tables, 800 chairs, a dais for the head table, a dance floor, and staging for the band. If sold for a 700-guest all-day meeting, the classroom setup requires 1,400 linear feet of narrow tables and 700 chairs. A short theater meeting setup for 1,000 requires 1,000 chairs, a podium, staging, and audio visual equipment. The same space accommodates a cocktail reception for 1,400 guests; this requires cocktail tables, portable bars, buffet stations, and so on. This all boils down to ensuring ample storage space for equipment not being used— at least 1,500 square feet.

Moving goods from the back of the house to the front requires careful planning to ensure that precious labour dollars are used efficiently. Are the rollaway beds, cribs, and high chairs stored near an elevator for quick delivery? The housekeeper closets should be centrally located on guest room floors to cut down on access time. A 6-foot, 2-cubic-yard garbage cart will not work if the elevator is only 5 feet deep. If ice machines are offered for guest self service, they must produce an ample supply (10 pounds per room per 24-hour period) for the number of guest rooms on that floor or floors. The ice machine room requires the proper utilities, including electricity, plumbing, lighting, and HVAC. Don't forget the sign on the outside of the room, which must meet ADA standards!

MODEL ROOM

Build a typical king and double/double guest room close to the site so you can review every single item in them. Are ample electrical and telecom outlets placed exactly where the TV, lamps, clock radio, mini-bar, coffeemaker, hair dryer,

Internet access, and telephones are located so the cords are hidden? Are spare outlets offered for guest use (computer, iron, etc.)? Is the closet rod hung so the ironing board organizer and iron board fit in the closet? Is the thermostat location convenient for guest access? Are the case goods (dresser, nightstands, headboards, chairs, etc.), designed for commercial heavy-duty use? Will they hold up to abusive use? Do they have sharp corners that will snag guest clothing? Does the bed skirt hang 1/2 inch off the floor? Do the bedside lamps give off enough lumens so guests can read in bed? Does the room meet or exceed every operator brand standard? These model rooms serve as sales tools for the sales and marketing staff selling group rooms up to three years before opening.

Pre-opening Staff Plan

The pre-opening staffing begins with an organizational chart with all positions. Once the titles and staff counts by position are finalized, then spreadsheets are created to include the position titles, start dates, pay rates, bonus, transfer allowances, and number of full-time equivalents (FTEs) for all positions. The pre-opening staff plan is a comprehensive document that states who is hired, when they start, how much they are paid, and whether or not they are allocated a relocation allowance and benefit costs. Each of these pieces is used to build the pre-opening staff plan budget. If hiring has already begun and the opening date changes, the budget must be amended. Hiring a position that does not conform to the plan, such as bringing on a renowned chef one month earlier than planned, also requires the budget be modified.

Pre-opening Budget

The OPM develops and manages the preopening budget. This budget typically consists of three major categories; labour cost (40 percent), sales and marketing efforts (40 percent), and miscellaneous (20 percent). The labour cost is taken directly from the pre-opening staff plan. Sales and marketing activities comprise advertising, collateral, public relations, and travel to see clients. Rounding out the budget are all of the miscellaneous items. These include office space rental before moving into the hotel, utilities (power, water, Internet, and telephone), human resources recruitment (ads, headhunters, drug testing, etc.), training materials, association dues, and licenses and permits (business, liquor, sales tax collection, etc.). If the hotel opening date is delayed for any reason, the pre-opening budget is affected. Additional costs include labour, office rent, utilities, and marketing efforts. If the opening date changes within three weeks of the original plan, major costs are encountered, as most of the staff is already hired.

Operational Supplies And Equipment (OS&E)

The largest and most complex aspect of the OPM's responsibility is specifying, quantifying, and budgeting for the operational supplies and equipment (OS&E) list. This budget typically pencils out to $8,000 to $10,000 per guest room for a typical four-star property. The list of goods typically exceeds 2,500 line items. Add a little more for a full-service resort; deduct a little for an in-city business hotel. The OS&E comprises all of the items that are not nailed down, with the exception of the furniture, fixtures, and equipment (FF&E).

The FF&E is typically specified and ordered by the interior designer. Typical guest room items include bedding (frames, box springs, mattresses, mattress pads, sheets, pillows, pillowcases, towels, etc.), clock radios, hangers, laundry bags, laundry tickets, iron, ironing board, ironing board organizer, luggage rack, guest amenities (soap, shampoo, lotion, etc.), hair dryer, shower curtains, and shower curtain hooks. Housekeeping equipment includes vacuums (guest room and wide-area units), carpet shampooers, carpet extractors, housekeeper carts, laundry bins, garbage trucks, valet delivery carts, and shelving, to name a few of many items.

Housekeeping must also keep an inventory of guest request items including humidifiers, dehumidifiers, cribs, high chairs, rollaway beds, bedboards, spare pillows, towels, amenities, refrigerators, laundry soap, and so on. Food and beverage front-of-the-house items include flatware (knives, forks, and spoons), hollowware (serving trays, serving utensils, chafing dishes, sugar bowls and sauce boats, punch bowls), glassware, table linen, napkins, skirting, salt and pepper shakers, china, plate covers, espresso machines, menu covers and the list goes on and on.

Banquet items include all of the above plus tables, chairs, staging, staging steps and railings, dance floors, carts, carving boards, ice carving trays, flags, podiums, portable bars, ice bins, pianos, and tray jack stands. The largest purchase order—typically over 100 pages long—is for a full-service kitchen and includes everything a chef needs to produce the menus being sold at the hotel. Every utensil, pot, pan, dish, and glass rack, ware washing chemicals, mops and buckets, specialty items (roller-docker, anyone?) must be reviewed by the chef, purchased, and delivered the day before the chef starts burning in the kitchen.

On the hotel administration side, the OPM specifies the office desks, chairs, cork and dry-erase boards, conference tables, filing cabinets, safes, bullet-proof window for the general cashier's office, fax machines, copiers, currency and coin trays, and a set of flags for the exterior flagpoles. One of the largest and most complicated purchase orders is for staff uniforms. Before quantifying uniform needs, many questions are asked. Do we need summer and winter uniforms? Will the uniforms be laundered by the hotel or the hotel associates? How many extra servers are needed for a capacity dinner function in the ballrooms? Is the intent to have a large percentage of parttime staff? Which uniforms need custom embroidery (restaurants, culinary, engineering, etc.)? What percentage of spare uniforms are needed in reserve?

Once these questions are answered, then the selection process begins. Operations and the interior designer review the look and feel the options available. Each position (housekeeper, bellperson, etc.) or similar position (front desk clerk/concierge) has different requirements. Housekeepers and bellpersons require durable uniforms that breathe and can handle lots of bending and stretching. The uniforms of the culinary and engineering staffs are often stained and must hold up to numerous launderings. The uniform order is placed 90 to 120 days before the first uniformed staff is hired. To quantify the sizes required, a typical bell chart sizing curve is used for the particular country or region of the hotel. The uniforms are delivered and sorted prior to the individual fitting process. On the line staff's second day on the job, each individual is measured for uniforms. An army of seamstresses then takes the pants, jackets, and dresses and alters each piece for each associate. The fitted uniforms are issued a few days before opening day.

Purchasing, Warehousing, Delivery, and Installation

In an ideal process, the 500 purchase orders are issued beginning six months prior to opening. Each order is tracked to ensure it is delivered to the proper location on the desired date. Most goods are delivered to a local warehouse and pulled for delivery to the site as the general contractor completes construction and turns over areas. Some goods are shipped directly to the site to eliminate double handling. These large orders include bed sets (21 40-foot shipping containers for the Kona project), televisions (3 containers), banquet chairs (2 containers), banquet tables (3 containers), and guest room safes (1 container). The linen order for guest rooms and F&B are shipped to an off-site laundry facility for initial washing.

Once the goods are on site, they are typically staged in the largest ballroom for unpacking and distribution. The unpacking process requires a plethora of workers. For example, each clock radio must be unpacked, the electrical twist tie removed, the 9-volt battery installed, and the time set. Then the unit is placed in a guest room on the nightstand. For the 525-room Kona project, this task required two people for three eight-hour days. Once they completed this task, they spent the next five working days installing the 7,000_ shower curtain hooks, 525 shower curtains, and 525 shower liners. Then they unboxed 30,000 glasses and placed them in glass racks for washing. These kinds of tasks must be carried out for each of the 2,500 line items. Once receiving and distribution begins on site, another element comes to the forefront: garbage. During the five-week Kona installation process, over 3 tons of packing material were generated every day! Making friends with the local waste-hauling service is a priority.

INTERIOR GRAPHICS PACKAGE

The project manager reviews the interior graphics package for errors and omissions. This package includes every sign needed to direct guests and staff in front and back of the house areas. The recent Kona project included 1,600 signs, 98 percent of which were one of a kind.The text must be correct, the directional arrows must point the correct way, and most are required to include raised Braille text, per the ADA. The OPM works with the marketing department to develop the identity for the unique areas within a property. These include the restaurants, bars, pools, spa, and retail areas. These logos are incorporated into the signage package, collateral (cocktail napkins, menus, check presenters, etc.), and uniforms.

Third-party Vendors

Many third-party vendors must have access to the property prior to opening. The project manager schedules and directs all of these vendors, including the soft-drink vendor (who installs soda guns for the bars and vending machines for the guest floors), the coffee company (which must install and test equipment), the pay-per-view TV vendor (who must connect every television in the building and test the signal strength), the warewashing chemical vendor (who must install and calibrate the dishwashing machines), and the office furniture installer (who must assemble all office equipment). Among the other vendors are those dealing in copier services, postage machines, telephones, fitness centre equipment, security systems, and first aid supplies. These vendors are constantly informed when they can install their equipment based on the general contractor's completion dates. When the construction schedule changes, vendors must be updated so they show up when the area they need access to is ready.

Human Resources

The OPM assists the human resources personnel during the last two months of preopening so that they have all of the tools they need to recruit and hire the staff. On average, the HR department interviews at least five applicants for every position. This works out to over 1,000 applicants for a typical 300- room four-star hotel. This process is referred to as the mass hire. The mass hire is typically conducted over a two- or three-day period six weeks before opening. To interview this many job seekers, HR requires office space, reception space for up to 200 at one time, rest rooms, and break rooms for the interviewers.

The OPM coordinates all of these details so that the operations team can focus on the recruitment. Once the offer letters are accepted, all line associates start work about three weeks out. The first few days on the job are dedicated to group training, operational philosophies, code of conduct, and other general policies. On day three, divisional training takes place. In the second week of training, the staff is broken out into departmental or job-specific duties. Departmental training includes teaching staff to make beds, clean a room, cook every menu item, the most efficient route to each guest room, and what to tell the guest en route to the room.

Opening Day

The activity during the last 72 hours before the opening ceremonies is chaotic. This is the time that all hands are on deck. Sixteen-hour days are the norm. Rooms are cleaned. Housekeeping closets are stocked. Liquor and food storerooms are filled. The general contractor completes all small details such as paint touch-ups. Artwork and furnishings are installed in the public areas. Rehearsals are conducted for all aspects of the operation, including serving test meals and cocktails, guest check-ins and check-outs, and even such easy to- overlook activities as valet parking and vacuuming the pool. As soon as the general manger cuts the ceremonial ribbon, the OPM knows what kind of job has been done. The next step is to find the next project and do it all again!

Chapter 2

Hotel Company Practices

The importance of electronic hotel-distribution routes has grown substantially in recent years. According to statistics quoted in the Horwath Worldwide Hotel Industry Studies, direct reservations fell from approximately 39 percent in 1995 to 33 percent in 1999, with the shift in sales going almost exclusively to electronic channels. While hotels continue to make extensive use of travel-agent-oriented global distribution systems (GDSs), consumer adoption of the Internet as a reliable and secure commerce medium has prompted a change in the way in which hotel rooms are being distributed.

The Internet has dramatically changed the way people communicate, research information, and buy goods and services. Travel products in particular have proven to be suitable for sale on line. The typical Internet user—an affluent, frequent traveler who spends more than the average on leisure and entertainment—is an attractive market for travel suppliers. Furthermore, from a consumer's perspective purchasing travel products on line has, in many instances, become faster, easier, and more convenient than contacting a travel agent or telephoning a supplier directly. As a result, on-line travel-related revenues are forecast to grow sharply.

For example, according to a recent report by Jupiter Media Metrix, on-line travel sales will more than triple in the next five years—from US$18 billion in 2002 to US$64 billion in 2007. Booking volumes are also forecast to climb. The Travel Industry Association of America (TIAA) estimated that by the end of 2002 between 6 percent and 10 percent of all travel reservations would originate on the web. If Jupiter's 2007 prediction comes true, travel will be the biggest selling online product, with a volume nearly double that of the current leading product, PC hardware.

Price is key to selling successfully on line. Studies by Internet analysts Gomez and PhoCusWright, and also a study by TIAA, all identified price as being one of the key motivating factors that encourages consumers to purchase travel on line.

For example, the PhoCusWright study found that competitive pricing is the best way to attract customers (Pastore, 2001). When travelers who haven't bought on line were asked what would encourage them to do so, 64 percent said that saving money would make them more interested. No other benefit—whether saving time, getting bonus loyalty-club points, more control, or obtaining better information—came close to this level of response.

HOTEL PRICING ON THE WEB

In a 2000 study that almost six out of ten leisure travelers now actively seek the "lowest possible price" for travel services. Similarly, a 2001 Forrester Research study found that 66 percent of all buyers had used an on-line discount in the previous 12 months to buy travel on line, and a study by the Joint Hospitality Industry Congress found a real expectation among consumers that Internet prices would be lower than those available in the "bricks and mortar" world. Such a perception has developed for several reasons. First, many of the best-known Internet retailers initially competed with traditional outlets based, to a large extent, on price.

Second, savvy consumers are aware that webbased distribution costs are lower than those of other channels. As Jack Geddes, Radisson Hotels Worldwide's managing director, sales and marketing Asia, has pointed out: "Consumers now understand that suppliers are cutting costs through this channel and expect savings to be passed on to them, as well as being rewarded for making the booking themselves". Such expectations are being reinforced by the budget-airline sector, which offers substantial discounts for online bookings. Companies such as EasyJet, RyanAir, and Buzz estimate that by avoiding telesales and travel agents, they can achieve savings of up to 30 percent—which they pass on to customers in the form of lower fares. Similar or even greater levels of savings can be made by hotel companies, as can be seen from the internal, which show how an 80- to 90- percent savings in transaction charges can be achieved by selling directly to the consumer on line.

Finally, many hotels (and airlines) use the web to sell last-minute deals—packages at relatively low prices but with short lead times. While such promotions can help dispose of unsold inventory, they have also resulted in the public's associating rooms sold over the Internet with lower prices. These factors have combined to make consumers associate on-line booking with good value, which in the consumer's mind translates into low prices. However, in the case of hotel brands' own web sites, industry practice frequently seems to be the opposite of theory.

In a 1999 survey, for instance, a colleague and I found that rates obtained from the web site were usually substantially higher than those obtained by contacting the central reservations office. That study was limited, however, in that it focused only on direct sales over hotel chains' own branded web sites. Electronic distribution is rapidly evolving for hotels, and a large number of other on-line consumer focused channels are now available, with most chains using multiple routes to reach the consumer.

The availability of numerous points of sale poses some interesting questions. Foremost among these is: Is there consistency between the room availability and prices being offered over each of the channels? Unlike in the physical world, where a potential customer would have to telephone or visit several suppliers, comparison shopping on the web can generally be accomplished relatively quickly. Research has shown that consumers shopping for travel on line almost always check more than one site before purchasing. According to Jupiter Media Metrix, just 10 percent of would-be guests visit only one site to book a hotel room, another 43 percent visit two or three sites, and 22 percent visit four or more sites.

Because they check prices in several places, on-line purchasers have become increasingly intolerant of inconsistent information, and may react unfavorably to a firm's disparate rates by booking with the company's competitor.

Two related questions, then, are:

1. If rates are not consistent across channels, is any one route consistently cheaper?
2. Is the company's approach to pricing logical from both the consumer's and the hotel's perspective?

Methodology And Limitations Of The Study

Previous studies of hotels' Internet use have been limited. Murphy et al. focused on rating the content of hotel web sites, while Van Hoof and Combrink attempted to measure managers' perceptions of and attitudes toward the Internet. Web reservations facilities were investigated in detail in the co-authored paper that I mentioned above. However, the issue of pricing over several distribution channels does not appear to have been the subject of extensive systematic research to date.

The objective of this study, therefore, was to analyze the room rates being offered to consumers over multiple electronic distribution channels. An exhaustive analysis of the rates being offered by all hotels would be virtually impossible. Those rates are constantly in flux, as hoteliers project occupancy rates and open or close rate classes accordingly (according to yield-management principles). Major international hotel chains' electronic-distribution activities are indicative of industry patterns, because recent research has shown that large companies are most active on the web—perhaps because their size often gives them an advantage in terms of technical expertise and financial resources.

As a result, decided to focus this study on the behaviour of the top-50 international hotel brands. While this strategy means that the findings are not representative of the industry as a whole (and, therefore, not generally applicable), it does allow establishment of an accurate benchmark of trends as they currently stand. The companies were chosen based on the ranking of the top-50 hotel brands published in Hotels magazine.

Two of those companies were removed from the listing because they operate resorts and distribute their rooms largely as part of packages, which means that their products are not directly comparable to the rest of the industry. Furthermore, another three companies neither offered on-line reservations on their own web site nor were they listed on any of the other channels studied.

Thus, the results discussed below reflect the findings from the 45 hotel brands for which consistent data could be found. Five major types of electronic business to consumer distribution channels were identified from the literature, and leading examples of each category were selected for inclusion in the study. In addition to a chain's own web site, these comprised channels that draw their data and reservations engine from the GDS; those that are based on the databases and reservation engine of the switch companies ; and pure web-based channels with an inventory and reservations database that is maintained on line.

While not collectively exhaustive, these represent the majority of hotel-reservation sites. Omitted from the study were the auction-style web sites, such as Priceline.com, which are not comparable to typical booking approaches. As another point of comparison, incorporated voice channels into the study by analyzing the rates offered by the toll-free number to the central reservations service (CRS).

Data were collected by repeatedly offering to reserve a standard double room for specified dates in a selected property from each of the brands using each of the distribution channels discussed above. Where the product requested was available on the system, both the number of rates displayed and the lowest rate available were recorded for analysis.

To help ensure consistency, you ignored rates not available to the general public, and analyzed only those rates that could be booked by a "normal" customer. After checking the web sites, you telephoned the hotel company's CRS to request the same booking. In that case, you recorded only the first rate quoted by the agent, and did not ask for a lower rate. Although better rates could probably be achieved by haggling, decided that negotiating would leave no systematic way of consistently determining the lowest rate, depending as it does on the caller's persistence. The above process was repeated for five sets of alternative dates to reduce the possibility of error due to system malfunctions or other exceptional circumstances.

Research Findings

As each of the major hotel brands uses multiple simultaneous distribution channels. The most commonly available channels were voice (via the company's CRS) and electronic. The company that did not make a CRS number available was in the economy sector. Offering hotel rooms via the company web site is almost universal, all but one of the brands surveyed offering on-line reservations in this manner. It is interesting to note that this represents a considerable advancement when compared to surveys made only a few years ago, which found that only approximately 50 percent of the major hotel companies provided on-line reservations. As hotel companies make less use of the other channels investigated.

Approximately four-fifths of the major brands used the GDS-based intermediaries Expedia and Travelocity, three-quarters used Travelweb, and barely one-third used World-Res. These findings are not in themselves surprising. Both Expedia and Travelocity draw their data from the GDSs, where the majority of the hotel brands represented in this study (being major hotel companies) can reasonably expect to be represented. Similarly, Travelweb draws its data from THISCO

(The Hotel Industry Switching Company), and thus any of the hotel brands that use this as their switch service could be expected to make inventory available for sale via Travelweb. The chains' low usage of World- Res surprising.

With the exception of a company's own web site, using WorldRes has the lowest potential transaction cost and thus would appear to be an attractive channel for use by hotel companies. Examination of its property database reveals a large percentage of independent hotels, bed-and-breakfast inns, and small hotel chains. An unresolved question is why the major brands do not exploit this distribution channel.

Rates Available

Each of the electronic channels offered multiple rates. As can be seen, each channel presented an average of five rates in response to the request, with more being offered to the customer by Travelocity than by the other channels surveyed. Presenting a variety of rates to the customer has both positive and negative implications.

From a positive perspective, it offers choices to potential customers, allowing them to match their needs with the products being sold. On the other hand, presenting a large number of rates without adequate differentiation between products can confuse customers regarding what they are getting for their money.

This is best demonstrated by an example encountered in the study, where a property offered 17 different rates for a particular date on Travelweb, with few (if any) discernible differences in the room descriptions. Clearly such a scenario would be confusing and frustrating for any customer wishing to book that property.

Mean Prices

It was difficult to make a general observation about which of the several channels is consistently least expensive on average, although Expedia's rates were marginally lower than those offered by other channels and WorldRes seemed to offer consistently higher rates than did the others. Indeed, all things considered, prices across each of the channels were comparable— with the average price for the Hotel company website 444 97% Expedia 38 84% Travelocity.com 35 78% Travelweb 34 76% WorldRes 14 31% requested room being in the range of US$163. It was interesting that Expedia's mean rates were lower, because as an on-line travel agency, it has a high distribution cost, and it would be logical to assume that rates offered over this channel would reflect the higher costs.

By the same token, since WorldRes's transaction costs are relatively low in comparison with those offered by the other channels surveyed, hotels could potentially offer cheaper rates over this channel. In other words, what found is that when selling hotel products on line, there does not appear to be a relationship between the cost of using the distribution channel and the rate offered. Illogically, the electronic channels with the highest transaction costs for the hotel seem to regularly offer the best value to the customer. As will be discussed, hoteliers need to rethink their current practices and take action if they are to benefit from the increasing market for on-line hotel-room sales.

Segment Breakout

The foregoing discussion was based on an overall look at hotel room sales distribution. If the brands studied are subdivided into classifications based on their targeted market segment, a different picture emerges. As hotels at the low end of the market are far more likely to offer consistent rates across all channels used. While it could be speculated that the reason for this might be that economy properties are more likely to have a single fixed price for their product irrespective of demand, it could also be due to a more consistent pricing strategy on the part of the hotel companies involved when addressing a relatively price-sensitive market.

Furthermore it can be seen that consumers at the low ends of the market are far more likely to obtain low rates through direct (company-owned) channels. For economy brands, direct sales over the company's own web site were lowest 26 percent of the time.

When coupled with the 46 percent of cases where the same rate is offered irrespective of the channel used, that means that a consumer reserving an economy room will find the cheapest rate on the hotel company's web site nearly three times out of four. With mid-price products, the chain's web site is even more likely to give the best rate, offering the lowest rate nearly half of the time. The situation is different at the upper end of the market.

Luxury-hotel companies' web sites gave the cheapest rate in less than 10 percent of cases. Furthermore, the company's web site quoted the highest rate in over one-third of cases. Overall, the evidence seems to indicate that if you want to stay in up-market hotels, you should avoid booking on these hotels' web sites if you are searching for good value. Instead, the on-line intermediaries offer the highest probability of finding the best rate available for high-end properties, with an average savings of 5 percent available by booking through Expedia rather than on the company's own site.

Haggling Required

It is also clear from the data that a hotel company's CRS is not the place to obtain the best rates, at least if one takes the first offer as did for this study. Irrespective of the market segment, there is a higher probability of being quoted the highest rate through this channel, and bookings through this route were almost never the cheapest available.This finding, however, is to a large extent driven by my methodology. Indeed, in many cases, as soon as indicated that did not plan to make a booking at the quoted rate, the CRS associate quoted another, lower rate. This anecdotal finding suggests that negotiation might have resulted in lower prices.

DAWN OF A NEW WAY

From the above discussion, it can be seen that both the range of channels through which hotels can be booked and the complexity of such channels have grown. This study represents a first attempt at documenting hotel companies' pricing practices over electronic routes. The study revealed that the majority of hotel brands now use simultaneous, multiple electronic channels of distribution, making their rooms available to a relatively wide audience.

While the use of CRS-based reservations has fallen slightly, there has been a growth in the availability of hotel companies' own web sites, and a vast majority of companies that studied now make their rooms available for sale in this manner. The differences between this study's findings and earlier published research indicate a major expansion in hotel chains' use of the web as a direct-sales medium, perhaps accompanied by a realization of the web's benefits in comparison with other, more traditional, electronic channels of distribution.

Most companies offer multiple rates to customers over each channel. It is interesting to note, however, the large number of companies that now offer consistent pricing across all channels. Previous research found less than 10 percent of companies had consistent pricing and cited the lack of integration among the various inventory databases used to manage inventory as a possible cause. Yet over one-third of the brands studied now offer consistent pricing across multiple channels, indicating progress in the industry's management of electronic distribution. Although no single channel consistently offers the lowest prices, in-depth analysis does reveal a link between pricing and the market being targeted.

First, the lowest prices can rarely be obtained from the CRS (absent negotiation), irrespective of market segment. As compared to the first-offered CRS price, a would-be customer can save at least 5 percent by booking over any of the electronic channels examined. From the data it can be seen that consumers are more likely to find the lowest prices on the hotel chains' own web sites in the economy and mid-price segments than will be found from those companies' CRS or third-party web sites. So-called upmarket hotel brands are, on the other hand, more likely to quote higher prices on their own web site than what they offer on other channels. Economy brands seem to be the only ones in the industry as a whole displaying a logical on-line pricing strategy (in terms of the relationship between the cost of using a channel and the rates offered there) and also in terms of actively managing their channels of distribution.

Implications

First, it is clear that for those with a taste for upscale products, the hotel brand's own web site is not the place to shop, as better value can be obtained in most cases through other channels. More interesting, however, is the fact that, in general, prices have become more or less equal across many of the channels investigated, and by implication, across many other electronic distribution channels as well. It is well established that time is a valuable commodity in today's society. Since the number and variety of ways that a consumer can book a hotel room has become undeniably manifold, the cost associated with searching through even a small number of the many consumer-focused channels currently available in the marketplace in an attempt to find a low price has increased.

Given that this study has found that many of the rates being offered over alternative channels are more or less the same for many hotels, customers should reconsider whether all that time and energy searching for the lowest rate is actually worthwhile. The implications for the hotelier are more pressing. Findings suggest that many hotel chains are not actively managing the room rates being offered in their portfolio of electronic distribution channels. Most companies offer multiple rates on each channel, which, as discussed earlier, can be beneficial as it gives a choice to the customer. Displaying too many rates, though, can be counterproductive, if the customer becomes overwhelmed.

Presenting a small number of tightly defined rates would be the most appropriate solution. However, most companies currently display about five rates in response to a customer inquiry, with others showing significantly more, usually with little or no apparent product differentiation. In addition, there appears to be inconsistency in terms of the rates being offered over electronic channels. In many cases, no clear or logical pricing strategy is apparent. The lowest prices are offered on channels with the highest transaction costs, and vice versa.

A small number of companies offer consistent pricing irrespective of the channel being used to make the booking. Informal follow up with those companies revealed that they follow this strategy as they believe in the principle of one "correct" price for each customer. In this way, they do not have to address the issue of customer dissatisfaction as a result of a person's being quoted a lower price for a room on a different channel after having already made a booking. However, such an approach ignores the issue of the cost of processing a booking over a particular channel. As was discussed earlier, such costs vary greatly depending to a large extent on the number of intermediaries between the supplier and the customer.

The greater the number of intermediaries, the greater the transaction cost and processing fees—and therefore the greater the distribution cost. This would seem to argue for having high rates on the channels that have high-cost structures and low prices on those with low cost structures. Coupled with this matter is the fact that customers have become more knowledgeable about and comfortable with e-commerce issues in general, are more aware that distribution costs are lower in the virtual world than the bricks-and-mortar one, and thus increasingly expect to find the cheapest prices over electronic, and particularly direct electronic, routes. Put simply, when they go to a hotel company's web site, they expect to find the best value there.

This study has shown that in many cases this is simply not the case, given that luxury hotels in particular tend to offer their highest rates over direct channels— and (ironically) their cheapest rates over the most expensive on-line intermediaries. Informal follow up to the study revealed that this may be due to the proactive approach of the on-line companies in contacting hotel companies on practically a daily basis and encouraging them to reduce their rates in return for better positioning on their search listings. In contrast, the rates on hotel companies' web sites go largely unmanaged, in many cases being set far in advance and not adjusted to reflect changing supply and demand. Irrespective of its root cause, the behaviour of hotel companies is driving Internet shoppers into the arms of the waiting on-line intermediaries, where in addition to consistently low prices, they also find wide product choice.

Because of this, it's likely that many hotels are losing potential bookings to competitors as a result of consumers' migration toward the on-line travel sites that offer relatively low rates from many different hotel chains. Instead of being presented with a list of a chain's properties on a company's web site, prospective guests see a much wider variety of options from the on-line intermediary and may be tempted to book a competitor's room (especially if price becomes an issue).

Once consumers conclude that they will usually find better prices on a third-party channel, they will make Expedia or Travelocity, for example, their first port of call for future bookings—threatening brand loyalty, driving up transaction fees, increasing reservation leakage, and strengthening the third parties' power to demand "special rates" or commission overrides for a company to gain premium positioning (or even inclusion) in their search listings.

Hotel companies need to take urgent action if they are not to lose control over the sale of their own product. At the very least, this means offering consistent prices over all channels, but more probably means providing customers the lowest rate over their own web site. This would decrease guests' motivation to book on alternative electronic channels, would help build web-site traffic, and should help to decrease distribution costs.

Customer Relationship Management (CRM)—a managerial philosophy that enables a firm to become intimately familiar with its customers—is currently gaining widespread popularity in many industries. Firms that embrace CRM strive to provide consistent and personal customer service over time and across multiple touch points.

At first glance, the lodging sector, with its emphasis on customer service and multiplicity of customer touch points, seems ideally positioned to take advantage of CRM initiatives. We believe, however, that the current structure of the lodging industry gives rise to a "data-ownership dilemma," which appears to be limiting the adoption of a comprehensive CRM approach.

The three parties typically involved in running a hotel—the owner, the management company, and the brand (Brand refers to the franchiser that flags a given property (e.g., Hilton, Marriott, Six Continents)—have partially misaligned interests and, as a result, often resist sharing customer data, a prerequisite for successful CRM. (The recent slew of lawsuits between brands and ownership groups that allege data misuse confirms the often conflicted relationship between the entities.) This paper highlights the data-ownership dilemma and outlines several possible future scenarios leading to its resolution. The first introduces the CRM concept and discusses the potential benefits and risks it engenders.

The second examines the current structure of the U.S. lodging industry and outlines the complementary role of the three major industry players—owners, management companies, and brands. The following demonstrates why the current structure of the lodging industry creates a barrier to successful CRM adoption by hotel companies. The effect of the "data-ownership dilemma" is discussed. The final of the article presents alternative scenarios as to how the dilemma may be resolved.

CUSTOMER RELATIONSHIP MANAGEMENT

Customer Relationship Management (CRM) is currently one of the hottest topics in the fields of business strategy, information technology, and marketing management. Put simply, CRM is a management philosophy that calls for the reconfiguration of the firm's activities around the customer. CRM differs from traditional marketing initiatives in that, while the latter take predominately a short-term, transaction approach, CRM focuses on maximizing revenue from each customer over the lifetime of the relationship by getting to know each one intimately. CRM is also, by definition, a cross functional philosophy that calls for substantial business integration.

Thus, to implement CRM successfully, a very different mindset is needed: The firm no longer markets to customers, but it fosters a relationship with them through programmes that span marketing, operations, information systems, accounting, and other organizational functions. One of the questions most often asked about CRM is, "why bother?" Changing an organization's philosophy and methods of operation is troublesome; developing and maintaining in-depth customer databases is expensive and the benefits of the approach are not guaranteed.

First, by developing a closer relationship with customers, the firm may gain a competitive advantage and, through increased switching costs, may be able to defend it. Over time individual customers typically educate a company about their individual needs, wants, and preferences—a costly process that they are reluctant to repeat with a rival (Peppers and Rodgers, 1994, 6). Thus, getting to know customers intimately creates a barrier to imitation of the leader's strategy.

Second, effective CRM can lead to increased customer satisfaction. Properly implemented, the customer-company dialogue facilitates the tailoring of products and services closely to individual needs, and the development of new products and services to meet changing needs or even anticipate future needs (Palmer, 1994). Third, using CRM techniques contributes to decreasing overall marketing expenditure. Acquiring new customers is estimated to be more expensive than keeping existing ones. Figures of between five and seven times as much have been quoted.

And, last, developing a closer relationship with customers is thought to increase customer loyalty, and loyal customers are thought to stay with the firm longer, buy more from it, and buy more often. An oft-quoted statistic is that companies can improve profitability by between 25 and 85 percent by reducing customer defections by 5 percent. While the value of loyalty is currently being debated, for some time now lodging firms have been fostering loyalty through frequent traveller programmes and CRM may be seen as the logical next step. The above arguments offered by CRM proponents suggest that CRM leads to higher profitability due to increased sales, declining customer acquisition costs, and increasing profitability of customers willing to pay a premium for "better" service.

The top row of effects leads to building relationships with customers and thus establishing customer loyalty. The bottom row lists well-accepted outcomes of data mining activities. Together those two sets of outcomes have stimulated many companies to invest in creating a database-driven CRM system. Some authors warn that substantial investments in CRM are not right for everyone. In a small or niche business, for example, it is relatively easy to keep in touch with customers' preferences.

But because of the significant increase in the amount of information that must be managed as the firm's scale and scope increase, successful CRM requires significant investments in technology, process redesign, and people. An airline or a major international hotel chain must manage substantially larger amounts of data than does a small inn to achieve a similar relationship with its customers. However, information technology (IT)—used appropriately— can help mitigate the problem. Between 1990 and today, the world has seen enormous transformations in the extent to which organizations can deploy computer power.

IT allows customer data to be collected, consolidated, manipulated, and analyzed on an unprecedented scale, and IT has been identified by many authors as one of the key success factors for CRM implementation. IT allows increased reach into new markets without high incremental entry costs, and facilitates specifically tailored customer marketing and increased responsiveness.

The role of IT in CRM efforts is so important that some writers, and many practicing managers and vendors, associate CRM with the technology that is used to support the approach. Many use the term in the highly specific sense of database marketing, where a range of demographic, lifestyle, and purchasing activities are recorded and tracked, and subsequently used as the basis of targeting differentiated products to selected customer groups. In turn, their response to each marketing contact is tracked and used to further refine the approach. However, CRM is a broader concept than just technology.

For example, CRM has been defined as "an enterprise-wide commitment to identify your named, individual customers and create a relationship between your company and these customers so long as that relationship is mutually beneficial". This definition highlights several key CRM concepts— that the company will actively seek out the right customers (and, by implication, will not target those that will not do business with them), will develop a long-term, mutually beneficial relationship with each customer by starting and maintaining a two-way dialogue, will strive to satisfy customers' needs and solve customer problems, and will support customers throughout the life cycle of their interactions with the firm.

This approach to CRM demands more than computer systems and information technology. The customer must become the focal point of the organization. All members of the organization must understand and support the shared values required for CRM, its philosophy must encompass not just marketing but the entire organization, and it must be used to manage all aspects of the customer relationship in a coordinated way. Although limited research about the effectiveness of CRM has been published to date, most observers agree that successful CRM is predicated on the ability to effectively capture exhaustive data about existing and potential customers, profile them accurately, identify their individual needs and idiosyncratic expectations, and generate actionable customer knowledge that can be distributed for ad-hoc use at each point of contact. The objective is to achieve a comprehensive view of customers, and be able to consistently anticipate and react to their needs with targeted and effective activities at every customer touch point.

CRM requires the firm to keep track of the information produced through each interaction so that it can "learn" on a continuous basis, get to know each guest better, and enrich its database of individual customer knowledge. Godin has likened CRM to "dating a customer," in that it is a long-term process that requires an investment of time, information, and resources by both parties. The result is an active, participatory, and interactive relationship between customer and supplier. Lastly, CRM is about customization, or the ability to consistently treat different customers differently. Relationships differ as they develop.

We do not treat old friends in the same way as new friends or good friends in the same way as casual acquaintances. Such consistent personalized interaction requires integration and synchronization of many organizational functions, from marketing to accounting to operations and information systems. Failure to understand the scope, essence, and magnitude of CRM is likely to result in problems, rather than its promised benefits.

THE POTENTIAL OF CRM IN THE LODGING INDUSTRY

Lodging-industry participants face an increasingly competitive market. In addition, the basis of competition is changing. Location, a key driver of business, is fixed in the short and medium term, and attracting and retaining customers based on facilities and amenities is becoming increasingly difficult as they have become increasingly standardized across competing brands. Price competition is unattractive, even more so as consumers are able to easily find and compare prices over the Internet. As a consequence consumers are increasingly displaying less brand loyalty, and CRM is becoming increasingly attractive as a way for hotel companies to differentiate themselves from their competitors.

The lodging sector is ideally suited to applying the principles of CRM. In few other industries is there such potential to build up a comprehensive and accurate picture of the client. In few other industries do customers provide the significant amount of information hotel guests divulge when making a reservation and during their hotel stay. Every interaction between the guest and the customer is an opportunity to refine knowledge about her or him and to further build a relationship.

By methodically collecting, consolidating, and analyzing both guest preferences and transactional data, hotel chains have the potential to develop a deep understanding of each customer's needs and preferences, provide substantially improved service levels, individually tailor the customer experience, and generally offer more personalized service. Providing outstanding personal service is certainly not a new concept in the hotel sector.

Companies such as Ritz-Carlton and the Savoy group historically maintained extensive manual guest-history systems recording guest preferences in an effort to better serve their best customers. However, when operated manually, such systems are expensive to maintain, are frequently inaccurate, and can only be used to track a limited number of clients at individual properties. Developments in information and communications technologies have enabled automation and efficiencies in these processes, reducing costs, increasing accuracy, and allowing comprehensive knowledge about each customer to be shared on a global basis.

As a result, many companies are turning to technology to improve customer service by implementing large-scale CRM programmes. Analysis of the lodging sector shows that, driven in most cases by pressure from the marketing function, many of the dominant hotel chains are in the process of deploying (or have already deployed) the technological infrastructure to support CRM. A recent study by Arthur Andersen and New York University found that over one-third of U.S. hotel chains had a data warehouse in 2000, with another 50 percent planning to install one in the near future.

Many chains have introduced information systems to improve the targeting of marketing and sales efforts. Such systems can help the firm to assess the value of each customer as well as their propensity to respond to various offers, and to market to them individually. As discussed earlier, while important, such initiatives do not imply that the company has adopted CRM.

In most cases, such developments focus solely on marketing objectives and lack the integration among functional areas that characterizes a CRM initiative. Only where the company reconfigures its operations to deliver a comprehensive view of the customer and to support consistent, highly personalized service at every customer touch point could it truly be regarded as CRM.

Few companies in the lodging sector appear to have progressed to such an advanced stage. Given the geographic dispersion of hotel properties and the role of brands in marketing and distribution, large-scale CRM initiatives seem most justifiable at the brand level. Implementing CRM at this level would help to increase consistency and personal service throughout the chain and at each customer touch point.

However, to achieve this, consistent and comprehensive information must be captured from all properties within the brand and then consolidated, analyzed, interpreted, and subsequently disseminated to each property in time to influence the next customer interaction. Two barriers currently prevent that from happening—a lack of standardization and IT system integration within each franchise, and the fact that at any one time there may be up to three parties holding a stake in the operations of a particular property (owner, management company, and brand).

The two issues are largely interconnected as the industry's generally reactive attitude toward IT has been exacerbated by its structural characteristics. The technical challenge is subsiding due to recent developments in technology, including the emergence of the application service provider (ASP) model.

(*Note:* When software applications are delivered using an ASP model, they are not installed on the computers at the property. Rather, they are accessed by remote users via the Web. Thus, IT resources under the ASP model are not bought but acquired as a service.)

A discussion of these technologies is beyond the scope of this article. Note, however, that, even assuming away technological challenges, we believe that the structure of the lodging industry creates severe obstacles to successful CRM. The remainder of the paper focuses on these challenges.

The Lodging Industry's Structure

Lodging is an important component of the tourism industry, providing accommodation (and associated ancillary services) to travelers while away from home. Lodging operations are diverse, ranging from small bed-and breakfast properties in rural locations to large hotels with several thousand rooms in major cities. The majority of the world's hotel properties are concentrated in Europe (55 percent) and North America (22 percent).

The exhibit also demonstrates that the average property size in North America is larger than that in Europe (56 versus 28 rooms), with chain-affiliated properties being more common in North America. Despite controlling only a minority of room stock (approximately 30 percent of total room supply) hotel chains dominate the lodging sector and tend to exert a disproportionate influence on industry operations and performance.

In addition to generally having higher occupancy and average daily rate, chain properties tend to be more profitable, delivering trading profit per room seven times more than their independent counterparts. As a result, the industry is expected to continue to consolidate, with an increasing number of mergers and acquisitions resulting in a small number of large companies dominating the marketplace. A differentiation must be made between hotel ownership, hotel branding, and hotel operations.

Historical developments with Real Estate Investment Trusts (REITs) in the United States gave rise to a situation where many owners could not operate their own hotels. Instead they must use a separate management company to oversee day-to-day operations, resulting in a split between hotel ownership and hotel operations.

The situation is further complicated by the widespread use of both franchises and marketing agreements that provide a consumer brand and require compliance with brand standards.

At any one time there may be up to three parties holding a stake in the operations of a particular property:

(1) The owner, who holds title to the assets, is responsible for mortgage payments and provides the capital for the operation;

(2) The brand, which brands the property and provides standards, distribution services, marketing, technology, and other services; and

(3) The management company, which provides management talent and operates the property on a day-to-day basis.

The exception of Wyndham International, the major brand companies own less than one-third of their branded properties, with various management companies operating the remainder on behalf of their owners.

Furthermore, within each management company the brand portfolio is quite mixed, with each company operating under a variety of competing flags in different geographical markets. The data lend support to our claim that in the U.S. lodging industry there are multiple stakeholders with, at times competing, interest in the operations of the property.

THE DATA-OWNERSHIP DILEMMA

As was discussed earlier, CRM's success is predicated on the ability to collect, analyze, and disseminate large amounts of timely and relevant information for customer-service operatives to act on to improve the experience at each point of customer contact. Thus, a CRM initiative cannot be successful without commitment among a critical mass of properties. Hotel chains cannot provide a consistently high level of personal service unless customer data can be garnered from most, if not all, of the affiliated properties, organized and synthesized in one central location, and subsequently redistributed to each property on an as-needed basis.

However, we propose that (technological constraints aside) this apparently simple theoretical proposition is difficult to realize in the lodging industry due to an inherent data-ownership conflict between the major industry stakeholders. In the following sections we present the main issues facing the brand, the management company, and the owner.

The Brand

For brands, the development of an effective CRM initiative is deemed an important competitive move as it would facilitate the development of a deep understanding of customer needs and preferences, potentially resulting in a high level of personalization, thus helping to improve service levels across the brand as a whole. As a result guests would have a strong incentive to remain loyal to the brand and patronize affiliated properties, thus increasing the value proposition for owners and operators through improvements in financial performance.

For the promised benefits of CRM to materialize, standardized information systems must be implemented throughout the franchise network to allow data to be obtained from all branded properties—a problem in the past, becoming less important as a result of recent technology improvements. Furthermore, the brand must be willing to share the customer knowledge generated by the consolidation of customer data chain-wide with the individuals that can take action based on it at each point of customer contact. Such data sharing presents the first dilemma. In some cases, the brand may be reticent to disseminate customer knowledge back to the property for fear that owners or operators might use it to poach high-value customers and divert them to competing brands within their own portfolios.

For example, imagine a management company that operates a hotel flying one flag (Brand A) in a particular market, and a competing flag (Brand B) in others. This company might be tempted to steer highvalue customers toward its Brand B hotels in markets where it does not operate Brand A hotels. Thus, Brand A is faced with a decision— either share the data it collects companywide to reap the benefits of large-scale CRM and risk the poaching of high-value customers by some of its partner management companies operating individual properties; or protect its customer knowledge from the interests of multi-flag owners and operators, thus forgoing the full benefits of CRM.

The Management Company

Management companies do not appear to have strong incentives to develop a CRM initiative for themselves. As such companies tend to operate a varied portfolio of properties, each flying different flags, on behalf of different owners. By definition a CRM initiative developed across flags is unlikely to generate brand loyalty and thus is of limited interest to most management companies. The question arises, however, as to whether management companies should actively cooperate with the collection of operational guest data by brand-level CRM initiatives. As most companies operate a varied portfolio of flags, if the management company participates in a brand-based CRM initiative, it will stand to gain only in those properties that carry that particular brand.

Conversely, participation will result in a competitive disadvantage in markets where it competes against the brand.

As a result, management companies have little incentive to support brand-level CRM initiatives by contributing data about customers that stay at its properties. In fact, by doing so, they would in effect be undermining their own operations in markets where the brand operating the CRM initiative is a competitor rather than an ally. Moreover, while the management company may not be interested in detailed customer data for branding purposes, it certainly finds value in customer data that allows it to create customer-value models and better target high-value prospects, particularly with respect to group business. Consequently, management companies have in effect an incentive to limit data disclosure and not cooperate with brand-level CRM initiatives.

The Owner

While owners, like operators, typically have many flags in their portfolio of properties, they have a different focus in terms of profitability. Many primarily view hotel ownership as a real-estate investment, and have a marginal interest in the question, "Who owns the data?" Where their properties fly the flag of a successful CRM initiative, they may have an advantage over other competing properties; where their properties fly competing flags, they may be at a disadvantage. Thus, the same dilemma facing the management company seems to affect the owners—whether to participate in brand level CRM initiatives, or to refuse to cooperate with the collection and consolidation of customer data.

The owners may also have interests that go beyond the use of the data strictly for operational purposes. Customer data may be used by the other entities (the brand and the management company) for marketing purposes and analyses that run counter to the owner's own interests (e.g., studying the feasibility of building new properties in the same geographical area).

Conclusions and Implications

In this paper we have drawn attention to what we term the "data-ownership dilemma"—the inherent conflict that various entities in the lodging industry face as they embrace CRM. We propose that the data-ownership dilemma represents a significant, yet often unrecognized, challenge to the success of CRM initiatives. As was discussed, CRM strategies appear most applicable at the brand level, but their success is dependent on the active cooperation of both the operator and the owner of each property. For CRM to succeed at the brand level, operators must supply the brand with in-depth customer data—a requirement with which operators in particular, and owners to a lesser extent, have little incentive to comply. Brands also face challenges in terms of maintaining control over the resulting customer knowledge and preventing its spread outside the brand network.

Because of this conflict, we believe that CRM in the lodging industry may never progress beyond its current, relatively limited, level of sophistication. While database-marketing techniques will continue to be used, we propose that few hotel companies will successfully implement large-scale, chain-wide, CRM initiatives. Only if significant change occurs in the structure or methods of operation of the sector are the full benefits of a CRM approach likely to be realized. In closing, we speculate as to what changes will have to occur for successful implementation of CRM initiatives. There are three possible scenarios: there will be a fundamental change in the way in which hotel brands are organized; a change in the nature of franchise agreements and management contracts; or there will be more cooperation among brands to take advantage of CRM's promised benefits. These three scenarios are further developed in the remainder of this article.

The first scenario is that the need for adoption of a CRM approach will induce changes in the ownership and management structure of the lodging sector. If CRM truly provides compelling benefits, the large brands should begin to pressure the management companies and franchisees within their network to provide the data needed for successful CRM operations. Those brands that manage a relatively large number of their own hotels will be in a good position to take advantage of these initiatives quickly, should face little resistance as a result of the data ownership dilemma, and should be able to easily reap the benefits of CRM.

Wyndham International's ByRequest initiative demonstrates that highly integrated lodging brands are moving quickly to embrace CRM. If these pioneers are successful in their effort and are able to attract and retain high-value customers, competing brands will have to follow suit and develop similar CRM capabilities. Such companies would have to resolve the data-ownership dilemma either by "integrating down" or by restricting the number of flags that the companies operating their hotels can fly. Integrating down implies that brands would move aggressively to take over the operational management of their branded properties. Such integrated companies should be able to standardize the IT infrastructure needed to support CRM, mandate the collection and consolidation of customer data, and provide each property with dynamic access to the central knowledge repository.

Since all operations would effectively be managed by the brand, there would be no conflicts of interest and no danger of high-value customers being poached, freeing the brand to take full advantage of the CRM initiative. Obviously, taking over operational control of their unit properties would be a dramatic and high-risk strategy. Thus, brands, particularly in the short term, may instead concentrate on restructuring their management and franchise agreements to minimize the barriers to success discussed earlier. Redevelopment should focus on two main areas— data collection and data use. While many franchise agreements require properties to feed its customer-folio data back to the central level, few specifically mention any other data collected about the guest.

As CRM is dependent on building up a holistic picture of the guest's needs and behaviour, this oversight may force brands to restructure contracts to force greater compliance with data needs. structured contracts could specify that all customer data generated at the property level be extracted and loaded to the brand's central data repository. Management contracts also need to be rewritten to offer protection to the brand as it disseminates customer knowledge back to the property level. Both of these measures mean that ties between brands and operators would be strengthened, which may ultimately result in further industry consolidation as owners and operators feel pressure to fly a limited number of flags. In an extreme scenario, each operator would effectively become aligned with one brand and fly only one flag.

The final potential scenario we envision is the emergence of an industry consortium that both develops and maintains the CRM infrastructure and standardizes customer-data collection and distribution. As it has happened historically with hotel e-commerce systems such as THISCo (The Hotel Industry Switching Company), HDS (Hotel Distribution Systems) and Avendra (an e-procurement marketplace), competing brands could cooperate to develop the standards and the infrastructure necessary to capture, store, organize, and distribute customer information. Such a scenario is attractive as joint development would mean that the infrastructure could be delivered and operated at a fraction of the cost of proprietary initiatives.

Thereafter, rather than being used as a basis of competition, customer data would be shared and companies would compete on the analysis, interpretation, and use of such data. For example, competing brands could use the same data to market to their chosen customer bases. Competitive advantage would come from how well they could use the data to identify, target, and build a relationship with each individual. We believe the latter scenario to be the least likely, even though it may optimize industry-wide performance. The likelihood of an industry consortium developing and managing customer information for the benefit of the industry as a whole is small, as the industry's belief in the proprietary value of customer data, the industry's structure, privacy issues, as well as a culture that precludes trust in this domain makes the cooperation necessary unlikely. We see a change in contractual agreements and in industry structure as far more probable. In any case, given the potential proposed for lodging-industry companies, careful consideration must be given to the data-ownership dilemma to avoid failure.

As part of our research, we investigated the CRM initiatives of large hotel chains. One such chain, Wyndham International, has made CRM a cornerstone of its brand strategy. We briefly describe the key characteristics of Wyndham's CRM approach to aid the reader in understanding the principal characteristics of large-scale CRM initiatives. Wyndham International is one of the five largest U.S.–based hotel chains, with a portfolio of over 160 branded properties. After converting from paired-share REIT status to a C corporation in 1999, Wyndham revised its corporate strategy in an effort to become a "world-class branded hotel operating company." Wyndham's differentiation strategy is nicely captured in the words of Andrew Jordan, Wyndham's senior vice president of marketing: "We said, okay, we are going to reinvent the Wyndham brand. We are going to say: We are all about personalized service.

We are going to say: We are the brand who really recognizes that guests are individuals, we know you have specific needs, quirks—you tell us about them one time and we are going to remember them." The cornerstone of Wyndham's strategy is its membership-based CRM initiative: Wyndham ByRequest. When a guest joins ByRequest, he or she completes a comprehensive profile including general and contact information, room preferences (e.g., room location, needed extra items, newspaper), credit card and express check-in/check-out preferences, airline frequent-flyer preferences, personal interests (e.g., activities, music, readings, spectator sports), and complimentary beverages and snacks (e.g., preferred wine, soft drinks, juice, snacks). The above information is compiled at Wyndham's headquarters and a pledge is made to the guest that, irrespective of which property in the Wyndham chain the guest travels to in the future, he or she can expect a consistent level of personalized service.

This includes a room that is located where desired and fitted with the required amenities, a welcome snack and drink that's of the guest's liking, and information that suits the traveler's interests (e.g., reading material, information about shows or sporting events). Key to the initiative's success is the realization that, while important, the technology underlying Wyndham ByRequest—including the website, the preferences databases, and integrated operational systems (e.g., PMS)—does not in and of itself deliver the ByRequest promise. As a result, Wyndham has designated staff members to support ByRequest and created a property-level position—the Wyndham ByRequest manager—who has responsibility over property-level execution, and Wyndham has developed integrated processes for delivering the ByRequest promise.

Overview

Spas are becoming such a significant component of the service menu for resorts and full service hotels that their absence, especially in amenity-rich resort environments, is glaringly obvious. Within the leisure industries in 2003, revenues related to spas ranked number four behind golf fees and dues ($19.7 million), cruise line revenues ($14.7 million), and health club revenues ($14.1 million). At $11.2 million, spa revenues outpaced amusement park revenues ($10.3 million), box office receipts ($9.5 million), and vacation ownership sales ($5.5 million). In this, we first examine trends that support a sea change in North Americans' attitude toward spa use. After evaluating spa demand demographics, we discuss the types of spas currently popular in the industry, development and operational considerations, the components of a spa experience, compensation issues, and trends in the spa industry.

SPA Demand

According to the International SPA Association research, between 2002 and 2003, 11 percent of the national population over the age of 16 made one or more spa visits. This statistic shows that one in ten Americans visited a spa during that period. Additionally, of these, 41 percent were visiting spas for the first time, indicating a larger population embracing spa usage. Age demographics show that 14 percent of clients are between the ages of 16 and 24, and over 50 percent are in the 25 to 44 age bracket.

An emerging national statistic is the number of male visits to spas. Twenty-three percent of spa visits and 29 percent of spa goers were men in 2003, trending toward special gender-oriented treatments and male-only spas being opened worldwide. Spa selection criteria are determined by a number of factors. An established and known environment—for instance, as a part of an established resort, club, or destination spa— often influences the decision, as does atmosphere, quality of treatment, and friendliness of staff. Additionally, among spa goers, nine out of ten respondents report they would return for a similar experience.

Most spa customers believe they received good value for their spa dollar. On a 10-point scale, services were given an average of 8 for value, with massage generating 8.8 on the value-for-service scale. Spa services demonstrated the highest and heaviest demand on weekends, followed by appointments after work on weekdays. Gender demographics also play a role in spa demand, as men are more likely to go for regular weekly visits after business hours or while traveling on business. Women, however, often visit spas during regular business hours. The International Hotel Resort Spa Association (IHRSA) reports that branded resort spas such as Canyon Ranch are opening in the day spa market, adding new competitive pressure on the independents. Nontraditional players are also adding product supply.

For example, corporations are creating in-house spa environments, hospitals are adding wellness as part of their repertoire, and medi-spas, with a primary focus on cosmetic surgery, are adding spa business as an additional profit centre. Health clubs are also trying to capture a piece of the pie by adding spa practices. The rationale in this market is that time-crunched patrons can benefit from the one-stop-shopping approach to fitness and wellness, but the health club operator also uses the spa as an enticement to join the fitness centre. As the day and destination spa markets become saturated, it will become imperative for survival that each operator differentiate from the competition.

The necessity for market segmentation to ensure clear communication with consumers will be a key to success in the maturing spa market. Another component of success will be a branding strategy that the consumer can immediately identify with respect to spa performance and the consumer's personal comfort level.

Health Issues and SPA Demand

Increasingly, spa goers are looking to create prolonged wellness that integrates and renews body, mind, and spirit. To that end, Eastern and Western lifestyle issues related to medicine, philosophy, and spirituality are becoming a mainstay of many spa/wellness experiences. To best deliver this, the wellness spa (located at day, destination, or resort environments) supports guest needs by creating an experience, not just a series of treatments. All the guest amenities, facilities, treatments, and programmes must be seamlessly integrated into a personally tailored guest experience. These experiences should be targeted toward couples, parents with children, and teenagers. In the early 1990s, spas were considered a natural outgrowth of fitness facilities and focused primarily on treatments related to body wellness.

As market sophistication evolved, the body-mind connection attracted consumer focus. In the beginning of the twentyfirst century, spas and marketers are overtly addressing body, mind, and spirit connections in order to respond to emerging market sensibilities.

Among the components one might find in a modern spa are services related to:

- Complementary and alternative medicine in mainstream lifestyles.

- Traditional Western medical and Eastern lifestyle/ wellness practices.
- A proactive approach to overall health and the quality of one's life.
- Action spas are attracting a greater percentage of men who are looking for a way to unwind and keep active. Because of this trend, an aggressive array of activities— including cardio-circuit courses, squash, racketball and tennis, free and fixed weights, jogging, and bike paths, hikes, and water spots—is still a basic spa/wellness requirement.
- As part of the wellness experience, medical affiliations are sometimes available to provide information and to check blood pressure, heart conditions, bone density, and so on.
- Exceptional food can be tailored to virtually any dietary restriction or request.
- When examining which body treatments to include, note that salt glows and exfoliant treatments are approximately four times more popular than any other body treatment. These items are a mainstay in successful spa services.
- Guests must be able to upgrade their experience with add-ons such as eye-firming therapies and mineral-enhanced hydrotherapy soaks. Further, it is important to sell services in several time blocks so guests can select services that fit their schedule and financial budget.
- Educational programmes at many levels include classes and clinics. These programmes personally empower the guest, expand the wellness center's demand base, and encourage repeat visits. Health and wellness issues encompass cardiovascular health, holistic childrearing, the integration of Eastern and Western medical practices, indigenous spiritual practices, aging, intimacy, transition/death, vitality,

strength training, cooking programmes (macrobiotic, vegan, vegetarian, indigenous), women's issues, and so on. Traditionally, educational programmes at spas have focused primarily on personal health issues.

- Mind-body techniques may include spiritual and cultural instruction. Examples include tai chi, visualization, progressive muscle relaxation and biofeedback, labyrinth walking, meditating and chanting, sweat lodges, and storytelling.
- Extensive yoga programmes should include Hatha yoga for body control, Ashtanga yoga for cardio workout, Iyengar yoga for balance and alignment, and Kundalini yoga for breath work.
- Comprehensive touch/alternative manual therapies including chiropractic treatment and deep tissue massage (rolfing, myofascial release, nueromuscular massage, acupressure/ shiatsu, watsu, Trager massage, etc.) are a necessary component of any wellness clinic. This modality is an extension of the basic massage offered at all spas and wellness/healing centers. Practitioners who provide manual therapies should be cross-trained in the areas of subtle energy work such as reiki, chakra balancing, and chi gung. Offering alternative touch/energy therapy as a component of traditional massage has the potential to accelerate market acceptance.
- Ayurvedic treatments are popular and provide an additional link between the East-meets-West philosophy showcased in many day spas. Elements of ayurvedic treatments can be incorporated into most touch therapies.

Spas and the Lodging Industry

As far back as 1993, a well-known study by David Eisenberg revealed that one-third of all patients had visited a practitioner of alternative health care in the past year, at a cost of $13.7 billion. This indicated to the medical community that the significant out-of-pocket expenses implied not only lost revenues to traditional (allopathic) doctors but also a broad dissatisfaction with mainstream medicine. A great number of people were taking the issues of health and well-being into their own control, thus setting the stage for the popularity of proactive wellness programmes.

In 1997, Eisenberg updated his study. He estimated the total number of visits to alternative medical providers at 600 million, representing an expenditure of over $27.1 billion. The number of visits to alternative care physicians in 1997 was greater than the total number of visits to traditional primary care physicians in the same year.

The increasing popularity of alternative wellness modalities, the aging of the population, and the strength of the economy are all factors that support the growth of this trend. As of this writing, it appears to continue to grow. The use of at least 1 of 16 (alternative) therapies during the previous year increased from 33.8 percent in 1990 to 42.1 percent in 1997. The fastest-growing therapies were herbal medicine, message, megavitamins, self help groups, folk remedies, energy healing, and homeopathy.

The probability of users visiting an alternative medicine practitioner increased from 36.3 percent to 46.3 percent. In both 1990 and 1997, alternative therapies were used most frequently for chronic conditions, especially back problems, anxiety, depression, and headaches. In general, it can be concluded that alternative medicine expenditure increased substantially between 1990 and 1997, and this can be attributed primarily to an increase in the proportion of the population seeking alternative therapies rather than increased visits per patient.

SPA Classification

Spa development and its attendant popularity have deep historical roots and vast potential for the hospitality industry. The term spa was once reserved for European destination resorts where guests went to "take the waters" and restore a healthy and balanced life. However, the term now is used to describe many types of facilities and amenities in the U.S. lodging industry. At one end of the spa spectrum are dedicated destination resort spas aimed primarily at those seeking a specialized combination regime of health, fitness, and pampering. Modalities and treatments include massages, unique treatments, custom dietary plans, lectures, and adventures that can include, but are not limited to, an array of activities ranging from nonsurgical facelifts to helicopter skiing.

Destination resorts, such as Miraval's Life-in-Balance and Canyon Ranch, with locations in the Berkshires in Massachusetts and the Arizona desert, draw demand because of their facilities and reputation. The primary reason for going to a destination resort spa is to enjoy the spa itself and its related activities. The destination itself is a demand generator. Closely related to a destination resort spa is the amenity spa.

The primary difference between an amenity spa and a destination spa is the scope and depth of spa services. Amenity spas, while sometimes quite extensive, support the resort environment, whereas destination spas are the focus of the resort environment. In situations where a full-service, high-end hotel is located in an urban environment and has a significantly large spa component, the spa can operate as both an amenity spa (to the hotel) and a day spa (to the local community).

Later in this chapter, we study the case of the Westin Los Angeles Century City's 35,000-square-foot Spa Mystique. This spa supports the needs of the hotel's convention and individual travelers while experiencing heavy local day spa use. Middle-market hotel properties now feel obliged to add a spa as an amenity; however, due to capital and real estate restraints, often they cannot provide a full-service location. As a result, this sector has seen an explosion in poorly conceived and executed spa additions that provide the owner the opportunity to add "...and spa" at the end of the business name. These are often no more than the result of subcontracting a massage therapist and converting the guest room closest to the swimming pool into an exercise room.

These spas seldom surprise and delight their guests and often reflect poorly on the spa industry overall. Fortunately, the sophistication of the industry is making it harder and harder for the "...and spas" to succeed. As the spa industry matures, certain development trends are emerging. In 2005, the spa industry was considered the fastest-growing segment of the travel, hospitality, and leisure market, showing 26 percent growth from 2002 to 2004. Spas are no longer considered a niche industry but rather an entity unto themselves.

The spa industry is made up of the following segments, each with its own characteristics and operational opportunities:

- Destination spas
- Resort hotel spas
- Day spas
- Medical spas
- Mineral springs
- Club spas

Destination Spas

A destination spa is one whose sole purpose is to provide programmes and facilities that support lifestyle improvements and enhance guest health. The services offered are professionally administered and include fitness, education, and lectures on lifestyle, nutrition, and disease prevention. Because of their healthful orientation, destination spas often provide programmes that support postoperative conditions, address various addictions, and provide tools to cope with serious, prolonged illness. The destination spa industry constitutes only 1.6 percent of the total spa industry, per the International Spa Association's Industry Study (Thacker, 2004). However, the growth in the development and use of destination spas reflects the market's trend toward wellness and health as a major component in spa menus.

Resort Spas/Amenity Spas

Resort spas are located on the grounds of vacation resorts where treatments for mind, body, and spirit are offered to complement other resort activities such as golf, tennis, horseback riding, skiing, and water sports. Healthful spa cuisine is on the menu as an option, complementing traditional offerings. In the evenings, guests can enjoy resort pastimes like dancing and live entertainment. Children's programmes are also offered.

According to the ISPA Spa Industry Study, the resort spa represents 14 percent of spa locations in North America but accounts for almost 41 percent of the total industry revenue, 27 percent of all spa visits, and 26 percent of the industry's employees. A luxury resort spa has the ambience of a secluded retreat on the grounds of a first-class resort. Set in beautiful surroundings, these resorts commonly have world-class golf courses and other excellent recreational facilities. Gourmet dining and exceptional spa therapies are not only expected but demanded.

Day Spas

Day spas are designed to provide a healing, beautifying, or pampering experience in a short period. Guests may book individual treatments that last as little as an hour or a package of treatments that take up to a whole day. Found throughout North America, day spas are freestanding or located in health clubs, hotels, and department stores. The day spa industry constitutes 72.2 percent of the total industry revenues, per the International Spa Association's 2004 Spa Industry Study.

The large percentage of day spas and their growth pattern reflect spa goers' time crunch. Day spas can be owner-operated or chain affiliated. Preliminary data from ISPA's 2004 survey show that industry growth is still robust. As of midyear 2004, there was a total of 12,000 spas nationally, of which 8,700 were day spas. These numbers reflect 25 percent growth in the industry in general and 20 percent growth exclusively in this market. The total number of day spa visits in 2003 was 81.2

million. However, only 13 percent of the general population had used a spa in the prior three-year period, indicating that the industry still has large growth potential.

Medical Spas

Medical treatments in various spa environments represent a significant trend in the scope, depth, and inclusiveness of numerous spas. Medical spa treatments can range from elective, reconstructive surgery to noninvasive Eastern modalities incorporating elements of Eastern philosophy that draw on the body-mind-spirit connection to create positive, measurable changes in the client/patient.

Slightly over half (51 percent) of the medical spas in North America have a partnership with a medical doctor, and 26 percent have a doctor on staff. The remaining configurations include being located in a doctor's office or having licensed staff members. Botox and microdermabrasion are the two most popular treatments, followed by chemical peels and laser hair removal. In North America, allopathic or Western medical procedures found in medical spas often incorporate Eastern-based treatments.

Day, destination, and resort/amenity spas are adding medical treatments to their spa menus. Part of this trend is directly attributed to market demand, and part is attributed to health insurance plans that reimburse for some procedures. According to the ISPA 2004 survey, medical spas are the fastest-growing spa segment with respect to number of locations. The average annual growth in medical spas by location since 1999 is approximately 45 percent.

Cumulative growth from 1999 to 2004 is 205 percent and from 2002 to 2004, 109 percent. Medical spas generated an estimated 1,900,000 visits in 2003, representing 1.39 percent of the total spa visits. However, this percentage of visits accounts for approximately 2.1 percent of the total industry revenues, reflecting the lucrative nature of this segment of the industry.

Mineral Springs Spas

Many mineral springs spas are considered to be the original spa prototype, where guests go to "take the waters." Mineral springs spas, by definition, are located at naturally occurring mineral springs, and by number of locations represent 2.8 percent of the total spa industry, or 1.3 percent of the total industry revenues, making this one of the more modest income producing segments of the spa industry.

The popularity of mineral springs spas is reflected in a cumulative growth from 1999 to 2004 of 143 percent. Growth from 2002 to 2004 represents only 15 percent, implying that the number of sites available directly affects the growth in this segment.

Club Spas

Club spas lack a lodging component, and their primary objective is to facilitate daily fitness activities. Many club spas' services complement the primary fitness component of the club by offering sports massage (deep tissue), chiropractic services, physiotherapy, and related treatments that address issues of pain management, flexibility, and mobility. By location, club spas represent 5.8 percent of the total spa industry in North America and account for approximately 3.7 percent of the industry's revenues. Growth in the club spa portion of the spa industry is the lowest of all spa segments. Between 2002 and 2004, cumulative club spa growth was only 3 percent.

SPA OPERATIONS

Spas as an Operating Department Historically, spa operations were treated by management similarly to other revenue departments, like catering and restaurants. These departments were simply perceived as an amenity needed to attract guests to the hotel. As long as the department broke even, or didn't lose too much money, their ability to increase occupancy was deemed sufficient justification for their existence. However, in the late 1990s, hotel spas followed the path of other operating departments and transformed from support facilities to profit centers. This trend is strong and continues today. In 1999, PKF Consulting identified only 30 hotels in the United States, thousands that report data to the PKF, extensive spa facilities and analyzed the financial performance of those properties and their spa departments. Dedicated destination spa resorts were not included in the analysis due to an insufficient sample. While spas were a relatively small source of revenues for the sample properties, spa revenues grew at a relatively strong pace. In 1999, spa revenues for the subject sample represented just 3.3 percent of total sales.

However, from 1998 to 1999, spa revenues grew 16.6 percent. This compares to revenue growth rates of 5.2 percent for rooms, 12.2 percent for food, and 3.2 percent for telecommunications, and a 0.3 percent decline in revenues for the beverage department. During 1999, the spa departments in the sample of hotels averaged a departmental profit margin of 30.7 percent. However, spa department profits did grow a strong 51.3 percent from 1998 to 1999. Spas mirror and enhance trends in the lodging industry. Drawing heavily from residential design and the use of technology, hotel designers and operators create a spa experience that:

- Complements the lodging experience
- Drives occupancy levels
- Enhances average daily rate
- Provides a distinctive marketing advantage North American spas are rapidly becoming more segmented, pursuing market niches well outside the traditional ladies-who-lunch demographic.

Adventure spas, fitness spas, children spas, family spas, and even pet spas are part of a new generation of spa facilities, spa programmes—and, most importantly, spa aficionados. Spas now attract a much wider demographic that includes men, women, couples, children, teenagers, and families. Since the early part of the twenty-first century, spas have been redirecting their menus to include stress relief and results oriented therapies. By focusing on the social benefits of hanging out in a safe, relaxing place, they not only address current market needs but also support the development of spa programmes that can be incorporated into virtually any leisure-oriented environment or level of lodging. In particular, destination spas and full-service resorts provide platforms that have both the infrastructure and the economies of scale to support cutting-edge spa treatments, sometimes also referred to as spa modalities.

Spas are no longer solely about frivolous self-indulgence and luxurious pampering. They are being reevaluated and repackaged with a broader emphasis on self-care, stress relief, emotional balancing, and preventative (as opposed to reactive) wellness modalities. This trend is being embraced by aging baby boomers as an adjunct to traditional health care. Because of this trend in health care, hotels and resorts have acknowledged and embraced the need for full-service spas as part of their amenities and facilities. The inclusion of a well-integrated spa can provide additional (and lucrative) sales and marketing opportunities.

Conversely, the exclusion of a spa facility may disqualify a property from consideration. Ironically, many hotel guests may dismiss a property out of hand for lacking a spa not because they require the services of a spa but rather because its absence may imply other areas of the hotel are also deficient in meeting current market expectations. Is it logical, then, that all full-service hotels and resorts without a spa should, without hesitation, incorporate one into their property? Numerous factors must be considered in developing or repositioning a spa, especially in chain environments where the lodging brand is already established.

Because spas are capital- and labour-intensive, they must materially enhance the property's revenue stream to be considered viable. In addition to creating spa revenue, a spa facility also must extend length of stay, drive room rates, enhance shoulder and low-season demand, augment food and beverage revenues, and capture new market segments.

Successful spa operations start with a standardized level of procedures and a prioritized sensitivity to guest needs. As it is for all departments in a lodging environment (or business models in the freestanding day and medical spa world), profitability is essential. Especially in a spa environment, a dynamic balance is essential to meet the fiscal requirements of the owners and the physical needs of the guest. A savvy spa manager continually monitors the spa and hotel operations to ensure that everything possible is being done to enhance the synergy of the two entities. Constant monitoring also provides an early warning system to the spa operator if revenues are falling or if expenses are not in line with anticipated revenues or budgeted amounts. Spotting these trends early enables the manager to take efficient, proactive steps to ensure that positive trends are enhanced and negative ones controlled.

Constant monitoring sets a standard of operations, which is an excellent way to train and motivate employees. It also puts employees on notice that the spa is a well-run business with extensive attention to detail, which should discourage any actions that might not be in the best interest of the spa's reputation and profitability.

Customer Service Training

A spa's reputation is easily made or destroyed by its level of customer service. Guests can forgive an occasional shortcoming if the level of service is exceptional. For this reason, it is essential that all spas have an integrated quality management programme that provides ongoing training to assist its employees in addressing customers' expectations. Customer service training (CST) helps ensure that guests' expectations are exceeded. In a spa environment, expectations are usually very high, and a trusting bond can be quickly established if the spa employees are sensitive to guest needs. The guest's arrival sequence, starting at the front desk, initiates the spa ritual that brings the spa guest to a place of trust, relaxation, and rejuvenation.

CST is proactive and provides employees with the tools they need to meet or exceed guest expectations. Guest CST is a never-ending, all-inclusive process that bridges textbook training scenarios with operational realities. The traditionally high turnover of spa employees in the hospitality industry requires that CST be introduced as a part of the orientation process and reinforced regularly. Nonproductive training time (time that does not directly produce revenue for the spa) is actually a minor expense when compared to the expenses related to employee turnover, poor service, dissatisfied customers, and, ultimately, loss of business and reputation. Budgets must include CST as a nonoptional employee expense. For long-term success, CST is vital when margins are tight, business is slow, and turnover is high.

There is a strong correlation between high employee turnover and low CST. Employees should know that the training programme is an investment in them. CST gives the employee the means to understand what is expected of them as a representative of the establishment and identifies what guests expect from their visit. Seeing the process from the guest's point of view helps employees meet or exceed expectations.

This minimizes the need to provide discounts or compensation in cases of service delivery problems. Discounting or "comping" goods and services is a knee-jerk response to poor service and should be reserved for the last effort in service recovery; CST should stress this. An inclusive training programme is the engine behind stellar customer service and guest loyalty. CST should be seamless; while it predominately addresses the needs of the guest, the programme also includes instruction on profitability and yield management, thus addressing the needs of the owner as well.

In order to meet or exceed profitability goals, customer service must be delivered in a fiscally responsible manner. Employees must understand customer service in the operational context of the property in which they are employed. Minimizing the expense of a CST programme starts with the proper selection of employees. While there is no steadfast guarantee that a potential employee will work out over the long haul, first impressions, prior work experience, references, and, above all, attitude and enthusiasm are indications of whether or not it is appropriate to hire and invest the time and money in an applicant.

Management's expectations of guest service delivery should be clearly articulated and integrated into the corporate culture and reinforced daily at all levels and in all departments. Employees, no matter what their responsibility, position, or tenure, must be treated with the same level of respect and dignity that management requires for their guests. Reinforcing the tenets of customer service within the corporate culture provides the employee with the tools to do the right thing—that is, to ask, "What do I need to do to make a spa guest happy? How do I exceed their expectations?" Sometimes the little details reap the greatest rewards. Employee empowerment is a key component in CST. As an employee's experience and skill base develops (and as management becomes comfortable with an employee's performance), levels of empowerment should be increased proportionately. Empowerment is a vote of confidence in an employee and a way to quickly resolve problems as they arise.

This situation is said by spa managers to increase job satisfaction, and the employee's ownership of his or her position. CST also requires a strong foundation in the technical skills of how a department runs. Routine procedures, appropriate lines of oral and written communication, and what is expected of each employee in the normal course of his or her shift help minimize problems. When problems do occur, a strong foundation in technical skills makes it easier for the employee to create alternative solutions for the guest. Training draws on employees' EQ (emotional quotient) as well as their IQ (intelligence quotient). CST requires that employees draw on their ability to empathize with the guest. This starts by training employees to suspend judgment of a situation, become attentive listeners, and know the right questions to ask. This allows them to understand what the actual problem is. Training employees in this type of customer service delivery assists them in focusing on the salient issues and creating ways to address them. Because CST is ongoing, employees can benefit from their peers' experiences.

Vehicles to exchange this type of information can be as informal as role-playing and round-table discussions, or as structured as an employee newsletter. Incentives, acknowledgments, and rewards for excellent customer service delivery are an integral part of the training programme. Successful CST supports a skilled and unified staff, which translates into profitable operations. CST is an investment in property that owners can't afford not to make.

Provide Value, Create

Value Spa aficionados are savvy. They are looking to be indulged, pampered, and nurtured, not fleeced. Setting price points with market sensitivity can create tremendous customer loyalty. Because spas are no longer a one-time indulgence but rather a lifestyle choice, it is important to price services competitively and provide incentives for customers to return regularly. Numerous variables are involved in the development and operation of a spa as part of a hotel or resort. Doing one's homework is essential to success.

When a spa is developed or repositioned correctly, it can be a lucrative and rewarding experience. When it is not developed correctly, it can be a financial liability that haunts the spa director and jeopardizes the hotel's market position. If spas and their programming are not an integrated part of the hotel's future development, the property may lose a significant competitive opportunity. Spa-less hotels or poorly run properties have an inherent competitive market disadvantage. Not only do they find it more difficult to penetrate the market but they also often lose market share.

Resort Spas

The ratio of guest rooms to treatment rooms is based on many factors, including the anticipated return on investment to the owners, the topography of the site, the scope and theme of the spa, and the competition. In a destination resort, where the reason for the spa facilities is the reason for the trip, there should be an average of 1 treatment room for every 4 to 5 guest rooms. At the other end of the spectrum, such as a casino hotel, the spa is definitely an amenity, and 1 treatment room should be built for every 50 to 100 guest rooms. The spas at lower-end hotel properties normally are limited in scope and are often between 3,000 and 6,000 square feet, whereas luxury spas at full-service, high-end resorts average between 10,000 and 35,000 square feet.

These ranges vary based on each hotel's specific circumstances, including seasonality, accessibility, meeting space, fill patterns, and local demand. Each market and each lodging product must be individually evaluated to assess the appropriate ratio of treatment rooms to guest rooms. Another matrix that measures the viability of a resort or hotel spa is the cost to build the facility. Once again, a number of factors support various outcomes in this process, including the amount of available land, the finishes of the spa, the finishes of the hotel (these should be compatible), and the need to develop a spa either vertically or horizontally.

Vertical spas are most often built in environments where land is scarce or the allocated footprint for the spa is too small for one floor. Vertical construction always raises the price per square foot, as load distribution, drainage, and the weight of equipment and water must be factored into the construction design and budget. The cost to construct a resort or destination spa can range from as low as $200 per square foot to over $450 per square foot. High land-value areas and plumbing-rich design schemes will send cost dramatically above this range.

Overview most spas dictates how the space is allocated and where the income is generated. Spas should aim to have at least 50 percent of their total space—their prime real estate—produce direct revenue. Secondary real estate is the support and public areas necessary for atmosphere and supporting functions that assist in delivering the spa services. Secondary spa real estate includes areas where people can prepare for or relax from their spa treatments. These secondary areas are an important component in the spa development plan, as they allow guests to prolong their experience, which enhances the perceived value. If guests are hurried from their massage or facial out of the spa and back onto the street, the magic that is created can be abruptly snapped and the overall spa experience is compromised.

Conversely, if a guest is allowed to soak and relax for hours after a body wrap is completed, emotionally speaking, the cost of the body wrap is amortized over the entire spa experience and not just for the time the client was enjoying the body wrap in the spa's prime real estate. Combination rooms account for about 36 percent of North American spa spaces, but because of the various treatments offered in them, a revenue percentage generated from these spaces is hard to predict.

Combination spaces allow the spa to address surges in demand for specific treatments and at the same time be flexible and respond to global market changes. Massage rooms account for approximately 27 percent of the total space in North American spas but 47 percent of the spa revenue. Given these factors, an operator would need a compelling reason to not include massage on the spa menu. Facial treatment areas reflect 19 percent of the total spa space and result in about 33 percent of the spa's overall revenue.

Wet rooms, often the most underutilized portions of the spa, account for 7 percent of the space and revenue. Because many spa modalities involve water therapies, many spa developers and owners believe that wet rooms are essential, even if they seem underutilized. Because wet rooms are one of the most expensive components of a spa, it is essential that they be utilized to their fullest extent. Packaging wet room treatments with other spa services is one way to better utilize the space and create value for the spa.

SPA TRENDS

On-Site Industry Trends Anti-aging treatments and products are driving much of spa menu and retail development. This calls for devoting a treatment room to outpatient medical procedures. Programming and spa menu items include sun damage treatments, chemical peels for skin renewal, and other rejuvenation techniques that build on repeat procedures. Commensurately, spas are developing retail product lines that can take the spa experience home and continue the wellness regime. Gift card sales are driving new users to spas. In the friends and family sector as well as the corporate gift-giving world, day spa certificates are creating demand that is not directly user driven. Third-party purchasing brings to spas clients who may not normally have chosen the location or treatment, creating a large but undefinable market demand.

Regional specialties that relate to indigenous and climatic influences continue to create unique spa experiences based on site-specific supply. This has excellent leverage potential for spa operators working to differentiate their product matrices in densely operated areas.

It is important to position services for stress relief, especially to the male business traveler. Spa programming that requires a limited amount of special equipment and minimal changes to a property's infrastructure can do this.

Impulse appointments

"Life is uncertain, but I want a massage (reflexology appointment, yoga class, etc.) now!" This trend may result in developing adjunct programmes for oncall staff resources. The as-needed portion of the programme limits a hotel's payroll burden and other related fixed costs. Of course, this implies existing core programmes and facilities where these programmes can be developed and supported.

Shift in perspective

Self-indulgence, pampering, and luxury are being reevaluated and repackaged with a new, broader emphasis on self-care, stress relief, and emotional balancing. This is reflected in spa programming, the menu of services, food and beverage outlets, and spa-related retail. The retail positioning and spa programming components represent huge untapped revenue opportunities.

Changes in demographic use profile

Historically, the greatest segment of spa goers was women between the ages of 35 and 55. More couples and families are expected to visit the spa together as an alternative social/ recreational activity. This trend has the potential to extend business-related stays, fill business hotels on the weekend, and create demand for destinations. It is important to understand this trend when evaluating ways to increase market penetration in a down market.

Medical affiliations

For some markets, an affiliation with a medical centre or group in the area can be established to provide treatments such as acupuncture, nutritional assessment, laser therapies (hair removal and wrinkle reduction), Botox injections, collagen treatments, chemical peels, laser resurfacing, body contouring, microderm abrasion, and vascular procedures. When creating these types of relationships, it is essential that spa owners thoroughly investigate the legal disclosure and liability implications of being an affiliated medical service provider.

Green environments

A spa can be ecologically sensitive by incorporating environmentally friendly features into the operation. By proactively supporting programmes and products that are earth friendly, the spa does something good for the environment, provides a service to the community, and creates a competitive advantage and a unique selling point that may provide significant returns, especially in a highly competitive market. _ Global Industry Trends Trends in day, destination, and amenity spas influence each other. According to Susan Ellis (2004), president of Spa Finder, a spa marketing company, after the rise of the medical spa and broadening spa participation by men and teens, spa use is expected to become more popular in 2005 and beyond. Spa Finder's trends to watch for are abstracted:

- Those personal elements that make the spa experience special will find their way into the design of personal living spaces in private homes.
- Private, gated living communities will develop around central spa facilities, much like golf and fly-in communities.
- Some spas will compete on the far outer reaches of luxury, with ever-increasing rare and proprietary products and services.
- Spas will make house calls. Legitimate spas will offer out-call services where spa technicians travel with appropriate equipment and personnel to a client's home, office, or hotel room.
- Destination spas and resorts will develop market segments focused on personal goals—everything from spiritual awareness to sexual health to detoxification.
- The spa travel segment will grow, with more clientele booking through online portals.
- Medical spas will continue to be popular and will add alternative therapies and couple traditional medical treatment with spa luxury and innovation.
- Day spas will not grow their exotic menus much more but rather focus on the traditional; destination/resort spas will be the businesses that experiment with more exotic services and products.
- Specialized cuisine developed for spa guest consumption will find its way into mainstream grocery/specialty food offerings. Restaurants may also add lines of healthy spa cuisine to their menus.
- Eco spas—those designed and operated around green principles of management— will become a growing segment of the industry.

The foregoing discussion and explanation of the service and amenity potential of spas of varying types strongly suggests that they will continue to maintain a position of importance in the inventory of hotel services. Even the most modest of spa offerings can enhance a hotel guest's lodging experience. Someday basic spa services may be arranged for at even moderately priced lodging properties.

Chapter 3

Selecting and Attracting the Right Customers

Maximizing long-term profitability comes from maximizing customer equity—firms must maximize the lifetime value of the customer, including revenues, referrals as well as costs of serving the customer. Customer acquisition and retention efforts must be guided by the worth of the customer to the hotel.

Maytag provides premium service to its premium customers—those who purchase the Neptune line of laundry machines. Neptune customers get a dedicated staff, a separate toll-free number and fast response on service calls. This is an example of the common business practice where firms allocate resources by the profitability and value of the customer. They utilize the opportunity in directly interacting with individual customers to determine customer profitability and allocate assets accordingly. And what are the benefits of the practice of differentiating among your customers?

Broadly referring to the practice as CRM can sometimes defeat its purpose by losing sight of the basic meaning of the term: managing customer relationships. Managing customer relationships would mean actively planning, organizing, directing, and controlling a firm's business relationships with its customers. The term might be "new" in its current usage, but the business practice of managing relationships with customers is certainly not new. What has prompted the increased attention to CRM is new technology: how well firms can practice CRM has been advanced by information technology in the new economy.

Technology brings with it the risk of missing the benefits of huge investment costs if used inappropriately, however. The benefits can seem so attractive that the costs are rationalized until the technology fails to deliver. The American Customer Satisfaction Index, a measure of customer attitudes toward about 200 companies from over 30 different industries, has actually shown a decline, while at the same time CRM technology investments had grown about five times. When used with a fundamental understanding of CRM's purpose, the benefits of CRM technology enabling the business practice of managing customer relationships are clearly powerful. Siebel, Peoplesoft, Oracle, and other CRM technologies are really customer information management or customer knowledge management systems. These systems gather data and convert it to knowledge that will help firms in their customer relationship management activities.

The most significant contribution of CRM technology to the practice of business is not the technology itself, of course. It is in what the technology does to the practice of managing customer relationships. Because technology has now made it easy to do all the tasks of gathering and analyzing customer information, firms have been able to discover and realize the incredible benefits in proactively managing customer relationships. For example, Continental Airlines' customer information system allows its staff to mine data on passenger profitability and is also able to suggest remedies and perks for special requests or complaining customers.

Customer benefits from relationships with firms have been conceptualized under three categories: social, psychological, and customization benefits, in a two-part study using interviews and surveys. Financial services such as brokerage and banking are heavy users of CRM technology. Deregulation and information technology have effectively blurred the boundaries between those two once-different financial institutions. They have had a heavy reliance on information because these are primarily knowledge businesses. "Signature"-level customers at Charles Schwab wait no longer than fifteen seconds to reach a customer service person, whereas other customers can wait ten minutes or more. Some banks have coded their customers so that customer service reps can decide on rates and fees depending on the customer's profitability code.

Centura Banks rates its customers on a profitability scale of 1 to 5. The most profitable customers get service calls from staff and an annual call from the CEO. Attrition rate at the bank is down 50 percent in four years, and—more interesting—the percentage of unprofitable customers has gone down from 27 percent to 21 percent. The hospitality industry was able to slash 50 percent of its promotion programmes and increase response rates by 20 percent with a good database of response behaviour from its mailing list.

CRM systems have provided firms with the data they need to determine the revenues and costs to serve at the individual customer level, allowing firms to prioritize their allocations of value-creating assets and resources to the more profitable customers. According to AMR research, the CRM market grew from $200 milllion to $1.1 billion between 1994 and 1997, and is expected to reach as much as $16 billion—an indication of how much firms want this technology to manage customer relationships. A firm's knowledge about its customers has allowed it to adjust customer value based on the profitability of the individual customer.

Just as with power, information technology has to be used judiciously. Discriminating against less profitable customers can seem unreasonable to all paying customers and could backfire with publicity. AT&T withdrew its minimum usage charges for its basic-plan customers who were unprofitable. GE Capital tried to charge credit-card users who were not accruing a minimum level of interest charges and ended up having to sell its credit card business. When used appropriately at the individual level, information technology can be very rewarding. Capital One's senior vice-president for domestic card operations, Marge Connelly, says, "We look at every single customer contact as an opportunity to make an unprofitable customer more profitable."

CRM systems are not just about profiling customers and loyalty programmes. To derive maximum benefits, one must broaden the thinking about CRM technology. The technology should be viewed as knowledge-based systems that seek to prioritize commitment of a firm's assets and resources to the more profitable customers while enhancing the relationships with ALL (right) customers.

Pricing may not be the appropriate means to deal with the unprofitable customer. CRM systems give the firm access to information that may reveal other ways to manage the unprofitable customer. Enabling the managing of customer relationships is the goal of the CRM system. Managing customer relationships is about selecting, acquiring, retaining, and enhancing relationships with customers by using an intimate knowledge of the customer's consumption domain to maximize the return on the firm's assets. With CRM systems, firms have the knowledge and the technological capability to identify, retain and enhance more desirable customer relationships.

This portion covers issues regarding which customers to acquire and retain for maximum sustainable profits. How do you assign value to customers and what is involved in that evaluation? Who is the right customer? Who should be in your customer portfolio? Firms look at customers as investments. How do you value these investments? Or, What is the equity of your customers?

SELECTING THE RIGHT CUSTOMER

Markets consist of customers with diverse needs and differences in customer profitability. When serving multiple groups of customers, the goal must be to maximize the profitability of the combination of segments. When different segments are targeted, the firm essentially has a portfolio of customer segments—just as investors have an investment portfolio that maximizes returns at a certain level of risk, firms manage customer portfolios for maximum profits. In other words, this is the selection of customers at any point in time, compared to other segments, from which the firm can generate maximum profits. Firms must attract these most profitable customers and then must establish systems and procedures to retain them.

Most firms serve different segments depending on how the definition of segment is aggregated. The "segment-of-one" used in common business parlance to refer to customization at the individual level is really a maximum disaggregation of a market segment. As we saw in the preceding, most firms facing fluctuating demand and experiencing peak, shoulder and low periods of demand find it inevitable that, at different times, different segments must be served. Of course, each of these segments must have a compatible fit with the overall corporate image as well as a compatible fit with the products, services, employees and other customers. The question is, are they selected based on their combined long term value to the firm?

Most firms forecast the volume and revenues from various segments at certain price points at different times in the purchase cycle. In the typical firm, sales and communications efforts follow these underlying assumptions in pricing and in messages targeting sales prospects. The typical firm then attempts to formalize advertising campaigns to reach as many people as possible in the case of packaged goods. In the case of business-to-business services, the salespeople focus on making a sale. Most firms then struggle to orchestrate all these messages for acquisition of the customer in a coordinated fashion.

Much less attention is paid to the retention of the customer. Barring the well-run operation, common business practice for many firms is short-term oriented. On the contrary, a customer-focused firm begins by approaching sales as acquiring the right customer. The customer-focused firm also approaches the acquisition of customers as only the first step in managing the relationships with its customers. Once acquired, the customer must be retained. But, not always retained at any cost—a necessary condition is that the benefits outweigh the costs of acquiring and retaining that customer.

Customer-focused firms align all their activities and processes in acquiring and retaining the right customer. They see their value-creating assets as most profitably leveraged by focusing on the most valuable customers. In principle, the value of the customer is determined by contribution to the firm's objectives over the lifetime of the customer.

The right customer is that customer whose inclusion in the firm's target market helps maximize returns on the firm's assets.

CUSTOMER EQUITY

Ask a manager, "What is your firm's most valuable asset?" Chances are that you will not get the response, "my customers." You will find even fewer firms that actually make an assessment of this value in any real sense. The valuation of the customer is implicit in sales figures—essentially, the revenues generated by customers of the firm. What is the flaw in using sales as a proxy in valuing a firm's customers? Consider this. Two customers with the same cash value of purchases may not be of the same value to the firm. There may be differences in the cost of serving these two customers. The true value of the customer to the firm, or the equity that the firm has in that customer, must include all revenues and also all costs related to that customer, as in financial investments.

A recent framework by a team of researchers defines customer equity as the "total of the discounted lifetime value of all the firm's customers." They articulate three drivers of customer equity: value equity, brand equity, and relationship equity. They define value equity as the objective assessment of the utility of the brand, and value equity is driven by quality, price, and convenience; brand equity as the subjective assessment of the brand above and beyond the perceived value, and brand equity is driven by brand awareness, attitude toward the brand, and corporate ethics; and relationship equity as the tendency of the customer to stick with the brand, and relationship equity is driven by loyalty programmes, special recognition and treatment, affinity programmes, community-building programmes, and knowledge-building programmes. Their framework—the customer equity diagnostic—is offered as a way to determine which customers to acquire as well as what will enable their retention.

If we define customer value as the value of the firm or a product as perceived by the customer, customer equity is the converse and refers to the value of the customer to the firm. If the objective is to maximize the returns from your investments—the customer portfolio—you must maximize customer equity. This makes sense because you can maximize sustainable return on assets by maximizing customer equity for the long term. To maximize customer equity, we must be able to measure it.

If customer equity is simply the value of a customer to the firm, we can articulate that value in the same way that customers articulate our value to them. Just as customer value is the difference between benefits and costs to the customer, conversely, customer equity is the difference between the benefits and costs to the firm in serving a customer. One team of researchers describes their method of measuring customer equity as follows: "we first measure each customer's expected contributions toward offsetting the company's fixed costs over the expected life of that customer.

Then we discount the expected contributions to a net present value at the company's target rate of return for marketing investments. Finally, we add together the discounted expected contributions of all current customers."

Evident in their metric are the following important points about customer equity:

- It is the sum of the equity of all of a firm's customers.
- It summates the gross contribution of each customer, taking into account benefits as well as costs of serving a customer.

- It includes consideration of future revenues and variable costs from each customer.
- It is a time-discounted present value of future benefits to the firm.

It becomes evident that the customer equity concept when disaggregated to the individual customer level allows us to look at the revenues and costs of serving an individual customer. It helps answer the question, which customer should we serve? The ideal customer to the firm is the one that gives it the maximum long-term customer equity, which theoretically you want as a brand-loyal customer. However, as we will see in the next, the converse is not true, because not all brandloyal customers provide maximum customer equity.

THE RIGHT CUSTOMER

The concept of brand loyalty is a well-researched topic. The notion of a customer having a lifetime value and the prominence of database systems in managing customers have spawned a renewed interest in relationship marketing. Just making repurchases doesn't make a customer brand loyal. There must be some commitment by the customer to the firm for relational continuity reflecting a positive patronage bias. Not all brand-loyal customers have a positive disposition to the provider—some relationships may be forced because of a lack of choice. Brand loyalty reflects a financial, social, or structural bonding with the customer. Relationship marketing seeks to enhance the mutual benefits from the relationship with the right customer—seeking brand loyalty from the right customer. To determine who the right customer is, we need to understand what benefits the firm expects from an ideal customer.

At the outset, it is clear that the stream of purchases from the brandloyal customer is the primary benefit. In truth, the value of a brand-loyal customer to the firm must go beyond the purchases made over the lifetime of the relationship with that customer. As revenues can be direct and indirect. Direct revenues are all of the customer's purchases, and indirect revenues are the cash value of all of the other benefits the customer accrues to the firm, in the form of direct revenues from referred customers.

Costs to serve are drastically reduced, as brand-loyal customers are generally easier to serve. The argument is that as customers get familiar with the firm, its processes and products, customers will require less costly assistance from the firm in purchasing and using the product. Loyal customers may even be able to open up ways in which to reduce the costs of serving the customer.

Other benefits of brand loyalty would include product improvement contributions, new product opportunities, ideal sources for market information, and favorable word of mouth. At an overall level, all these benefits add up to a degree of stability and potential growth for the firms. Those brand-loyal customers who are committed in their patronage recognize their benefits from the firm and show commitment in the provider firm.

To select the right customer, the firm must be able to measure the value of the loyal customer from all these benefits as well as the costs of acquiring and retaining that customer. It is not easy to quantify all of these benefits. But it is possible to calculate the direct and indirect revenues from each customer. It is also possible to calculate the acquisition costs and relationship maintenance costs. Information technology has allowed us to obtain that data and made it easy to calculate the lifetime value of a customer.

The Calculus of Lifetime Value

A commonly used practice inherited from the direct marketing industry experience is called RFM (referring to "recency, frequency, and monetary data")—a method to determine whom to send promotions from among your customers. It takes into account the value of a customer's purchases, how recent they were, and how often they were purchased. As with the danger of any one approach, RFM has been used without much consideration for other important dimensions of the most valuable customer, such as how profitable the customer really is.

RFM is therefore not a proxy measure for the lifetime value of a customer. Indeed, if the costs of serving different customers show a variance, then the RFM method could attract the wrong customer. As there are three main factors in calculating the lifetime value of a customer. It is not just a simple product of the value of each purchase and the number of times the customer will purchase the product over that customer's lifetime. The lifetime value of a customer should also include referral value. And, it should include the lifetime costs as well. CRM technology has made it possible to do this, but, how many firms actually use this understanding in how they design and implement their CRM solutions?

Lifetime Revenues

Lifetime revenues is the sum of all purchases that the customer will make. An assessment of the progression of purchases over the lifecycle of the customer is a key point to be made here. For instance, consider what a college student's financial lifecycle would mean to a bank. First, it is a savings or checking account with a debit card and perhaps even a credit card. The college student may also be a good candidate for an education loan. Once graduated, this ex-student is now in the market for a car loan, and quite soon a home mortgage.

Once other life events such as marriage and children occur, there are more car loans, mortgages, home equity loans, trusts, custody accounts, education loans for children, and associated financial products that a typical family would need. USAA, the life insurance and financial services company, follows marriages, births, and other life events so that it can advise customers on changing needs. Every firm should attempt to develop such a long-term consumption profile for the typical customer in each segment, charting their potential purchases over a lifetime to take into account the life events of the customer—a customer lifecycle analysis. A similar case may be made for business customers based on an assessment of growth potential, so that any B2B firm has to project the growth of its customers and factor that into a lifetime value calculation.

Not all customers become brand loyal. We have seen that superior customer value is a prerequisite for brand loyalty. What percentage of new customers find the firm's customer value to be superior? The lifetime value of a customer must also factor the probability of the acquired customer becoming brand loyal. Thus, the lifetime value of a customer is the first purchase, plus the probability of repeat purchases for the duration of the relationship with the firm. The probability consideration takes into account that a customer may not be a good fit, that a competitor may have been able to provide a better fit, or that the need situation changed for the customer, such as in the case of relocation of the consuming unit.

Lifetime Costs

An activity-based costing approach allows a firm to account for direct costs that the firm incurs in the relationship with a specific customer. Once again, with information technology it is possible, where it makes sense, to attribute marketing and operating costs to individual customers. To obtain the full benefit from CRM investments, it is important to track costs at the individual customer level as well. Costs include acquiring and remarketing to the customer over the lifetime of the customer.

Costs also include value creation and delivery costs of serving the customer. Thus, the costs after acquisition include not only the costs of serving the customer, but also relationship maintenance and development costs such as the costs of cross-selling or upselling, called remarketing costs. Once again, the costs related to the first purchase are separated from that of lifetime purchases so that the probability of repeat purchase is taken into account when calculating lifetime costs.

Referral Value

The indirect revenue of referrals from a loyal customer is an often overlooked aspect of customer equity. The typical

CRM solution and database marketing approaches ignore the referral power of a customer in calculating the lifetime value of a customer. Most firms do not even capture this data, partly because it is difficult to obtain information when knowledge systems in a firm are not configured to obtain it. The other reason may be that firms are not proactively looking for referrals from their loyal customers in any systematic way.

How is the value of referrals from a customer calculated? To answer this question requires looking at the process and mechanics of how referrals work. Who provides a referral? Customers who are satisfied and who have a certain degree of loyalty are the ones who are likely to convey favorable messages about a firm and its products and services. A key piece of information needed here is what level of satisfaction a brand-loyal customer needs to have before being likely to refer a customer. The next obvious question is, who receives the referral? Customers are likely to convey this information to family, friends, and colleagues.

However, not all who receive the referrals are appropriate customers for the firm. What proportion of the customers who received the referral are good candidates for the firm? Out of the ones that are appropriate for the firm, not all are likely to be suitably influenced by the referral to make the first purchase. Finally, if a purchase is actually made, what proportion of referred customers makes repeat purchases? Those that are moved to try the product may not all turn into loyal customers, but if they do, then their lifetime purchases add to the value of the customer making the initial referral.

MAXIMIZING LIFETIME VALUE

Maximizing the collective lifetime value of its customers should be the goal in managing customer relations. By increasing the number of customers and by increasing the lifetime value of each customer, firms can maximize their long-term profitability.

From it becomes clear that to maximize the lifetime value of customers, you need to:

- Maximize lifetime revenues
- Maximize lifetime referrals
- Minimize lifetime costs

Maximizing Lifetime Revenues

Potential customers in a target market are by definition not yet customers. They may or may not be aware of or inclined to purchase from the firm. Firms have tc nurture customers' dispositions to the firm through a number of stages before they can benefit from the loyalty of those customers. The acquisition process of customers could begin at any of the different stages on the road to loyalty. Customers may or not be aware or have an understanding of the features and benefits of the product. If the knowledge of the product is favorable, customers may have a liking or preference for the product. Some customers may even have purchased the product but may not be repeat purchasers, may not be loyal to the product, or may have switched to a competitor. The right customers from any stage need to be moved toward a state of loyalty to the firm and its products. Can CRM technology be configured to capture information about the customer's stage in this process?

Once the appropriate customers are acquired, firms must look for increased usage and frequency, cross-selling opportunities, and trading up to premium versions. Retaining customers requires proactive customer management. Customers are likely to be indifferent to the firm, and a heavy user may become impatient and switch to the competition. Proactive customer management seeks to increase interest in the light user and treat the heavy user with appreciation and respect. Thus, the goal of maximizing lifetime revenues is achieved by maximizing the average purchase per year as well as the duration of the customer's relationship with the firm.

Maximizing Lifetime Referral Value

Referral customers have very low acquisition costs, since your brandloyal customers did the marketing for you. Following the mechanics of the process of word of mouth, that maximizing lifetime referral value requires maximizing the number of referrals from each customer and maximizing the lifetime value of each referred customer. To maximize the number of referrals, one must maximize the drivers of referrals from a customer. In other words, firms must attempt to increase the probability of a customer making a referral of profitable customers. Firms must move loyal customers to become advocates of the firm.

When word of mouth is seen as a powerful customer acquisition tool, firms will find a way to stimulate referrals. Many firms are not proactive in stimulating referrals, assuming simply that "good word of mouth will happen if we do a good job." What must firms do to increase the value from referrals?

First, firms must identify the current and potential advocates of the firm. Firms must proactively look for individuals and organizations that are likely sources of referrals and stimulate and reward them for the right kind of referrals. Satisfied and loyal customers are not the only ones who can stimulate positive word of mouth. There are opinion leaders: such individuals and organizations as consumer reports, firms such as Gartner and Forrester, who might be considered experts in the field, and most important, the general and trade media. Other ambassadors for the firm include players in often overlooked sources such as suppliers, resellers, employees, and other stakeholders such as investors. Community chat rooms on the Web are rich sources of information for the firm about what word of mouth is transpiring among its stakeholders.

Second, firms must attempt to stimulate referrals. Any new customer acquisition activity should record information on how the customer was moved to deal with the firm. When the firm obtains and records this information in the consumption profile of any customer, it is able to use it to calculate the average number of customer referrals made by each current customer of the firm. Customers and advocates with similar profiles need to be approached about playing a referral role. Since some customers may be amenable and others not, firms must explore what it would take to move suitable customers to play an advocate role.

Finally, from Equation C it is also clear that the better the fit between the referred customer and the firm's products, the greater the lifetime referral value. Research has also shown that the customers referred to by satisfied customers tend to be a particularly good fit with the firm and its products and services. The fit is better than with those customers attracted and acquired through marketing messages such as advertisements and coupon mailers. Brand-loyal advocates bring in like-minded customers. To get referrals to actually make a purchase or try the firm's offerings, it is necessary to get some incentives into the hands of the referred customers.

Minimizing Lifetime Costs

Reducing the costs of acquisition, costs of serving, and the cost of remarketing per customer can increase the lifetime value of a customer. Reducing costs to serve means that you need to be more efficient in the yield from your value-creating assets. Costs to serve per customer is reduced when you increase the cost efficiency or the capacity utilization efficiency. To reduce costs of acquisition and remarketing you need to be more effective in your marketing, both to new and to current customers. CRM technology can be used to continually learn from experience and utilize knowledge to reduce operating and marketing costs at the individual level.

ATTRACTING AND REMARKETING TO THE RIGHT CUSTOMERS

To maximize the total lifetime value of their customers, firms must proactively manage customer relationships. Proactive customer relationship management should seek customer appreciation from the heavy user and attract more interest from light users with better value bundles if they can contribute more in their lifetime value to the firm. This is in contrast to the firm that may have good customer service, for example, but in its reactive mode will leave the light user relatively indifferent to the firm and the heavy user susceptible to a competitor.

Most loyalty programmes involve some kind of reward for the continued patronage of their customers. Referred to as frequency marketing, continuity programmes, awards or points programmes, or simply loyalty programmes, the goal of these programmes is to market and manage relationships with customers. First instituted by American Airlines in the 1970s to get around government regulation that prevented price competition, now many firms' programmes attempt to solidify their relationships with its customers.

The rewards or awards, as they are called, may come in the form of free products and services at the firm, or sometimes even free products from other firms. The smart firms impose restrictions on the use of these rewards, so that they are used to increase demand when and where needed. For example, the hospitality industry blocks out certain dates so that the promotions are targeted at different segments to entice customer utilization at low demand periods. The problem is that many of these programmes are misguided in design and implementation. One obvious omission is evident when the lifetime calculus is compared to the criteria for the rewards.

The rewards focus on revenues for the most part. That costs are taken into account is not clear at all. A recent Harvard Business Review article offers data that would be a surprise for managers who have not considered costs of serving the customer. Brand-loyal customers are not necessarily profitable customers. In their knowledge of their own value and indispensability to the firm, the brand-loyal customer could make costly demands of the firm.

The firm, in doling out the goodies along with the product and other business favors, may actually be spending more than it recognizes as costs of serving that customer. The only criterion for these (brand) loyalty programmes should be that they should maximize the customer equity for each customer, based on the calculus of lifetime value that we have discussed. To be meaningful and powerful in managing relationships with the right customers, these customer acquisition and loyalty programmes must specify the following:

- Objectives of the programme
- Market and customer scope of the programme
- Value for customer scope of the programme
- Impact scope (costs, timing, impact on people, process, physical assets, other customers, publicity opportunities, etc.)

The objectives of the programme need to be stated in the context of customer relationship management. What is the expected value of the programme to the firm? What specifically must the programme accomplish? Perhaps it is to shift demand from peak to low periods, to attract new segments, to get light users to become heavy users, to promote a new product offering, or some other specific objective. Without a known objective, no programme can be assessed on merit.

The next specific decision for customer relationship programmes is to specify the customer that the programme is intended for. Often, frequency programmes are so loosely formulated that the rewards are earned by the wrong customer. Consider this example of the unfortunate consequence of a poorly guided programme. One Mr. Phillips logged 1.25 million frequent flier miles—about $25,000 worth of airline travel—with an investment of 50 hours of his time and $3,140. Mr. Phillips took advantage of an offer he found on the package of a Healthy Choice frozen entrée: 500 American Airlines miles for every 10 UPCs, with early birds receiving a double count of miles! A Mr. Fisher participated in the same programme and got 12,000 Northwest Airlines Miles.

Even if the airlines got an awfully good financial deal with Healthy Choice, one must ask who the loyalty programme attracts—whether the airlines are in the grocery business or in the airline business. How do their returns from this investment compare with the returns that they would have achieved with programmes that targeted the frequent flier instead of the frequent grocery shopper? The objectives of the programme should determine the appropriate segment or customer for the programme. The problem with most programmes is that they don't take into account the profitability of the customer. Who should be the target of the programme? Not every customer is right for the firm, as we have seen, nor is every customer right for every programme. The best programme is one that tailors the award to the target customer.

Thus, giant supermarket retailer UK-based Tesco mails 100,000 variations of promotions to its loyal customers. Further, some customers may be more costly to retain, while others may be increasing their profitability to the firm. It is evident that firms need to look at the acquisition costs and retention costs of its customer base when determining the focus of their retention efforts. The calculus of the lifetime value of a customer is clear in its indication of what needs to be factored into deciding to which customer to target the promotion.

Low acquisition costs and low retention costs are realized from your most profitable customers. At the other end are your customers who were costly to acquire and cost you a lot to serve. Given the acquisition costs, the firm must keep a close eye on the customer's cost of retention. If the firm misjudged a customer's lifetime value or committed more resources to the acquisition of the customer than the revenue stream would justify, the firm has to either reduce retention costs or stop serving the customer if possible.

For the chosen customers, the firm needs to decide what they would do to motivate the customer to act. Customer knowledge should indicate what the customer is sensitive to, so that the value of the promotion can be appropriate for the specific customer or segment. The value of the promotion may be in the form of additional product, a complementary service, a straightforward price-break, or a discount for future purchases or a gift, among other things. Software firms are able to use lead customers in beta-tests and other benefits about new and innovative offerings before the rest of the market will find out, giving these B2B customers early mover advantage in their value chains in their industry.

Of course, a projected cost/benefit analysis is a must—what additional revenues have been realized and at what cost? For service firms, and where the programme is about service components, it is imperative that the promotion take into account what it would do to the demand patterns of customers. The last thing you want is for customers to strain your operation if your programme ends up drawing more customers during peak times when you are already at optimum levels of served customers.

Any programme must consider the impact on other customers, on the staff, physical assets, and the delivery system or process. For example, a shortage of airline seats infuriates frequent fliers who, as brand-loyal customers, having diligently set aside miles for use on family vacations, find they are not able to use the miles because use of awards is limited to a certain proportion of the volume on each flight and are restricted to certain times and dates. Estimates are that about 10 percent of all miles flown on a carrier can be from people cashing in on these rewards. Does it make sense for frequent flier awards to range from personal digital assistants to designer watches? Are the costs and impact of these awards assessed? Another less obvious criterion is the potential for publicity in a promotion. A promotion that is newsworthy could attract the attention of a large number of potential customers and other stakeholders.

Firms must prioritize the management of customer relationships as a firm-wide imperative. Dell Computer, for example, has a "customer experience council" consisting of senior executives from each division or business line and major function that reports to a corporate vice chairman, no less. The council oversees measurement of several aspects of customer behaviour, including the effectiveness of its loyalty programmes.

Dell even measures all the costs its customers incur in purchasing and using their products, including such things as shopping, ordering, installing, operating, servicing, and disposing of products. The real value of tracking these revenues and costs over the lifetime value of the customer is that it allows firms to understand their brandloyal customers and anticipate their future needs. Such management practices will be able to deliver benefits to the heavy user to maximize their lifetime value.

FRAMING THE CUSTOMER-FOCUSED ANALYSIS

The lifetime value of the customer must be calculated for each customer—an assessment of revenues and costs over the lifetime of the customer's relationship with the firm. The investment in acquiring and retaining a customer must be made based on the customer's lifetime value to the firm. A continuous monitoring of up-sell and cross-sell opportunities could increase the lifetime value of the customer.

The potential customer equity from each segment or customer should determine the extent of value-creating adjustments to be made in terms of delivery process or product outcome customization in terms of value or other benefits to the customer or in terms of adjusting the price and other costs to the customer. These changes in promotion offerings to acquire a new customer or remarket to a current or inactive customer will impact both costs and revenues and their effect on the lifetime value of the customer will determine subsequent investments in acquiring and retaining customers.

Chapter 4

International Trade Theory, Practice and Policy

The choice of free trade versus protection policy that has dominated issues of trade policy over the last few decades has been debated with even greater intensity in developing countries than in developed countries. In order to assess the policies of developing countries toward trade, it is useful to return to "first principles" and examine trade theories, with the objective of understanding the implications of theory for trade policy. Since in both developing and developed countries there are typically various perspectives on the extent to which the country should engage in trade, it is appropriate to begin any discussion of trade with the fundamental question, "Why do countries trade with each other?" The answer to this question lies in the analyses of the eighteenth and nineteenth-century classical economists, the "neoclassical" theories developed more recently by twentieth-century economists, and newer classes of trade theories introduced by economists and business scholars only during the last few decades.

ABSOLUTE ADVANTAGE

It is well known that the first important classical trade theorist was Adam Smith. In his 1776 treatise, The Wealth of Nations, Smith suggested that countries would gain from trade, both exporting and importing, as long as each country had an absolute advantage in the production of a particular good. Such an advantage would be recognized in that country's ability to produce the good more cheaply than every other country. This conclusion was interesting at the time because it disagreed with the prevailing notion of mercantilism in which each country emphasized the advantages of exporting over importing.

Since countries received gold as payment for their exports during the period of mercantilist philosophy (circa 1500-1800), this trade strategy allowed countries to expand their holdings of wealth in the form of gold. Smith's theory of absolute advantage, on the other hand, disagreed with the mercantilist philosophy of national wealth. Instead, he suggested that a country's wealth was reflected in the living standards of its residents. Consequently, importing was not only necessary but also beneficial to a country if it imported goods that other countries could produce more efficiently.

Using an illustration that corresponds to the reality and imagery of the era in which Smith developed his theory, let us assume, that England and France had equal quantities of productive resources and that England could produce with all its productive resources either 100 units of machinery or 40 units of wine, and France using all of its productive resources could produce either 30 units of machinery or 120 units of wine.

Under these conditions, with England having an absolute advantage in the production of machinery and France an absolute advantage in the production of wine, England should specialize in machinery, France in wine, and both countries should export their surplus production and import the wine or machinery that their residents demand.

In this example, note that the potential welfare of both countries clearly improves after trade. If there were no trade between these countries and they each decided to split their productive resources equally between machinery and wine, their combined production would be 65 units of machinery and 80 units of wine. If, on the other hand, both countries specialize in the area of their absolute advantage, recognizing that they can export their surplus production and import the good that they desire but do not produce, their combined production increases to 100 units of machinery and 120 units of wine. Joint production has increased by 35 units of machinery and 40 units of wine, and both countries can increase their consumption of machinery and wine. Thus, the case for specialization and trade is clear in the context of the theory of absolute advantage.

COMPARATIVE ADVANTAGE

Implicit in Adam Smith's theory of absolute advantage is the suggestion that a country that can produce all goods more efficiently than any other country should never import. Of course, were this to be the case in a world of two countries, no trade would ever take place. This seems like a very reasonable conclusion: Why should a country import a good that it can produce more efficiently than can the country from which it would be imported? The Principles of Political Economy and Taxation, and indicated that the apparently reasonable conclusion was wrong. In so doing, Ricardo developed the theory of comparative advantage.

In his theory of comparative advantage, Ricardo argued that trade between any two countries was beneficial as long as these countries produced goods with different relative efficiency. In the Ricardian framework, differences in relative efficiency were based on differences in the productivity of labour across countries. The concept of producing goods with different relative efficiencies is best explained by an example.

Suppose that the world comprised two countries— Bolivia and the United States—and that both countries could produce two products: computer software and shoes. Suppose further that the United States used four units of resources to produce a unit of software, and ten units of resources to produce a unit of shoes, while Bolivia used twelve and fifteen units of resources, respectively. According to absolute advantage, since the United States produces both goods more efficiently (with fewer resources) than does Bolivia, the United States should import neither product from Bolivia. According to comparative advantage, however, this example meets the test of a situation where two countries can benefit from trade.

The United States and Bolivia produce two goods with different relative efficiency. The United States has a comparative advantage over Bolivia in the production of computer software relative to shoes because it produces computer software three times as efficiently (with one-third—4 units/12 units—of the resources) as Bolivia, while it produces shoes only 1.5 times as efficiently (with two thirds—10 units/15 units—of the resources) as Bolivia. It is important to note that—based upon these figures—although Bolivia has an absolute disadvantage in the production of both products, it has a comparative advantage over the United States in the production of shoes relative to computer software.

To see the implication of these relative differences in efficiency, think of what happens if the United States gives up shoe production (its area of relative inefficiency) in favour of computer software production (its area of relative efficiency). If the United States produces one fewer unit of shoes, it releases ten units of productive resources that can be used to produce 2.5 units of computer programmes. Since Bolivia would use thirty units of productive resources to produce those 2.5 units of computer programmes, the same as it would use to produce two units of shoes, it would be willing to give up two units of shoes in exchange for the computer programmes.

Consequently, the result of the United States releasing shoe resources in favour of producing computer software is to increase the supply of shoes that both countries produce by one unit while holding constant the supply of computer software. Theoretically, this process of shifting resources should continue until the world's output can no longer be increased by an internal shift of resources in either the United States or Bolivia.

Since "world" production has increased, both countries have the potential to benefit from this specialization and trade. Both countries might not benefit. The United States might be able to negotiate with Bolivia so that it receives all of the extra unit of shoes. The important point to note, however, is that, in the context of the assumptions of comparative advantage theory, the world cannot lose from trade and that both countries have the potential to gain from trade.

Note also that the possibility of gains from trade does not require one to assume that the countries have equivalent quantities of productive resources. The basis for trade lies in differences in the ratios of productive efficiency not in the quantity of resources a country has available. If, for example, Bolivia had 300 units of productive resources available, while the United States had 3 million, this would reduce neither the desirability of trade nor the direction of trade.

It would only reduce the amount of trade. Although Bolivia would continue to specialize in shoe production, the United States may be unable to completely specialize in computer software production because Bolivia, with its limited resources, might be unable to supply all of the U.S. shoe requirements or consume all of the U.S. excess computer software production. Thus, in this two-country world, the United States might continue to produce shoes but only after it has imported all of Bolivia's excess shoe production, which, in this two-product world, is equivalent to the exporting of all of its excess computer software production.

Not only is trade not dependent upon countries having similar quantities of productive resources; it is also not dependent upon them offering similar payments to the factors of production, including wages to workers. In fact, differences in real payments to the factors of production, land, labour, capital, and enterprise can be expected when there are differences in the productivity of the countries' factors of production or in the relative availability of, and demand for, those resources.

In the previous example, the greater productivity of factors of production in the United States relative to Bolivia would suggest that these factors of production would generate higher incomes in the United States compared with Bolivia. These differences in payments to factors of production, including wages paid to workers, do not reduce the potential gains from trade.

One of the important neoclassical advances to comparative advantage theory was developed by two Swedish economists, Eli Heckscher and Bertil Ohlin, writing in the twentieth century. Together, they developed the factor endowments base for international trade. Using simplifying assumptions, they developed what has come to be known as the Heckscher-Ohlin theory, which suggests that a country has a comparative advantage in the good that uses intensively the factor of production of which it has an abundant supply.

The theory is based upon the proposition that different products require productive factors in different proportions and that countries have different endowments of these productive factors. Thus, the theory suggests that a country with a large pool of capital will find that capital is cheap relative to other factors of production and, therefore, such a country should have a comparative advantage in capital-intensive products. Similarly, a country with abundant supplies of labour will find that labour is relatively cheaper, providing that country with a comparative advantage in labour-intensive products.

Classical trade theories and, to a lesser extent, neoclassical theories rely upon assumptions that diverge from reality. At issue is whether this divergence affects the generalizability of the theories.

ASSUMPTIONS OF COMPARATIVE ADVANTAGE THEORY THAT DIVERGE FROM REALITY

There are certain assumptions of the simple Ricardian model of comparative advantage theory that do not correspond to reality. Some of these assumptions are easily incorporated into neoclassical versions of the theory and may be viewed as weakly realistic; others are unrealistic and are not easily incorporated into classical or neoclassical trade theory.

Multiple Countries, Multiple Products

The assumptions most easily dispensed with are those of a two-country world in which there are only two tradeable goods. The Ricardian model easily expands to take into account multiple countries producing multiple goods without any loss of generality.

Mobility of Factors of Production

The Ricardian model also assumes that factors of production are completely mobile within a country and completely immobile across countries. Of course, neither assumption is correct; and both inaccuracies reduce the power of the model. Since resources are not freely mobile within countries, it is more difficult for countries to specialize by switching from the production of one good to the production of another. In the foregoing thought experiment using the United States and Bolivia, some of the labourers used in the production of computer software in Bolivia might find it difficult to switch to shoe production. Alternately, factors of production move more easily across countries than the theory suggests. Thus, some of the highly productive computer software experts in the United States might be willing to take their professional skills, their capital, and their entrepreneurial abilities and relocate to Bolivia.

Although both assumptions about factor mobility are inaccurate, however, they are also closer to reality than their extreme opposite assumptions. Thus, factors of production within a country are more mobile than immobile, especially over the long term. Further, factors of production, especially land and labour, find it relatively difficult to move among countries. Thus, these assumptions reduce the doctrinaire prescriptions of the theory without reducing its underlying explanatory and prescriptive power.

In some cases, these reality checks can be incorporated formally. Thus, the reduced mobility of factors of production within a country is incorporated into neoclassical trade models by assuming that each productive resource that is transferred from one use to another will be transferred at increasing cost. (In the jargon of the economist, the production possibility curve becomes concave from the origin in contrast to the use of a straight-line production-possibility curve.)

Transport Costs

The simple Ricardian model ignores transport costs, but these are also easily incorporated into the theory. The result, however, is that for certain types of goods with high transport costs, the benefits of specialization are negated by the costs of transporting goods across countries. Other unrealistic assumptions of comparative advantage theory present much greater threats to the explanatory power of the theory.

Demand Factors and Consumer Tastes

Classical and neoclassical comparative advantage theory is concerned principally with production and supply issues. There are two important assumptions with respect to demand. The first is that there is assumed to be sufficient demand for goods that are produced. Second, it is assumed that consumers in different countries have similar tastes in goods. Of course, neither of these assumptions reflect reality. Consumer demand constrains the extent of specialization, although it does not affect the direction. The United States may have a comparative advantage in the production of commercial aircraft. The resources it places into commercial aircraft production, however, are likely to be constrained by the demand for this product, even worldwide demand.

The other significant demand-related assumption is that of monolithic consumer tastes. Clearly, consumers around the world do not have the same tastes in goods despite apparent trends to create global products and markets. These differences in taste may provide an opportunity for production and sale of a good to be based on an ability to identify the particular tastes of consumers rather than be based only on least-cost production, as is true of export production according to classical and neoclassical trade theories.

Constant Returns to Scale

If firms produced according to constant returns to scale and did not benefit from a learning curve, then the early identification of a market segment interested in a different type of product would not represent a competitive advantage. Once this market was identified, other firms could seek to serve it, thus forcing competition to return to least-cost considerations.

Because these assumptions do not hold, there are advantages to being the first company to move into new markets. Firms do not produce according to constant returns to scale; that is, as the firm increases production, the cost per unit of output does not remain the same. On the contrary, in most industries, firms benefit from increasing returns to scale or economies of scale; that is, as output increases, there is a decline in the unit cost of producing that output.

Experience-Learning Curve

A concept that is related to increasing returns to scale is the learning curve, or its first cousin, the experience curve. Both curves convey the notion that as a firm learns more about a production process because of its experience producing the product, it will be able to reduce the costs of producing the product. In contrast to the message of these curves, comparative advantage theory assumes that there are no cost-reduction benefits associated with experience and learning in the same way that there are none associated with volume.

Each of these three unrealistic assumptions significantly reduces the explanatory and prescriptive power of comparative advantage theory. The prescriptions that have built upon the intellectual underpinning of comparative advantage theory include the notion that rational governments should specialize in the goods they produce most competitively based on their natural endowment of factors of production.

Further, it is said that they should maintain open borders that allow the export of their surplus production and the importing of the other goods their residents demand. Implicit in comparative advantage theory with its traditional factor-endowment focus is a pattern of trade in which most of the trade flowing across national borders would be in dissimilar products and between dissimilar countries, that is, countries with different factor endowments.

TRADE PRACTICE AND NEW TRADE THEORIES

In fact, the practice of trade is quite different from the prescriptions implicit in comparative advantage theory. Most countries restrict trade using a plethora of techniques. In using these techniques, countries seek to "create" comparative advantage instead of relying on nature's endowments.

Where trade does take place, a significant proportion takes place among countries with similar factor endowments (e.g., some 80 percent of world trade takes place among industrialized countries). Further, instead of the interindustry trade that is implied by comparative advantage theory, much of worldwide trade is of the intraindustry variety. For some products, the degree of intraindustry trade is particularly high. In the mid-1980s, for example, Yoffie reports that some 70 percent of worldwide exports of antifriction bearings, a critical component in most manufactured products, went to countries that also exported antifriction bearings.

New Theories of Trade

While classical and neoclassical comparative advantage theories do not explain these worldwide trading patterns, they are explained by new theories of trade that have attempted to build trade models that incorporate more real istic assumptions than those of comparative advantage theory. These models, developed by economists and business scholars such as Paul Krugman, Ray Vernon, and Michael Porter, suggest that increasing returns to scale and product differentiation furnish a basis for trade independent of comparative advantage. Increasing returns to scale and the learning curve phenomenon suggest, unlike comparative advantage, that a country's pattern of trade may be determined by acquired expertise rather than naturally endowed factors of production.

The Product Cycle theory, for example, places special consideration on the impact of demand factors in determining trade patterns. It argues that products tend to be developed to meet the needs of a market close to the home of the producer. The idea is that firms do not have perfect information on all markets around the world and that they are most likely to respond to the opportunities close to home. Further, not all countries are likely to spawn innovating firms. Rather, they are likely to emerge in countries with plentiful supplies of skilled labour that can be employed to produce the product and high-income consumers that are likely to purchase the innovative good. It is usually the developed countries that meet these criteria.

Thus, innovations will be spawned in a developed country; and during the new product stage of the product cycle, these products will principally be sold in that home market with exports beginning to other developed countries. As the product matures, exports will increase and will include exports to developing countries. Over time, the product becomes standardized and competition becomes driven by cost. In many such cases, the product may be produced in developing countries to take advantage of lower costs and be exported back to the original innovating country.

This view of trade patterns suggests that comparative advantage is driven by demand as well as supply and that it is not static. A country's relative ability to produce a product can change over time and is as dependent upon acquired skills as it is on natural endowments. This theory—with its recognition of the probability of product differentiation—also explains the reality of intra industry trade.

Generally, product differentiation furnishes a basis for trade independent of comparative advantage, and this trade may well be intra industry trade. Station wagons, for example, are more popular in the United States than they are in most other countries. Demand factors within the United States are particularly conducive to this type of automobile. Americans have access to a very well-developed interstate highway system, the country is large, and Americans travel extensively by automobile. While there are individuals in other countries that purchase station wagons, the largest concentration of consumers of these automobiles resides in the United States.

Consequently, the Japanese automobile company, Honda, builds station wagons in the United States, close to its most demanding customers, and exports these to Japan. At the same time, Honda builds sedans in Japan and exports them to the United States.

Increasing returns to scale and learning also furnish a basis for trade independent of comparative advantage. A country could become competitive in a particular product because of a historical accident or because the product appealed to its consumers. Once the firms in this country begin producing the product, the country's "first-mover" advantages become quite significant because of increasing returns to scale and the ability of these firms to climb a learning curve. These firms will be able to lower their unit production costs because of their ever-expanding operations and their continuous learning about how best to produce the product.

These cost advantages will allow firms in this country to out compete their rivals elsewhere. One should note that in trade theories that rely on increasing returns to scale the direction of trade is indeterminate; that is, it is not possible to predict based on any characteristics of any two countries which country will eventually export or which will import. That is entirely dependent upon which country happens to be the "first mover."

A final set of new theories surrounds the role of multinational corporations. These corporations dominate several industries in which there is a significant level of international trade. In fact, trade among affiliates of multinational corporations amounts to some 40 percent of worldwide trade flows. In such cases, contrary to the assumptions of comparative advantage theory, trade cannot be assumed to be a series of discrete arm's-length transactions.

Rather, international trade, in these cases, results more from the competitive strategies of these companies and the strategic actions of governments in these countries than it does from the inherent characteristics of a nation, whether these are supply characteristics or demand characteristics. This leads

Yoffie to suggest that "when industries become globally concentrated, visible hands rather than anonymous market forces emerge to guide trade."

For example, Wells points out that bauxite is mined in Ghana and that Ghana is the site of a world-class aluminum smelter built and operated by Kaiser. Ghana imports alumina from Jamaica to feed its aluminum smelter, and it exports bauxite to North America and Europe for conversion and smelting in facilities that are owned by the same companies that own mines in Ghana—this, despite the fact that each step in the conversion process cuts the weight to be shipped by one-half.

These trade effects that would not be predicted by traditional trade theory are explained by the actions of companies operating in oligopolistic industry settings. Much of the world's bauxite is mined and processed by a few vertically integrated firms. These firms, argues Wells, opted to separate their mining and smelting facilities as a hedge against nationalization. It is this set of corporate strategies that explains some components of trade patterns in this industry.

These are the new theories of trade. Note that these theories do not displace comparative advantage. Rather, they complement comparative advantage; that is, countries specialize and trade with other countries because of differences in factor endowments, but they also trade with other countries because they were or were not able to capture the economies of scale and learning in a particular industry, because their consumers have tastes that differ from those of consumers in other countries, and because of the corporate and governmental strategies pursued by firms in highly concentrated industries.

These new versions of trade theory are captured in the recent work of business scholars. Porter adds to factor endowments the effect of demand patterns, of the competitive structure of industries, and of linkages among industries in explaining patterns of trade competitiveness. Yoffie argues that country based factors, such as factor endowments and demand patterns, are appropriate for explaining trade patterns in competitive and fragmented industries in which government intervention is low.

In oligopolistic industries where scale and learning effects are critical, however, and in industries in which there is a significant amount of government intervention, it is the dynamics of the global oligopoly, the strategies of these global firms, and the strategies of national governments that will determine the nature of trade flows.

The role of national governments is a particularly controversial one with respect to the impact on trade patterns. There are certain industries, such as commercial aircraft, where the late-mover disadvantages were so great because of the significant economies of scale and steep learning curve that it was inconceivable that a firm could challenge the dominance of the U.S. aerospace industry without government support. It was this argument that, of course, led the European governments to establish the Airbus Consortium in an effort to compete with U.S. firms, Boeing and McDonnell Douglas. It is the subject of the government's role in trade policy to which the remainder of the chapter is devoted.

IMPLICATIONS OF TRADE THEORY FOR TRADE POLICY IN DEVELOPING COUNTRIES

Independent governments in developing countries had never felt particularly comfortable with classical and neoclassical theories of trade. They looked around at developed countries and noted that, without exception, all of these countries were also industrial countries; yet it seemed that comparative advantage trade theory would consign them to forever following their "comparative advantage" in minerals; agricultural products; and light, labourintensive manufactured goods.

In the 1950s, under the intellectual tutelage of Raul Prebisch, Hans Singer, and other economists that spawned the dependency school of development, many developing countries decided to ignore the dictates of comparative advantage and instead to restrict trade in an effort to develop their industrial base. The theoretical contribution of Prebisch and Singer was the development of the concept of the declining terms of trade.

A country's terms of trade represents the relationship between the price of a typical unit of exports and the price of a typical unit of imports. Trends in the terms of trade over time are identified by comparing export and import price indices calculated using the same base period. Prebisch argued that developing countries exported primarily mineral and agricultural commodities with low income elasticities (i.e., products for which demand, and therefore price, increased less than proportionately to increases in income).

Developed countries, on the other hand, manufactured and exported goods with higher income elasticities, which saw greater price increases over time. Consequently, developing countries faced declines in their terms of trade. Prebisch's policy advice was that developing countries should seek to avoid this situation by moving into the production of manufactured goods.

Prebisch's analysis found a ready audience throughout the developing world. Jamaica's former prime minister Michael Manley writes in his book, The Poverty of Nations, for example, that when Jamaica became independent in 1962, a tractor could be financed with the proceeds of 18 tons of sugar; by 1980, it took 60 tons of sugar to finance the same tractor. Even though evidence is sketchy and this issue is hotly debated along North-South lines especially, it does appear that there has been a long-term decline in the terms of trade for nonfuel commodities.

During the period of Prebisch's original analysis, Prebisch calculated that England experienced a 36-percent increase in its net barter terms of trade, implying that the countries with which England traded—primarily colonies producing agricultural commodities—experienced a decline in their terms of trade. Between the mid-1950s and 1980, there was little change in the terms of trade for non petroleum-exporting developing countries. Between 1980 and 1990, however, there has been a relatively significant deterioration in the terms of trade for non petroleum-exporting developing countries.

Some analysts would explain away any apparent declines in the terms of trade by suggesting that manufactured products have changed over time. Thus, they would argue that it is inappropriate to compare, as Manley did, a ton of sugar—which is essentially the same in 1980 as it was in 1962—with a tractor that may have changed significantly over the same period.

One suspects that Prebisch and his supporters would have said that whatever the cause of the declining terms of trade, the fact that declines are taking place lends support to the idea that developing countries should move away from commodities and move toward goods that are more likely to increase in price over time. This could be accomplished either by further refining, and thereby adding more value, to resource-based products or by shifting from resource-based products to manufactured goods.

Many developing countries did follow the prescriptive advice of Prebisch and the dependency school and engaged in attempts to develop their economies by shifting from an open trading strategy in which they imported manufactured goods and exported raw materials and commodities to an import-substitution development strategy. In a programme of import substitution, countries placed high tariffs on imported goods in an effort to stimulate the production of domestic goods that would substitute for imports. This trade strategy was exactly the opposite of the open trade strategy prescribed by comparative advantage principles.

This strategy tended to occur in phases. The first, known as the easy stage of import substitution, involved the substitution of domestic production for the import of consumer goods. The development strategy of import substitution was accomplished through the trade strategy of protection. Governments throughout the developing world placed tariffs on imported goods. In the heyday of the import-substitution strategy, these nominal tariffs were often as high as 100 percent on consumer goods.

These nominal tariffs, however, actually understated the extent of protection. This is because governments often allowed firms to import the raw materials that would be used for the assembly of the final products at low or, in extreme cases, zero rates of duty. Such a combination had the effect of making the degree of effective protection much higher than the rate of nominal protection.

Effective protection measures the protection afforded to the value that is added in the production or assembly process locally, compared with the value added to this process overseas. Essentially, it identifies to what extent the sum of local labour, materials, and other local costs can exceed the value that would have to prevail if the firm faced open competition from world markets.

Thus, for example, if a product faces a nominal protection rate of 100 percent, if the imported raw materials that are used to produce this product face no import duties, and if the value that is added in the country granting the tariffs is 50 percent, then a nominal duty of 100 percent translates into an effective rate of protection of 200 percent. That is, if e is the effective tariff rate, n is the nominal tariff rate, and v is the amount of value added internationally, then

$$e = n\ (1/1 - v).$$

To take this example further, if a local company was producing a car for $10,000, in which 50 percent of the production cost represented local costs, then a 100-percent duty on car imports, coupled with duty-free entry of imported raw materials would allow this company to increase its local costs from $5,000 to $15,000 and still remain competitive with imported cars.

During the period when import substitution was a popular development strategy, rates of effective protection in developing countries were, in fact, quite high. Average effective rates of protection were at about 200 percent for India and Pakistan during the 1960s. In the early 1980s, the average effective rate of protection in Indonesia was 124 percent for all sectors; but for the manufacturing sector, effective protection was an astounding 305 percent.

Not surprising, in retrospect, the development strategy of import-substitution industrialization had many unintended consequences. Firms producing in domestic markets with the high effective rates of protection that prevailed in most of the developing countries that undertook this strategy had little incentive to operate efficiently. Indeed, many of the firms that benefited from this protection and operated inefficiently behind high tariff walls were foreign firms invited into developing countries by governments following the path of import substitution by invitation.

Further, these firms invariably stayed at the easy stage of import substitution, rarely developing backward linkages to other sectors because of the attractiveness of the consumer goods sector. Consequently, imports of raw materials continued to burden the balance of payments of developing countries. Last, in concert with the import-substitution strategy, many developing country governments maintained overvalued exchange rates that made it less costly to import raw materials; but that hurt those entities seeking to export to world markets.

This was not an automatic consequence of an import substitution industrialization strategy, but most countries that pursued such a strategy maintained overvalued exchange rates.

By the 1980s, most developing-country governments were admitting that import-substitution strategies had not been particularly successful. That is not to say that there were not pockets of success. Particularly in large countries, import-substitution strategies created a rather broad industrial infrastructure.

India, for example, has probably the broadest and deepest industrial infrastructure in the developing world, producing a range of products from pins to satellites. In part, this is because of the intensity with which India pursued an import-substitution strategy, maintaining extremely high nominal and effective rates of protection for decades.

Although India achieved a measure of self-sufficiency through this development strategy, the Indian experience also points to the inadequacies of this strategy. Some forty years after the initiation of an import-substitution strategy, Indian industry continued, in large part, to operate quite inefficiently by world standards. For example, in the late 1980s, most automobiles driven in India were produced within that country, a feat matched by only one other developing country—Korea. In contrast to Korea, however, Indian cars were produced based on 1950s automotive technology.

Other data reported by the World Bank indicate a strong positive correlation between productivity growth and open trade strategies in a sample of developing countries in the periods of 1960 to 1984 and 1977 to 1988.

The mounting evidence pointing to the problems associated with a highly protectionist trade strategy in pursuit of development through import substitution has led many countries to reconsider this strategy and to move, instead, to a strategy of development via export promotion. The principle behind this strategy is to promote exports from the developing country by putting in place certain elements. One important element associated with an export-promo propriate point on the industry learning curve before they are able to penetrate export markets.

Indeed, this is no more than the classic infant-industry argument for protection. The countries of East Asia that are held out as models of export promotion—particularly Japan and South Korea—did, in fact, use protectionist trade be at the loss of another. A significant concern also is that developed countries are restricting their markets at the same time as developing countries are seeking to increase their exports.

Chapter 5

The Measurement of Efficiency and Productivity

OBJECT OF PRODUCTIVITY MEASUREMENT

In many Operational Research studies, it will be found either that the effective working of the unit studied is being limited by a shortage of one or more resources (e.g. manpower, plant, working capital), or that other evidence suggests that even though such resources do not form a bottleneck it would be desirable to get more output for a given input of one or more of them. (By output is meant here any measure of the achievement of the unit: for example, physical production, profit, casualties inflicted on the enemy.). It's convenient to use the term "productivity" for any measure of physical output per unit of an element of input of several elements of input. Much of this chapter will apply to measures of output without restriction as to their nature.

Defining a measure of output does not, of course, by itself lead to useful knowledge. Knowledge of the performance of one plant or other operating unit at one time is of little interest, except possibly as evidence (weak, but better than nothing) of the resources that would be required if the plant were to be expanded or a similar plant built. Productivity studies have been directed rather to finding the variations in productivity, relative to one or more elements of input, either between a number of comparable plants, or from time to time at the same plant, or between comparable bits machines, working teams, etc. of one or more plants. It is a matter of definition how many of these studies should be classed as Operational Research ; since, however, the methods and approach are likely to be of use to Operational Research workers, they are described here.

Such studies of variation of productivity have two main classes of use :

(i) They can throw light on factors affecting productivity : on how far different types of equipment, different systems of organisation, different types of supervision and so on, affect the output of a given productive unit. At the crudest level, the observation that, for example, some plants have outstandingly high or low productivity makes them worthy of closer consideration. This is not to say that the plant of high productivity is necessarily better; but it is likely that the reasons why it stands out will be helpful in improving others. And though low productivity and low efficiency are not synonymous, it is likely that study of plants with low productivity will point to cases where efficiency could be raised.

(ii) By the analysis of figures for a number of plants or a number of periods, or both, target figures for requirements of labour, raw materials, plant, etc., may be deduced which will lead to better production planning and forecasting. In particular, some of the more sophisticated methods of analysis may lead to information about the rate of exchange between one input factor and another (for example, how much labour will be saved per unit increase of equipment of specified type). When such information is combined with cost data, the way is open for finding the optimum combination of resources for a given output.

Study Made by the Shirley Institute

The classic example of the study of a large number of comparable units is the work of the British Cotton Industry Research Association (commonly known as the Shirley Institute) on productivity in cotton spinning. In 1945 the figures were collected at a number of spinning mills of the production (in pounds) of yarn of different counts.

More recently, the European Productivity Agency (a branch of the O.E.E.G. formed in 1953) has made comparisons on an international basis between cotton spinning mills.

The research team of the Shirley Institute collected the number of man hours worked, together with many technical details of the types of machinery used, the staffing of the various sections of the mill and so on; the figures of output were taken not only for the final spun yarn, but also for various intermediate stages for which records were obtainable, as the cotton progressed from the initial stage of the bale of raw cotton to the final yarn.

It was convenient in these studies that although any mill would make yarn of a range of counts, that range was, as a rule, fairly small ; thus it was not unfair to take for each mill at each stage the total production as being at the mean count of the range produced. It was therefore possible, by taking the figures for production and for man hours, to get simple figures for output per man hour. In fact the Shirley Institute found it convenient to work in terms of labour cost, that is to say, operative hours per unit of output (in this case 100 Ib. of yarn). This will be known hereafter as O.H.P.

The mere variation of O.H.P. from mill to mill is itself illuminating. It was clear, however, that not only for the overall production of yarn but also for production at each of the various intervening stages O.H.P. depended strongly on the count of yarn spun. When the figures for the various mills in the sample were plotted on a graph giving O.H.P. against count, the points were found to lie in a fairly coherent strip through which a mean curve could be drawn, but there was considerable variation about this, the highest O.H.P. at any count being about two or three times the lowest. It was therefore natural to seek for causes of this variation.

The striking thing that emerged from the attempt to find other factors that might account for the differences was that, for the mills taken as a whole, nothing that was suggested appeared to show a significant effect. It was to be expected, for example, that yarn made with poor quality, cheaper cotton, or yarn which had been more highly twisted, would take more labour to make it.

The variations in O.H.P. due to these factors, however, were either zero, or so small that they were completely masked by other factors of organisation, personality, or whatever one may like to call it, so that only count appears to be relevant. In the analysis of figures for particular processes, however, it was possible to isolate certain technical features of machine speeds and settings and to attribute effects to them also.

Nevertheless there was still a large residual and unidentified variation which was attributed to a "management " factor. Studies in other places have suggested what sort of factors may be relevant in this connection. For example, studies in the shoe industry have shown strong effects of such things as production planning and incentive payment systems. More detailed studies of an academic nature have shown the effects of certain human factors such as types of foremanship and degree of close supervision.

It may be of interest that the Shirley Institute have recently made a repeat survey of a number of firms and have used the information from the earlier survey to remove the effect of changes of count between the two surveys.

The figures show on the average some improvement between the surveys in productivity in ring spinning (the commoner process). However, in those parts of the spinning process for which the effect of technical factors can be allowed, it has become clear that almost all the improvement lies in better technical settings. There is on the average no improvement on the residual side. The other thing that is striking is that firms have considerably altered their order of relative productivity. There is evidence from a number of places that firms vary in their relative productivity, from time to time, and indeed that the fluctuations may be comparatively rapid.

A second example of productivity measurement and analysis is given by the work of Stafford Beer at Samuel Fox & Co. This work, which was intended to improve production planning and control. In this example in a single firm two things were achieved. First, figures were obtained which provided a basis for gauging machine capacities and for estimating the dates of fulfilment of orders with a good deal of confidence ; it was also possible to plan out what targets should be set as an indicator of efficiency. Secondly, there was a drill for a rapid calculation of these dates and for the regular scrutiny of the production records to see if efficiency was rising or falling.

These two cases between them exemplify most of the uses to which productivity measurement may be put, and most of the problems which arise in the course of trying to carry it out. These may be classified under three headings : reducing output to some sort of comparable measure, defining input, and the search for the factors which may cause productivity to vary from time to time or place to place. Of these the measurement of output has probably given the most trouble and the most references in the literature.

The trouble is, of course, that output is very seldom any simple thing that can be measured in a constant unit from point to point, although such cases do arise : for example, refined sugar, coal, and flying hours have turned up in productivity studies and have been measured in tons of sugar, tons of coal, and hours, without any problems arising of comparing one sort with another. (Coal, of course, does vary considerably in type and quality, but many studies have been made on the assumption that this variation can be ignored.)

The Need for a Comparable Measure of Output

In most cases a variety of goods or activities will be produced which have in some way to be made commensurable. In some simple cases one or two qualities may be sufficient to group the products so that to each group a unit of output can be put in a fair relationship to other units. For example, in the Cotton Industry study described overleaf, the only thing that appeared to have a recognisable effect on productivity in spinning was the count of the yarn spun.

It was therefore reasonable to draw a smooth curve to lie evenly among the points representing the average man-hour requirements per unit output for mills spinning particular counts of yarn. Any individual mill could then be compared with a notional mill spinning the same count and with a requirement lying on this curve. Various suggestions have been made for getting such factors for particular products, some of more validity than others. In the steel rolling case mentioned above, it was possible by detailed Statistical study to get target figures for machine hours per ton rolled for various types of steel and these figures could be given with some knowledge of their limits or error. It has been suggested, from time to time, that for many engineering operations the figures produced by time study could be of value. On the other hand this view has been strongly attacked.

Whether such figures are usable almost certainly depends on the type of comparison that is to be made. For comparisons from time to time at one factory or other unit where the market basket of goods produced will vary only slightly, and where the same men are making the time studies (so that one of the biggest sources of variation is eliminated), it is probable that time study figures are quite good enough for comparisons. Errors in the weights when the market basket is varying only slightly will have a trivial effect. On the other hand, for comparison between productive units, figures produced by time study are likely to be doubtful in view of the known variability of the rating technique, even if they are produced by the same observer, and if produced by different observers they are almost certainly valueless.

The conclusion of the special committee of the I.C.W.A. and I.P.E. was that in the present state of the art of time study, the variations in standards and consistency of time study officers made standard times set by these means no basis for inter-firm Comparison of productivity. Tests by Winston

Rodgers, Kinniburgh and Vallance and other workers have shown a very low consistency in rating. These tests have been attacked on the grounds that the officers tested were not chosen to be highly skilled in the art; certain firms claim that by internal training and testing they can get a high degree of consistency ; unfortunately no results on which to check this claim have yet been published, nor have any tests been made to show whether time study officers showing consistency within firms would also show consistency between firms in rating the same tasks.

The I.C.W.A./I.P.E. condemnation of the use of time study for interfirm comparison therefore appears still to be justified. Within a single plant, for reasons given later, average times either as measured or corrected by rating are probably a usable basis for inter-temporal comparisons. For comparisons between branches of one company all making the same sort of output, it is a matter of internal testing whether raw times, times corrected by rating, or other measures can be used for comparisons.

Another attack on this problem has been made by the British Boot, Shoe and Allied Trades Research Association (S.A.T.R.A.) by reducing the products to one standard product. It is clear that this method is applicable only when the goods vary but little among themselves. In the S.A.T.R.A. studies a number of factories all making the same general type of shoe were considered for example, twelve factories making " Goodyear " welted men's shoes.

Such shoes were reduced to comparability by translating the factory figures to those for a "standard " shoe, made by the basic operations required to make a pair of shoes of the particular type. If the factory used extra operations they would be ignored, their times not counted in. If operations were done by a non-standard method an attempt would be made to translate these figures into those for the standard method by any means available, but usually on the principle that the piece rates in the factory for the standard and non-standard methods would be proportional to the basic amount of work involved.

Thus S.A.T.R.A. was able to produce for each factory, and for each operation, a number of man minutes per dozen standard pairs involved to show the range of variation between firms and to go a long way to identifying factors that were usually associated with high or low productivity.

The method used by the Bureau of Labour Statistics is a variant of that for which standard weights are applied to the products. In the development of its methods the Bureau was undoubtedly influenced both by the fact that initially its aim was to get figures which could be combined into a global index for the United States economy and also by the need for a method which could largely be applied by the accountants at the firms studied. In its approach to an industry it would draw up not only a sample of firms in the industry but also, after discussion with the firms, a list of standard products.

In the base year it would find the production of these products and the number of man hours required to make each of them. In subsequent years it would take the quantities of these products made and the number of man hours required to make the total output of them; one could then compare the number of man hours required for these with the man hours that would have been required at the productivities for the individual products of the base year. The B.L.S. then used these figures to show scatter within the industry from year to year and trends for the whole industry.

DEFINING INPUT

To turn now to the question of inputs, these are in general more easy to identify, and the problem is rather that of deciding what to do about the relationship of the productivity of one factor to that of another. In some cases one factor is so clearly the important one that it is sufficient to take productivity in terms of that one factor alone. For example, during the war, in studies of the relationship of flying to the bottlenecks limiting it, it was found that as a rule maintenance manpower was the sole limiting factor except for certain particular operations and types of aircraft.

Flying hours per maintenance man were therefore the thing that was particularly studied in the development of planned flying though it was realised at the time that in other circumstances different limiting factors might be important. Most American industrial studies also concentrate on output per man hour almost exclusively, probably because of the tradition in the States of a relative labour shortage arising from an open frontier to which labour could always go.

However, the emphasis on labour to the exclusion of everything else has come under strong attack in Europe. Clearly raw materials, fuel and capital may all be important. Two approaches are then possible. One is to measure the productivity of each of these factors (output per man hour, output per kilowatt hour, output per ton of coal, etc.), look at the fluctuations of these from place to place and from time to time, and see if there are any correlations between them. The other possibility is to try to get some sort of a joint production function by statistical or other means. These two, of course, merge into one another. Methods for dealing with them probably have to be developed ad hoc, but it is worth drawing attention to two particular cases.

First, in the study of production functions for farms, J. O. Jones has made a number of statistical studies which are a somewhat simplified approach to multiple correlation analysis, in which the type of analysis is designed to show up differences in type of relationship from one end of the scale to the other and changes from straight line to curvilinear regression if these should appear.

Roughly speaking, his method has been to take the output of the farms and to relate it to a number of factors such as acreage, man hours put in over the year, tenant's capital, expenditure on fertilisers. These figures were used by classifying the farms into groups on two of the factors and looking for trends in each group for output per unit of a third factor. By this means Jones was able to develop production functions with a high degree of confidence. One of his results was distinctly unexpected, namely, the lack of apparent effect of tenant's capital on farm output. This result seemed inescapable from the figures he used, surprising as it may seem ; it gives room for a good deal of conjecture as to its possible cause.

A number of writers have attempted to develop productivity indices that will somehow take all factors into account. For example, Sir Ewart Smith and Dr. Beeching have suggested the estimation of all the man hours that have gone into a product (including those required in making all raw material ; bought out parts, fuel and power used in the manufacture, and those which are notionally consumed by the depreciation of the capital used in its manufacture), and comparison of output with this overall figure. The estimation of such a figure presents formidable problems and little has been published to show how it could be done in a practical case. One attempt at such a calculation has been given by W. Langenburg. He remains, however, slightly sceptical about the value of such an overall figure when it has been obtained.

It has already been pointed out that the usefulness of a productivity figure is not its indication that a firm should be praised or blamed, but its spotlighting of the parts of the firm, or the particular firms, that should be looked at, or the light it throws on the causes of variation from place to place. The trouble about such an all-embracing figure, even if theoretically impeccable, is tha. it is so very difficult to interpret.

For example, the figures which show how output per man hour, output per unit of fuel, output per unit of raw material and so on all vary, may throw a good deal of light on the exchange rate between one of these inputs and another, but the overall index which manages to bring all the inputs nearer into one denominator will hide this and it is very difficult to see what one can learn from the figures. Frcm the businessman's point of view, of course, there is one way of lumping together all inputs, namely, by the prices at which they may be bought.

Clearly, it is of interest to get as high an output as possible, preferably in terms of selling price per £1 worth of input. The inputs are put together on the basis of their cost; but cost accountancy has not usually been considered a branch of productivity measurement. This is perhaps a pity; the combination of the study of the real causes of variations of output per unit of labour or raw materials and of costs would probably be most valuable to production engineer and cost accountant

Identifying the Factors which cause Variations in Productivity

To turn to the third group of problems, that of identifying the factors which cause productivity to vary, one can only say here that a wide variety of types of factor have been studied. Which factors are looked at will depend partly upon the working hypothesis of the Operational Research worker, but partly also upon which factors show possibilities of being changed. Working conditions, capital equipment, technical process, training of the worker, organisation, state of trade, length of run, human relations in the firm, design of product, all these factors may affect the productivity of the firm.

Theoretically it is possible to try to cover all factors, and this is in fact being done in a study at present being carried out on three firms by a team at the Oxford Institute of Statistics but to attempt to cover all factors at once requires extremely detailed first-hand study for a long time, and even then it may be very difficult to see the wood for the trees. It is certainly not something to be attempted in every case where it is thought that efficiency may be varying from time to time or from place to place.

It is impossible to go here into all the various things that might be studied, but a few cases may be mentioned as being suggestive. The cotton spinning studies referred to above produced a good deal of information about the effect of machine speeds and settings on labour productivity. The S.A.T.R.A. studies also took into account the effect of quality, factory organisation, and systems of payment. The Building Research Station's analysis of the costs of building on sites showed up effects of number of houses, size of house, features of design, and degree of subcontracting.

Using the number of houses on the site as a parameter, their results tally with those found for a number of other industries, in which productivity continues to rise as a small power of the total production of a particular product, for an astonishingly long time. J. A. Mark has made studies of the effect of age on labour productivity and C. D. Harbury has compared urban with rural workers.

It may be possible to study the effect of such imponderable things as human relations even where no numerical measure of productivity is available. A good deal of work at the University of Michigan and at Oxford has been devoted to studying the effects on productivity in a firm of the relationship between the foreman and his team and organisation in the firm. Their method was to get pairs of teams such that both teams of each pair were doing work generally agreed to be comparable and such also that there was general agreement which of the teams was of the higher productivity.

Then it was possible to look for measures of statistical association between high productivity and such characteristics as authoritarian or democratic relationship between foreman and men, degree of training given by the foreman, the extent to which a foreman kept the men in his confidence, and so on. These results, though containing no numerical measure of productivity, are probably perfectly valid.

Many warnings must be issued: since the time of the Hawthorne experiments at the General Electric Company it has been known that worker performance may depend quite largely on the attitude of the workers, notwithstanding changes in conditions. In the Hawthorne experiments the conditions of a group of workers were changed and it was found that every change effect to a rise in productivity, even though some of the changes were of previous ones, and it appeared that the operative factor was the feeling on the part of the team studied that they were worthy of individual attention and hence people who had some special contribution to make. This effect on their attitude to work was far more important than the changes in physical conditions.

There is not as a rule room for elabourate statistical methods in studying the factors that may affect productivity; far more important are first-hand observations that will lead to useful hypotheses about likely factors and the collection of sufficient material for these factors to have a chance to show their effect.

One plausible statistical approach, (or other input) used day by day and the corresponding outputs of a list 'products and using regression analysis To find the input required per unit of each product, has proved to lead to nonsensical results in several studies (all, perhaps understandably, unpublished communications). It is likely that the variability in productivity from day to day on isolated jobs, and the tendency for records to pick up errors of their own, introduce too much randomness into the figures for them to stand such detailed treatment.

A good account of the difficulties produced by errors, arbitrariness, omissions and other peculiarities of works records is given by Luttrell ; it cannot be over-emphasised that the origin and meaning of any figures found in firms should be scrutinised very carefully before they are used for purposes other than those for which they were intended.

It must always be remembered moreover that productivity is liable to vary from time to time and there is probably room for investigation of the causes of this fluctuation. Several studies have shown that if firms are ranged in order of productiviiy not only will the range from highest to lowest, for any particular input factor, be quite large, but also that within this range the particular firms are liable to change their order from time to time in quite short periods. There is room for study of the reasons why these variations, from time to time, in the order occur, and why also some firms appear to be able to survive in competition with others which are great deal more efficient technically.

It may be that those which seem to be most efficient Fall back after a time and some of the less efficient climb up in response to the goad of poor results or for other reasons, or it may be that changes in trade conditions favour first one firm, then another.

There is room for investigation here, though this should probably be regarded rather as industrial economics than as Operational Research, except possibly if it is carried out within a multi-plant firm which requires the information for immediate business decisions and is concerned rather with the operations of the components of one firm than with a general study of the variations in efficiency within industry as a whole.

Chapter 6

Ultimate Goal of Operations Research

The ultimate goal of Operations Research is to measure the relative worth of alternatives on the basis of reasonably accurate estimates. Such measurements can never be substituted for decision making by the qualified manager, who remains the one responsible for risk taking. As stated by Peter F. Drucker: "To try to eliminate risk in business enterprise is futile. The main goal of a management science must be to enable business to take the right risk" and by D. N. Chorafas: "In fact, in engineering and in management, the main objective of operations research, and of the allied methods for system analysis, is to provide the executive with a rational basis for making decisions/'

Such decisions are to be based essentially upon one of two possibilities. In some cases, Operations Research provides the tools by which several alternatives may be tested on a trial basis. This makes it possible to select one of the alternatives that have been tested or even may stimulate the thinking of those involved toward another alternative, that can in turn be tested. This is basically the approach of the Simulation Techniques. In other cases, Operations Research uses mathematical methods to determine the most desirable alternative among all alternatives that could be considered.

Because the value of any alternative, as a whole, is based upon the effect of the interrelationships between all factors involved, only a few of these factors or maybe none of them can be optimized on their own, while the others are ignored completely. This is why what has been called "suboptimization" (which is an attempt to optimize only some of the factors involved) cannot be practiced effectively unless full attention is given to the whole picture.

STEP 1. SELECTING THE FACTORS

Before a decision can be made, one has to know which factors should be considered as pertinent. Recent developments in Operations Research have called attention to the possibility of considering factors which either would not have been recognized as deserving attention, or would have been deliberately ignored for various reasons, such as the inability or the prohibitive cost of evaluating them.

One of the main problems of production planning, the determination of the economic-lot size, will illustrate. The conventional approach takes only three factors into consideration: the set-up cost, the size of the inventory that is needed to satisfy the customer demand over a one-year period, and the cost of carrying such an inventory. In recent years, the problem of the economic-lot size has been the subject of extensive research work.

Attention has been called to the need for considering such factors as material handling costs, cost of equipment idleness resulting in some cases from the fact that large lots, because of material handling problems, are less schedulable into sequences which maintain high equipment utilization, quantity discounts, in-process inventory, interrelation of several parts that are required for the same assembly, cost of deliberately failing to meet delivery dates, and the impact of what has been called the "learning curve" and is also called the "manufacturing progress function.

These are only a few of the many factors that, in recent years, have been proposed in addition to the three conventional ones for the purpose of determining an economic-lot size. Furthermore, the economic-lot size is only an illustration of what has been a general trend toward increasing the number of pertinent factors to be selected before making a decision. Essentially, there are three reasons why Operations Research started this trend. One reason is that groups of specialists, operating as a team and sometimes meeting in brainstorming sessions, have an opportunity of merging their skills, each of them focusing his attention upon the aspect of the problem with which he is most familiar: marketing, psychology, or electronic engineering, for example.

None of them, if left alone, can think of all the factors they will list when operating as a group. Another reason is that, without using the new methods of model making and mathematical computations (these methods are reviewed later as Steps 3, 4, and 5), it would have been unrealistic to consider measuring the very complex interrelationships of so many factors. Last, but not least, new approaches have been offered to provide a quantitative evaluation for some factors which in the past were considered as not measurable and, for this reason, had to be ignored deliberately. This brings us to Step 2.

STEP 2. EVALUATING THE FACTORS QUANTITATIVELY

Some of the new methods offered for evaluating the factors in quantitative terms are well established, others are still controversial. Whenever factors are considered as having "some influence" upon the results to be obtained in following one course of action rather than another one, difficulties are encountered which arise because three conditions exist:

1. Some factors are intangible items.
2. Some are tangible, but their actual measurement would be impossible either for technical or economical reasons.
3. Some are partly under the control of another party and the data, even if existing, are not within reach.

Operations research has made a special effort to overcome these three obstacles, by evaluating intangible items, making extensive use of statistical methods, using the Monte-Carlo technique, and applying the game theory. These four approaches will be reviewed briefly.

Evaluation of intangible items

This is one of the most delicate aspects of Operations Research. Although this approach can often be very helpful in providing reasonable guidance, there is always the pitfall that the evaluation of the intangible deviates substantially from the true value, which may never be established or may later be discovered on the basis of wisdom of hindsight. This is true in many cases, but especially so, when human factors become involved. To a certain extent, the objections that can be made in such a case are related to a certain concept of human nature. This concept is in op position to the idea that a human personality can be rigidly defined or quantitatively measured.

At the same time, it is a fact that intangible factors have to be evaluated whenever possible. Even if the evaluations are not 100 per cent accurate, they provide a very useful guidance as long as they are reasonably accurate. Specifically, they provide a standard of measurement for costs that are tangible but not measurable from the point of view of their effectiveness.

To illustrate: such costs as the cost of scheduling, of subcontracting, or of keeping inventory at a high level either throughout the year or during part of the year in a seasonal business, are tangible ones, whether the costs are recorded or reasonably easy to estimate if they are not recorded. How can they be compared to the resulting benefits, such as the ability to meet customer's demand, or to maintain employment at a steady level in the plant? These benefits are not recorded. In fact they are intangible.

As a result, the decisions made are often unwarranted. For instance, the tangible costs are greatly reduced while the resulting increase in intangible costs is ignored, thus saving money at a cost that exceeds the savings. Sometimes the reverse is true. The intangible costs are overestimated. This leads toward undue increase of tangible costs on the basis of unwarranted assumptions.

Operations Research has, in many cases, solved this dilemma by offering the quantitative evaluation of what can be gained or lost by making the decision. For instance, the cost of scheduling, of subcontracting, or of keeping inventory at the high level throughout the year or part of the year, which are tangible costs, have been related to other costs, that are intangible, but nevertheless have been measured. Some of these measured intangible costs include the cost of failing to maintain a steady employment, the cost of cancelled orders, and/or the loss of goodwill resulting from the failure to deliver on time.

The methods followed to assign a quantitative value preferably using the dollar as a unitary from case to case.

They may be based upon extensive research, including, for instance, an evaluation of the probability that the demand will be in excess of the sales forecast and a measurement of the cost of failing to deliver in relation to such a probability. The methods used may also be based merely upon asking such a question as: "How much would management be willing to spend outright in order to change this factor or eliminate that risk?"

Extensive use of statistical methods

Statistical methods, and, specifically, the probability theory, the sampling method, and the waiting-lines (or queuing) theory are being used extensively. They make it possible to provide a quantitative evaluation of factors, the direct measurement of which would otherwise be impossible or impractical for various reasons.

The probability theory provides the ratio of the chances favoring an event to the total number of chances for and against it. Such a ratio can be used in a great variety of circumstances so as to determine the optimum conditions of operation, For instance, for the purpose of production planning, its application makes it possible to evaluate the number of parts that should be ordered in excess of the number of parts needed for assembly to provide a given probability that this excess will compensate for and not exceed too greatly the rate of rejects by quality control.

The sampling method is based upon the random selection of some of the units under consideration. The selected group, the "sampled population" is easier to measure because it is only a fraction of the total group, the "target population." The transfer of conclusions from the sampled population to the target population is based upon an evaluation of the probability of the degree of validity of the transfer (confidence limits). This requires common sense as well as mathematical ability.

The sampling method is not expected to provide absolutely accurate information. In some cases, its use is justified by the cost reduction involved, for instance, for the purpose of quality control in manufacturing. In other cases, the sampling method makes it possible to obtain quantitative information which otherwise would not be available, for instance, a market survey, based upon the interviewing of a few hundred individuals, reflects the attitude of thousands of customers who could not be approached one-by-one.

The waiting-line (or queuing) theory deals with the fact that services cannot always be made available at the precise time they are needed. The question is: what is the quantitative relationship between an improvement in the service and the reduction of the waiting line? This makes it possible to determine how much more money should be spent to improve the service. To illustrate; after World War II, the Bell Telephone Labouratories started the development of a new telephone-switching system. A new group of circuits was designed to select available lines at the time the caller lifts the receiver and is waiting for the dial tone.

The question was: how long could the customer afford to wait, not only on the average, but at times when telephone calls are most frequent? Ultimately, the decision with regard to the adequate system was based upon an evaluation of the waiting time for the dial tone and the impact of this waiting time upon the telephone customer versus the cost of a given system as compared to the cost of an alternate system.

The queuing theory has been used in manufacturing, for instance, to decide what can be spent in preventive maintenance for the purpose of avoiding the loss due to the waiting time related to machine breakdown, or to make an evaluation of machine waiting time so as to determine the most economical approach to be followed when several machines are operated by one man. The queuing theory has also been used to evaluate the size of the inventory required to optimize the cost of waiting for delivery of goods.

Research recently has been started at General Electric which is considering the use of the queuing theory to determine the optimum plant layout by comparing the cost of more machines to the benefit of less in-process inventory. This research work, which is still in the preliminary stage, was reported in 1959 at a General Electric Simulation Seminar and Workshop by H. B, Carter, Manager of Plant Layout and Material Service of the Manufacturing Engineering Service.

Use of the Monte-Carlo technique

The Monte-Carlo technique makes it possible to obtain approximate evaluations in cases where even the sampling method could not be considered, either because of the complexity of the situation, or because only hypotheses are to be tested. The Monte-Carlo technique originated with the mathematical study of the perambulation of a drunkard. His "random walk" was simulated by the random selection of n two-digit numbers out of a table including one thousand two-digit numbers, and the preparation of a model using the selected numbers to compute the distance he would cover after having walked n steps.

To illustrate: in 1954, the United Air Lines applied the Monte-Carlo technique to study problems of aircraft routing and maintenance. An airport station simulation model was set up on an electronic computer, an IBM 704. The simulation varied the input of such items as manpower, facilities, and schedule or maintenance policies, and indicated as output such things as idle manpower, utilization of maintenance docks, schedule delays, and, maintenance, working, and waiting time. The relationship between input and output was based upon the use of the sampling technique, but and this is characteristic of the Monte Carlo technique and its simulation the sample was not taken from an actual population, but from an "analog" population, selected because it was expected to reflect the same kind of probability as the conditions of operation.

Application of the game theory

In spite of their wide diversifications, the factors-evaluation methods, described up to this point, have one thing in common: they deal with factors that are accessible. Operations Research has attempted to go even further by considering methods that are intended to evaluate quantitatively the inaccessible factors such as decisions already made but unknown, or decisions expected to be made by competitors on the basis of what they know. Such methods are based upon Von Neumann's ideas, his minimax principle which tends toward the minimization of maximum loss and upon the game theory that developed as a result of these ideas. Although these concepts have received increasing recognition, their application is still a controversial issue Step 3. Interrelating the Factors in a Model

For the purpose of decision making, it is meaningless to consider each pertinent factor on its own without relating it to all other factors that are considered pertinent. To spend $100,000 a year to operate quality control in a given plant manufacturing instruments of high precision may be a very reasonable cost with due regard to the conditions of operation. In another plant, where the volume of production is lower or where plastic toys are being made, $10,000 may well prove to be an undue amount. The cost of quality control, unless considered in relation to the conditions of operation, is, by itself, meaningless. This illustrates that it would be useless to evaluate quantitatively all factors that have been considered as pertinent (Step 1 and Step 2) unless they can be quantitatively related to each other. The problem does not arise so much because there is a great number of factors involved; it is essentially that the factors considered as pertinent are so diversified that the nature of their interaction varies greatly from one group to another.

For instance, eighteen finished items include a minimum of 120 parts and a maximum of 630 parts per item. Some parts go into one item only, some go into all of the eighteen. A total of 777 parts is being used. It happens that five of these parts are not available on time because of an unusual rate of reject by quality control. Scheduling had not expected it. As a result, unless the decision is made to do something, we will fail to deliver on time the orders placed by three customers.

To make the decision, the cost of failure to deliver on time must be compared to the cost of overtime that will be needed to set up and operate ten of the fifteen machines used to manufacture the five parts which we are short of. The complexity of making the comparison is even greater if one considers that it also must be related to many other factors, such as the possibility of subcontracting or the possibility of delaying the delivery of other orders, or the revision of engineering specifications.

The challenge, therefore, is not only to measure quantitatively all the factors considered as pertinent, but also to evaluate the interaction between the factors and to do so in spite of the fact that many of these are fundamentally different from each other. The approach followed in operations research to meet this challenge is the construction of a model.

By definition, a model is the representation of something to be made or already existing. This representation may be either an approximate, possibly simplified reproduction, or it may be an abstract presentation of symbolic character. Both approaches are followed by operations research. Some models use logical and mathematical symbols. They can be called "Mathematical Models." Other models provide essentially a working analogy and for this reason can be called "Analog Models/' Let us review briefly these two fundamental concepts.

The mathematical model is intended to reflect, in quantitative terms, the relative influence of each factor upon the whole situation and the impact that a change in one or another of the factors would have upon some or all of the others. The mathematical model provides the framework within which the relative worth of alternatives can be determined by proceeding with computations which are based upon both the quantitative evaluation of the factors and the quantitative evaluation of each factor's influence. Many of the mathematical models offered in operations research basically attempt to relate the factors under consideration to each other by taking advantage of the fact that some factors can be related to each other in linear functions and that the linear equations thus determined can be grouped into the rows and columns of matrix algebra. This is the fundamental approach of linear programming.

Mathematical models are generally used for the precise computations involved in such fields as production planning, inventory control, warehousing problems, and distribution of sales effort between various marketing areas. It has also been suggested that they be considered to prepare reasonably simple formulas that can be used on a routine basis applying the simulation techniques.

The Analog Model, in spite of the fact that there is no standard terminology available to designate clearly a type of model, can be considered as providing a concrete and simplified visualization of the system under consideration. For instance, a given process of manufacturing may be represented by a model that shows graphically the sequence of operations and also the possible alternatives in this sequence. Actual data related to the performance sequences are to be part of the model.

The analog model does not attempt to provide the kind of precision that is expected from the mathematical model.

Because it offers an analysis of the system which, by definition, is based upon the selection of the factors considered as essential ones, the analog model often provides a better understanding of the situation than a completely accurate, and, therefore, not selective model, could provide. For this reason, analog models are being used extensively when the simulation techniques are being employed.

How rigorous must the model be and how rigorous can the model afford to be? This is the fundamental problem that requires a balance between two extremes.

There appear to be certain inadequacies in much of the earlier and current research into organization. In one type of approach, experimental control has been emphasized. Ease and simplicity of experimentation have been obtained by almost complete sacrifice of realism. The results have been rigorous but limited and, in the main, are incapable of being used for extrapolation to problems in real ongoing organizations. On the other hand, there have been thorough observational studies of particular organizations. The results of these studies are rich in detail, but lack the generality required in the development of theory and methods for solving problems in organizations other than the ones studied.

A balance must be struck between these extremes, one which retains the necessary experimental rigor without sacrificing consideration of the essential forces and interrelations that characterize all organizations. A balanced approach appears to stand the best chance of success in making a direct attack on organizational problems. In recent research work, more attention has been given to the need for such a balance. This is especially the case when operations research considers information handling and the impact of decision-making practices within the organization structure from the point of view of an integrated system concept.

The restrictions or boundary conditions exclude solutions which would be provided by such computations as the ones related to matrix algebra but would be antagonistic to the conditions of operations. For instance, if a contract has been signed which requires the delivery of 15,000 units of Item No. 123, any solution that provides for less production of this item during the period under consideration will be excluded even though it may prove to be the most economical one in relation to the production capacity and the sales forecast of other items.

Such routine restrictions as the number of working hours per day or the fact that some factors, by definition, are non-negative ones also must be included. Routine restrictions will automatically exclude solutions which would be mathematically sound but completely illogical, if, for instance, they require thirty-seven hours of work per man per day, or the manufacturing of not twenty-six, but minus twenty-six Parts No. 12345. Other restrictions are less obvious, but also must be taken into consideration. For instance, if some parts are of such physical dimensions that it is impractical to store large numbers of them between successive operations, then a part cannot be produced at any given time unless it can be processed without delay to the next operation.

STEP 5. UTILIZING THE MODEL MATHEMATICAL PROGRAMMING SYSTEM SIMULATION AND INDUSTRIAL GAMES

Some models are used, for the most part, to determine, on the basis of mathematical programming, which of the alternatives under consideration provides the most profitable solution. This purpose can be served by mathematical models and by some kind of analog models. Other kinds of analog models are considered as system simulation and are used either for training purposes or to clarify a problem and thus stimulate the thinking of operating executives and supervisors prior to decision making. These two approaches will now be reviewed.

Mathematical programming

Whenever two linear functions related to the same variable are under consideration, the optimum solution can easily be determined either by simple algebraic computations, or, in some cases, by a graphical presentation which will locate the point where the two functions have the same value. This is, for instance, the case of the determination of the "Limit Point L" when selecting a given piece of equipment among several ones considered for purchase.

Whenever a few non-linear functions, possibly associated with linear ones, none having an impact upon the structure of the other ones, and all related to the same variable, are being considered, they can be combined into one non-linear function. Using the conventional methods of calculus in equating to zero the derivative of this single function, it is easy to determine the optimum solution. This is, for instance, the case of the computation of the economic-lot size in accordance with the conventional method, where the cost of the setup per unit, the cost of inventory keeping per unit, and the cost of production per unit in relation to the lot size are combined into a cumulative function.

This cumulative function, the variable of which is also the lot size provides the U-curve, the minimum value of which is established by equating its derivative to zero.

Such methods do not apply to the complex models of operations research, matrices, or other models. New methods of computation have been offered to derive the optimum solution. One of them, the simplex method, is probably the most widely used in linear programming. Actually, the computing procedures available are very complex, and it is generally recognized that they should be simplified. As stated by Professor P. M. Morse, of Massachusetts Institute of Technology: "Techniques of solution are not simple and many of them require high-speed computing machines; much further mathematical research is needed to simplify computing procedures in linear programming computations."

It is to be expected that the needed simplification in present computing procedures will characterize the evolution in the field in the years to come. In the meantime, present computing procedures should be understood at least in general terms by the student who wants to appreciate the value and the possibilities of modern techniques in the determination of the relative worth of alternatives.

There is no established trend toward the simplification of computing procedures. One approach that has been suggested is to simplify the structure of the model whenever possible. As stated:

In order to translate the scheduling problem into a mathematical problem of minimizing a cost function, we need a mathematical form that is both sufficiently flexible to approximate a wide range of complex cost relationships, and sufficiently simple to allow easy mathematical solutions.

To a certain extent, the most recent developments in the field of electronic computers have helped in handling the delicate situation created by the use of very complex computing procedures. The statement was even made that: "with the wide variety of computer programmes that are now available, the method of finding solutions fades into secondary importance to the problem of formulating the model for the average practitioner."

In fact, there are instances where electronic computers determine the cost of each of the solutions under consideration, using what is known as iteration methods. This is not the case when mathematical models have been constructed for the purpose of determining the optimum solution, which implies the choice between a very large number of alternatives and requires the use of electronic computers for working out a linear programming solution. It can be the case, however, when an analog model is being used and when the choice has to be made between a relatively small number of alternatives. In such a case, the electronic computer can provide an estimate of the cost of each alternative. This automatically indicates which is the most profitable one. This is an approach widely used when applying the simulation techniques to be described now.

System Simulation and Industrial Games

The system simulation and industrial games constitute an approach somewhat different from mathematical programming. Most of the time the model used will be an analog model, including of course the necessary data. The model may be purely hypothetical and even deliberately far away from the conditions of operations, the substance of which it intends to represent. In such cases, the model is actually an educational game to be used either for research work or for training. In fact, in recent years, games based upon simulation processes have been extensively used by industry, universities, and professional associations for the training of students and supervisors as well as the presidents of companies.

Following another approach, the model may be a direct representation of the conditions of operation, for instance, the plant where a scheduling problem is being considered. In such a case, the working model, also called the "simulator," includes a recording of all information on magnetic tape and a time-measurement device that is part of the simulator. The model includes only carefully selected machine centers, not all machines, and is based upon approximate data provided by existing records. In such a case, simulation shows the direction that should be explored in more detail and in a more accurate manner.

It also provides an opportunity to test various hypotheses. The use of electronic computers makes it possible to evaluate in dollars the cost of any alternative that is being tested on the basis of suggestions made by the participants. For these reasons, it has been found that the simulation techniques can be used not only for the purpose of training the participants and increasing their interest in a new system, but also for the purpose of stimulating their thinking. The game may throw light on some aspects of the problem that had not received the attention they deserve, and may develop better solutions than the ones that would have been arrived at without using the system simulation as a research device.

Like most of the new techniques, simulation can be misused. As stated by D. N. Chorafas: "The increased emphasis on simulation studies and the corresponding lack of experience from the part of some people who attempt to apply the method can lead to pseudo-simulation." At the same time, experience has shown that, if properly conducted, simulation can be very useful. The case of General Electric will illustrate.

Simulation at General Electric

At General Electric, simulation is being successfully applied in manufacturing planning, plant layout, and production control. The typical steps followed in establishing and utilizing a mathematical model have been as follows:

First: Data gathering by two or three manufacturing engineers over a period of several months.

Second: One or two good mathematical modellers applying the techniques of computer analysis to the solution of the manufacturing problems. This typically takes one to three months.

Third: Two computer programmers take about two to four months to prepare the instructions in machine-sensible language.

Fourth: One or two programmers may take one to three months to make corrections and changes in the programming so that it functions properly and efficiently.

Fifth: The time for applications by the operating personnel depends upon the selected course of action.

At General Electric, by using simulation, the manufacturing personnel have found answers to such questions as:

- Is the new shop layout right and scheduled correctly to obtain the best use of the men and machines?
- Can we really meet the delivery promises we have given the customer?
- Is the amount of inventory tied up in the factory really justified?

- Why does it take two weeks to produce a product with only a day's direct labour in it?

Dynamic computer simulation seems to offer many of the answers to these important but perplexing questions. It provides an opportunity to gain "experience" beforehand and use this valuable hindsight in planning the new operation.

At General Electric, in one of the Departments engaged in motor production, one of several coil-manufacturing areas was simulated on a large computer. Four months of operation took only fifteen minutes, a reduction of roughly 3,000 to 1. This sort of speed permits economical exploration not only of various scheduling and product mix plans, but also of machine tool selection and layout possibilities, or even better maintenance planning. Capacities and limitations of the shop under various scheduling combinations are readily determinable.

Improvements in this coil-manufacturing area showed annual savings of $100,000 in direct and indirect labour costs and, in addition, a 50 per cent reduction in the manufacturing cycle, a 20 per cent reduction in work-in-process inventory, and a 20 per cent improvement in scheduling accuracy.

These improvements were primarily due to changes in scheduling methods and also in the methods to be followed for dispatching when the schedule, for one reason or another, could not be met exactly.

The same Department next simulated a new manufacturing to aid them in preparing their layout. A variety of product mixes was tested, and the layout that had already been made by conventional means, but was still at the stage of a model, was substantially changed, thus avoiding subsequent costly rearrangements of actual equipment. In another department, manufacturing a variety of transformers, a model was prepared and the situation run on a medium-sized computer. The information gained made it possible to obtain the following results:

- Maximum capacity was found to be substantially greater than originally estimated
- Work-in-process inventory was reduced 42 per cent
- The manufacturing cycle was reduced over 50 per cent
- Additional equipments that were considered for purchase were found to be unnecessary
- At General Electric, simulation has become an accepted, essential tool to management planning.

STEP 6. FOLLOW-UP AND CONTROL

Last, but not least, this step, follow-up and control is to be considered as part of the over-all process of operations research. Most of the data used, and most of the evaluations made, as previously mentioned, are evaluations rather than actual, precise measurements. A follow-up procedure is obviously needed as soon as it can be carried out without requiring unwarranted research. The follow-up will verify whether or not the evaluations are within reasonable limits of accuracy. The same procedure applies to the model that was constructed. In addition, changes are bound to occur in the conditions of operation. Whenever these changes are of substantial magnitude their impact should be evaluated.

Addition of New Pertinent Factors

Some factors that have not been taken into consideration may require attention after a certain period. The fact that they have not been considered as pertinent may be due either to: failure to select them at the right time, or a change in the conditions of operations. As an example of the latter case, when new items are added to the line of products being manufactured and their manufacturing cycle is much longer, the factor "in-process inventory" which had been deliberately ignored must now be taken into consideration.

Elimination of Existing Factors

Factors, at times, may have to be deleted from the model. For instance, a change in the line of products may lead toward the elimination of "in-process inventory" as a pertinent factor,

Re-evaluation of the Factors

It can happen that a substantial increase in competition clearly indicates that the value assigned to the failure to deliver on time should be reconsidered.

Re-evaluation of the Interaction of the Factors

This affects the structure of the model. Reevaluation may be made necessary, for instance, by changes in the plant layout or the sales-district structure, or the warehousing facilities, or by the opening of a new plant. It may also be required because substantial discrepancies are discovered between the actual performance in the plant and the expected one. If the variance is excessive, it indicates, possibly, that the model used for scheduling was not adequate. Other factors, such as an unexpectable breakdown may of course be the cause. This should not be ignored.

These considerations indicate the need for a control procedure that will make it possible to evaluate actual performance in relation to the estimates that were made and to detect the need for revisions. A balance must, of course, be kept between the two extremes. One extreme is failure to adjust the various factors or the model itself. The other extreme is to make changes, having to pay the high cost that such changes involve, when the variance should be considered as negligible.

Chapter 7

Identifying Sources of Operational Risk

Risks like market and credit risk can often lurk undetected in hidden exposures of a company. Operational risk seems to suffer the reverse malady—the concept itself is so broad that operational risk can be found in just about everything. For this reason, identifying op risk in general should not be the goal of the firm. Rather, identifying meaningful operational risks that can have a significant impact on the value of the firm is the task at hand, and it is not an easy one.

Operational risk identification is more art than science and can get sticky for several reasons. First, the definition of operational risk and its distinction from business risk at any particular firm depends strongly on the risk management and business strategies of the firm. A company in Operational risk identification is more art than science and can get sticky for several reasons. First, the definition of operational risk and its distinction from business risk at any particular firm depends strongly on the risk management and business strategies of the firm.

A company in the commodity export business, for example, bears a number of supply chain and logistic risks—crop spoilage, processing plant malfunctions, quality verification problems, truck breakdowns, worker strikes. As an expert on supply chain issues, the firm may well consider all those risks as normal business risks well within the purview of its expertise. If those same risks faced a bank, it might be tempting to call them op risks. But when facing the commodity exporter whose main business is dealing with those aspects of supply chain management, differentiating between business risk and op risk is tough.

A second complication to operational risk identification arises from the linkage between the risk and loss. Operational risk-related losses are quite often driven by market, credit, or liquidity risks. The failure of Barings to catch the huge position build-up by rogue trader Nick Leeson was in some sense an operational risk management failure. It was a failure of processes (i.e., internal audit and control), people (i.e., Leeson was defrauding the firm and others), and systems (i.e., a consolidated global position-keeping system would have revealed Leeson's rogue positions). But in the end, Barings went bust because Leeson's positions went underwater as a result of their market risk. Operational risk management may have failed to catch the process, personnel, and systems problem, but market risk sank the firm.

Most operational risks ultimately translate into potential losses for a firm because the operational risks expose the firm to market, credit, or liquidity risk. Separating op risk-driven market risk losses from normal business-related market risk losses, for example, is complicated to be sure.

Yet a third reason that op risk is a slippery thing to identify is driven by the different organizational processes that firms use to address operational risk. Some firms address op risk on an ad hoc basis, whereas others have appointed Heads of Operational Risk Management. Similarly, banks and nonfinancial corporations tend to view op risk through different lenses. For banks, op risk is an internal risk that is only recently being addressed in any formal context. But for nonfinancial firms like Schindler Elevator or Boeing, the operational risks associated with product management and potential product liability captured the undivided attention of risk management personnel long before market and credit risk did at many firms.

The wide gulf that separates one firm from the next in its degree of op risk management preparedness and awareness is in large part cultural. Firms like Schindler have a risk culture that leads to zero tolerance for operational faults on its elevators, but its risk culture may not have absorbed the same philosophy for interest rate and exchange rate risk. Conversely, banks like Barings may claim to have little tolerance for naked market risk exposures, but their cultural disposition to risks like internal control failures and fragmented IT systems obviously was not one of low tolerance.

STAGES OF EVOLUTION IN OP RISK MANAGEMENT

The BBA/ISDA/RMA (1999) survey notes that companies typically evolve through five stages of operational risk management maturity. Any given company may have a very different conception of op risk depending on the stage at which they are and thus may tend to define its tolerance for operational risk accordingly.

The first stage of op risk management is called the traditional baseline stage. This is the most informal treatment of op risk that a firm can exhibit. The firm has no processes or personnel dedicated to op risk in particular, but rather manages op risks on an ad hoc basis through other business processes like internal audit. Tolerance for operational risks likely will be determined at such firms on an entirely reactive basis—once encountered, managers will make a case-by-case determination of whether the uncovered op risk is a risk with which the firm can live.

In the second evolutionary stage of op risk management, firms enter into awareness that op risk must be explicitly addressed. Personnel are appointed with op risk-specific responsibilities, and senior managers and directors begin to craft policies and procedures for the systematic identification, measurement, monitoring, and control of op risks. The ownership of op risk management is clearly defined in this stage to be at the level of individual business units, and op risk exposure tolerances—albeit still vague and ad hoc—will start to be defined at the business unit level.

The third stage in the evolution of op risk management is the monitoring stage. At this stage, the notion of explicit and formal risk tolerances for op risk first begins to emerge, albeit on a largely qualitative basis. The business begins to focus on tracking internal risk indicators, op risk scoring systems, and business unit performance measurement adjusted for op risk. Senior managers and directors define and express their tolerances for op risks based on these qualitative and pseudo-quantitative criteria and in the context of the business and risk management strategies of the firm.

In the fourth stage of op risk management evolution, a firm finally develops a quantitative system of some kind for the formal measurement of op risks on a business unit basis. Only at this stage can senior managers and directors begin to articulate their tolerances for operational risk along a dimension that can be consistently and regularly compared to an actual measure of current op risk exposure. Also at this stage, a firm is presumed to have developed an operational risk management function, either independent or within an EWRM unit under the CRO.

Finally, a firm matures into the integration stage where op risk becomes a fully integrated part of a comprehensive EWRM process. Quantitative op risk measures are then integrated into other risk measures and reports, and the risk tolerances of the firm become defined at much more general levels—for example, firmwide VaR inclusive of integrated market, credit, liquidity, and operational risk sources.

In all five of the above stages, the company's risk culture and risk management strategy will play a paramount role in helping the firm understand and articulate its risk tolerances. As noted, nonfinancials used to operational risk management in product line areas will find the progression in many ways much easier than financial institutions whose business is more directly tied to financial risk. But despite the difficulty of shepherding the evolution of op risk management through these five stages, it is an important risk, and stakeholder tolerances thus must be defined as a precursor to any effective risk management process.

MEASURING OPERATIONAL RISK

Very few firms have evolved to the full maturity end of the op risk management spectrum. Consequently, op risk measurement methods and their integration to a broader op risk management process are diverse and vary widely across firms and industries.

One major reason for the huge disparity in op risk measurement methods is the lack of data on operational losses at many firms. Experience with large losses owing to operational risks may be infrequent, and the firm may not have tracked those losses that did occur. Because op risks are inherently firm-specific, the absence of such data is a real obstacle in sound op risk measurement.

ISDA (2000) characterizes four basic types of op risk measurement regimes, each of which is summarized next.

The "Basic Indicator" Regime

A basic indicator op risk measurement regime typically relies on one or two risk indicators that are coarsely defined. A basic indicator risk measurement regime is usually accompanied by a reasonably decentralized and ad hoc op risk management process that emphasizes existing control structures like internal audit to facilitate op risk management.

Several basic indicators may be used for op risk measurement in this kind of regime. An industry or regulatory measure of op risk, for example, can allow the firm to incur essentially no effort to measure its own, unique op risks but instead at least to rely on standardized operational loss information about broad classifications of firms, industries, and sectors.

One type of basic indicator that firms should not adopt is a residual earnings volatility approach. This method of op risk measurement entails calculating a firmwide EaR and then subtracting risks otherwise attributable. The residual EaR after subtracting earnings at risk due to market, credit, and liquidity risk, for example, would be a basic indicator of the firm's op risk.

The residual earnings volatility approach is fundamentally flawed for several reasons. Most importantly, residual earnings op risk measures presuppose that every other risk facing the firm is measurable and has been measured properly, including the strategic and business risks that are not included in op risk. Many firms have no reason to quantify and manage their business risks. Consequently, the residual EaR likely will lump together op risk with any number of other risks that a selective risk manager has chosen to tolerate rather than measure and manage.

Residual earnings-based op risk measures also de facto assume independence between market, credit, and op risk. But as noted earlier with the example of Barings, these risks clearly are not independent.

Finally, residual earnings volatility is inherently historical in nature, so that op risks to which the firm is exposed that have never impacted earnings will also be omitted. Just because a massive flood or fire has never destroyed the firm's assets and systems does not mean that op risk can be ignored, although in fact it would be ignored in a historically calculated residual earnings basic indicator of op risk.

The "Standard Lines of Business" Regime

The second op risk measurement regime identified by ISDA (2000) is accompanied by more structure along all dimensions. The op risk management process is more clearly defined and less ad hoc, and the firm is presumed to have articulated some basic set of op risk tolerances at the business unit level. Accordingly, op risk can be measured at the business unit level in this regime.

Common forms of op risk measurement within this regime include industry-level indices of risk categorized by business line type, as well as selfassessments of business-unit-specific op risks. Surveys and other techniques may be used to help the firm develop a Risk Map of op risks at the business unit level. Online risk measurement facilities like

Measurisk.com often provide standardized op risk surveys to help firms give more structure to these self-assessments.

The "Internal Ratings" Regime

Called the internal risk regime by ISDA (2000), internal ratings better conveys the intent behind this type of op risk measure given our discussion of such internal ratings methods for credit risk measurement. In a manner similar to the use of internal ratings for credit risk, op risk internal ratings are subjectively determined quantitative ratings that are assigned to specific op risk factors in individual business units.

An internal ratings based approach may or may not be dependent on historical operational risk and loss data. Even firms with sound and welldefined, comprehensive op risk management processes may not have a decent time series of historical loss data from which to draw probabilistic inferences about future op risk-related losses. Consequently, expert systems like those found in credit risk management are common sources of internal op risk ratings.

The "Internal Models" Regime

Again akin to the use of the term, the internal models approach to op risk measurement typically represents the most advanced available op risk management tool. Such systems are usually based on institution-specific loss data and may rely either on structural econometric models (like credit scoring models) or analytical-and simulation-based VaR-like constructs.

Most op risk measurement models bear great similarity to some of the models for credit risk measurement. Indeed, a goal of op risk measurement is to generate a figure essentially similar except for operational risk losses instead of credit losses. As in the cases of market, credit, and liquidity risk, the objective then is yet again to come up with an estimable probability distribution.

Like downgrade or migration risk, operational risk often has two distinctly different sources of randomness—the random arrival of events that lead to losses, and the random size of the loss. As discussed already, the latter is usually dependent on market, credit, or operational risk.

In other words, the probability density function for total loss S_n is the integral of the joint distribution of the size of losses with the occurrence of losses, or, equivalently, the conditional density of loss size given occurrence of losses times the marginal density for the probability of n losses occurring.

Depending on the structure of the distributions involved, the probability densities for loss magnitude and frequency sometimes can be combined into named distributions. Jorion (2000) shows, for example, that if the frequency of losses is geometrically distributed and the severity of losses exponentially distributed, the total loss is also exponentially distributed. If the resulting distribution is not named, then parametric statistical inference may not be possible and simulation methods may have to be used.

One source of op risk noted is fragmented IT systems and excessively decentralized IT application and data architectures. Ironically, to achieve an internal model level of sophistication in op risk measurement, this particular source of op risk arising from systems must be virtually negligible already. In other words, if the op risks typically associated with fragmented IT infrastructure are a real problem for a company, then that company almost by definition will not be able to implement an effective internal models-based op risk measurement system.

OPERATIONAL RISK MONITORING

ISDA (2000) has set forth six fundamental principles to which any institution should adhere in developing an operational risk management process. The monitoring of op risks vis-à-vis the firm's tolerances for those risks should occur against the firm backdrop of these six principles.

First, ultimate accountability for the management of op risk should lie with the board of directors or the security holders whose welfare is being enhanced by the risk management process. The degree to which op risk is tolerated should be defined on a top-down basis, and business units should accept whatever tolerances and guidelines are articulated by senior managers, directors, and other key risk management process stakeholders.

Second, senior managers and directors should ensure that operational into a formal process and framework as quickly as possible. Even if the op risk management process at the firm is relatively immature, organizational responsibilities and lines of reporting concerning op risk should be well defined and known throughout the organization.

Third, senior managers and directors should ensure that the op risk management process includes an exhaustive internal classification of all types of op risk facing the firm. A catalogue or Risk ID/Risk Map of internal processes, people, and systems and external factors that can create operational risks must be developed and serve as the backbone for the administration of the op risk management process.

Fourth, the firm should produce a set of written policies and procedures that outline the operational risks facing the firm, the tolerances of stakeholders for those risks, and the suggested means by which those risks will be managed. These policies and procedures should be consistent with the risk management strategy of the firm, as well as its overall business strategy.

Fifth, business units and back office support areas should be represented and have a voice in the op risk management process, in a manner reflective of any sound EWRM process.

Finally, line management should develop a tactical implementation plan for the day-to-day management of operational risks in a manner consistent with the overall risk management process of the firm. In other words, op risk management should involve identification, measurement, control, and realignment phases just like the comprehensive EWRM. As firms evolve from earlier stages of op risk management maturity to later ones as discussed in the prior, the op risk management process will simply fold into to the firm's EWRM process.

Ironically, the Bank for International Settlements (1998) reports that as of today, more banks monitor operational risk than measure it—at least not in the sense of using internal ratings or models. Banks regularly monitor indicators like business unit volume and turnover, settlement fails, delays, errors, and the like.

In this sense, operational risk is being managed even without the usual processes of op risk identification, measurement, and comparison to tolerances. As the rest of the discussion in this chapter has suggested, however, adding even a degree of formality to ad hoc monitoring processes could provide significant marginal benefits to financial and nonfinancial institutions alike.

The nature of the legal risks that firms can face in their risk management process depends on whether the firm is a risk controller, efficiency enhancer, or risk transformer. Many sources of legal risk are transactional— arising from legal and/or regulatory issues concerning specific transactions. Risk controllers can face such risks through their use of financial instruments, while risk transformers face such risks through their supply of financial instruments. Apart from transactional legal risks, firms also can face legal and regulatory risks at a broader firmwide or strategic level.

Legal risk has so many different dimensions that it is difficult even to categorize, much less discuss. This chapter considers risks that arise primarily because of the actions of the firm engaged in risk management or one of its counterparties. We then summarize how the interaction between laws, regulators, and market participants can exacerbate certain uncertainties in the risk management process.

Although firms must strive to manage legal risk, it is perhaps the one risk in the risk management process where risk tolerances and the measurement and monitoring of risks relative to those tolerances is not practical. Firms should strive to minimize legal risks on an ongoing basis, but quantifying and systematizing that process is a nearly insurmountable task. Unlike the other risks, this is the one risk that probably can be managed as well as possible without the aid of formal quantitative risk measurement and monitoring vis-à-vis explicit tolerance levels.

DOCUMENTATION RISK

Documentation risk is the transactional risk that a firm will incur a loss if a contract contains terms in its documentation that are either unenforceable or enforceable in a different manner than the firm had in mind. Examples include the lack of written confirmations for OTC derivatives, ambiguous language or misunderstandings regarding the treatment of holidays in OTC derivatives or other commercial contracts, the enforceability of close-out bilateral netting, the enforceability of multiproduct netting, and the like. All of these documentation risks share the common feature that they are transactional risks—risks arising from one or several specific deals, rather than the broad positioning of either the firm or a body of law.

A number of industry associations around the world have sought to bring a level of operational uniformity to documentation in OTC derivatives transactions. The International Swap Dealers Association was formed in 1984 as a trade association designed to provide a forum for the pursuit of issues of common interest to all swap participants. Although ISDA is neither a regulatory nor a self-regulatory body, it exercises a significant amount of influence over the practices of industry participants, both domestically and internationally. In 1993, ISDA changed its name to the International Swaps and Derivatives Association, Inc.

For some years, derivatives transactions were legally governed almost entirely by disparate contracts that were bilaterally negotiated on a product-by-product basis between counterparties. For a number of reasons, this heterogeneity of contracts led to a considerable amount of uncertainty regarding the enforceability of the various provisions in those contracts. Of particular concern was the ability of counterparties to enforce close-out netting provisions.

To moderate uncertainty surrounding enforceability, as well as to lower transaction costs for participants in derivatives activity, standardized forms of documentation for CTC derivatives transactions began to evolve. Such documentation is generally offered by ISDA and other industry associations, including the British Bankers Association, the Australian Financial Markets Association, a loose confederation of German bankers, and the Association Francaise des Banques.

In 1987, ISDA formulated its first set of standardized contracts, known as the ISDA Master Agreements, which were substantively revised in 1992. Although the development—and exhaustive legal review—of these pro forma documentation templates has greatly reduced documentation risk for derivatives, misunderstandings still occur. Consider the following examples.

Delays in Obtaining Written Transaction Confirmations

When OTC derivatives like interest rate swaps first became popular, oral confirmations tended to precede written confirmations by a surprisingly long interval of time in quite a few transactions. A survey by the Global Drivatives Study Group (1993) of market practices indicated, for example, that only 39% of respondents normally received a trade confirmation (confirm) from a dealer on the day of the transaction, and only 36% normally received a confirm on the next day. Even fewer reported normally receiving same-or next-day confirms from end users.

Failure to obtain a written confirm expeditiously exposes the firm to the risk that the counterparty has a different understanding of the deal than the firm. Such misunderstandings are often small but important. Interest payments in rate swaps, for example, are calculated on settlement dates based on some "day counting" convention to determine the size of the payment. Popular day counting conventions include Actual/360 Actual/365, Actual/ Actual, and 30/360 where Actual denotes the actual number of days between settlements and where the denominator references the number of days in the money market year underlying the reference interest rate.

A U.S. dollar swap whose floating leg settles to six-month Libor, for example, likely will have interest payments calculated on an Actual/360 basis because the U.S. money market year contains 360 days rather than 365. If a counterparty mistakenly—or deliberately—marks the trade confirm as Actual/365 days, the firm will not know this until the confirm is received.

In recent times, the time gap between oral and written confirms of OTC derivatives has narrowed. Nevertheless, especially for nonfinancial transactions like commercial purchase and sale agreements, documentation backlog remains an issue to which attention must be paid.

Holiday and Weekend Payment or Exercise Conventions

When counterparties in different legal jurisdictions negotiate contracts with one another that involve optional delivery or payment dates, ambiguous documentation can lead to serious problems. Consider a forward purchased by European Firm Rousseau from U.S. Dealer Paine. The documentation must clearly delineate one of three business day conventions: preceding, following, or modified following, all of which relate to the possibility that the value and/or settlement date occurs on a holiday in one jurisdiction—say, Thanksgiving in the United States.

"Modified following" means, for example, that if the date of maturity is not a business day, payment of principal and interest required to be made on such date will be made on the next business day with the same impact as if made on such date. No additional interest shall accrue as a result of such delayed payment. Misunderstandings or ambiguities about these business day conventions can lead to serious disagreements on swap and OTC option transactions, in particular.

Even when a transaction is well-documented and clearly specifies a mutually satisfactory business day convention for normal settlements, further problems can arise if abnormal activities occur on holidays. Suppose that Broker Burke is clearing futures trades for a wealthy Chinese private banking client, Mr. Fang, who is located in Hong Kong. At the peak of Chinese New Year, Mr. Fang's positions take a radical turn for the worse and a request for margin is sent to his office.

Because he is celebrating the holiday, he neither receives the margin call nor the notice that Broker Burke is blowing him out—liquidating his positions at the market. Even with clear documentation allowing Broker Burke to take such an action, Mr. Fang likely will be not be happy, especially if prices reversed after the blow out and moved in his favour.

CAPACITY AND SUITABILITY RISKS

Some concern remains about the legal authority or capacity of certain entities—most prominently municipalities—to enter into OTC derivatives transactions. In a well-publicized 1991 case before the U.K. House of Lords, it was determined that the Hammersmith borough of London did not have the statutory capacity to enter into the numerous swap transactions that it had been negotiating since 1981. The Law Lords held that a local borough of London had no power to enter into a swap transaction, thereby rendering the contracts ultra vires. That ruling of the House of Lords invalidated swap agreements between more than 130 councils and 75 major banks, and it reportedly resulted in over $1 billion in total losses to counterparties.

Some concern persists in the marketplace that counterparties to certain types of financial transactions, still including many swaps, may not have the legal capacity to enter those transactions, thereby giving rise to fears that the Hammersmith experience could be repeated in the future.

These days, a bigger concern than the capacity of firms to enter into certain transactions is the suitability of certain types of firms to do so. Especially following on the heels of the highly publicized so-called risk management failures at the Orange County Investment Pool (OCIP) and Procter & Gamble (P&G), some politicians and regulators have attempted to promulgate regulations regarding a swap dealer's obligation to assess the suitability of their counterparties.

Institutions like OCIP and P&G, some contend, are just not capable of assessing the risks of derivatives on their own, and implementing requirements for suitability assessments like those that exist under U.S. securities laws, liability for failing to assess suitability, and/or a formal industry "code of conduct" was proposed as the solution.

The OTC derivatives industry, in particular, however, has done a good job over time policing itself, leading others to conclude that calls for regulation are both precipitous and unnecessarily costly. As an example, the ISDA promulgated in 1996 an addendum to its master agreements that attempts to deal with "Representation of Relationship Between Parties"— the suitability issue—by explicitly requiring each counterparty to attest that it is "capable of assessing the merits of and understanding (on its own behalf or through independent professional advice), and understands and accepts, the terms, conditions, and risks of [the transaction]. It is also capable of assuming, and assumes, the risk of [the transaction]."

RISKS ARISING FROM INSOLVENCY

A variety of legal concerns remain concerning how insolvency law affects existing commercial transactions and risk management transactions such as derivatives. These risks range from the enforceability of contracts under local insolvency laws to the impact of particular contract provisions on their participants in the event of a failure.

Close-Out Netting and Cherry Picking

A particular problem is the lack of enforceability of bilateral netting under certain local insolvency laws, which can lead to "cherry picking." This is a notorious form of risk vexing companies that rely on close-out bilateral single-and multiproduct netting clauses in their master swap agreements, some of which include regular commercial transactions as well as derivatives. When netting is not enforceable under the law, stipulating it in a contract may not be enough.

If a Malaysian bank negotiates a simple interest rate swap under London law with a British bank, for example, the insolvency of the Malaysian bank may create a situation where local insolvency law supercedes the London law governing the open contract. If the Malay bank owes the British bank a payment of $100,000 and the British bank owes the Malay bank a payment of $50,000, unenforceable netting and cherry picking could occur if Malay law allows the receiver for the failed Malay bank to demand the $50,000 payment even if it cannot make the $100,000 payment that it owes under the same transaction.

Liquidity Risks

The risks associated with unexpected shocks to cash balances. Liquidity risk includes both the risk of cash flow problems and the risk that forced asset liquidation will be costly. The nature of a counterparty's problems and the options selected in master agreements with that counterparty can exacerbate these liquidity risks.

Under the 1992 ISDA Master Agreements, the obligation to make or receive payments for the life of the contract is terminated if a counter party experiences an "Event of Default" or a "Termination Event." Events of Default under the ISDA Master Agreements include failure to make payment or delivery on a settlement date, counterparty bankruptcy (including the appointment of a conservator or receiver), or "cross-default, " wherein the default-based termination of any specified contract between two counterparties constitutes an Event of Default for all transactions between those counterparties. Termination Events are events not based on default that result in early termination of the contract. They include changes in the law governing the contract, tax code changes, changes in counterparty credit resulting from a merger, and so forth.

An "Early Termination Date" may be designated by the non defaulting party under the ISDA Master Agreements, so that some time after the occurrence of an Event of Default, no further scheduled payments or deliveries between counterparties are made. For default-based termination events, cross-default provisions of the Master also apply, resulting in early terminations of all transactions. Even though an Early Termination Date can be specified as early as the date of the Event of Default, the non defaulting counterparty can wait up to 20 days to give notice of early termination. If the counterparty waits, however, the notice of early termination only may be given if the Event of Default is still continuing at that later date.

Alternatively, counterparties may opt at the time of the contract's inception for "Automatic Early Termination." If this option is chosen, any Event of Default will result in the automatic specification of an immediate Early Termination Date upon the occurrence of the Event of Default.

Liquidity risk in swaps can manifest itself when Automatic Early Terminations occur unexpectedly on out-of-the-money transactions, thus necessitating an immediate payment to the counterparty of the replacement cost of the transaction. If the firm planned only for the next net cash payment in its cash balance forecasts, funds may not be on hand to honor the replacement cost payment associated with an Automatic Early Termination.

This problem can become particularly acute when a company is relying on "cross-default" provisions in its master agreements. Such provisions can result in Early Terminations when a firm defaults on any of its outstanding swap obligations. In the extreme, an operational failure that leads to a cash imbalance and a skipped swap payment can trigger an Automatic Early Termination. This in turn can trigger other Automatic Early Terminations, and a liquidity crunch can rapidly move from bad to worse.

Walkaway Clauses

Once a default-based termination has occurred and an Early Termination Date has been set, the ISDA Master Agreements stipulate that counterparties engage in close-out netting as of the Early Termination Date. The Master Agreements require, moreover, that counterparties choose at the time of the contract's inception a method by which close-out net values are calculated. Under what is now known as the First Method, the non defaulting party may terminate a contract with no payment obligation to the defaulting party, regardless of the market value of the transaction.

In other words, under the First Method, a defaulting party has no right to receive payment from a non defaulting counterparty when the contract represents a net entitlement to the defaulting party. This payment provision is often also referred to as a limited two-way payments (LTP), or walk away clause. In November 1992, a New York federal court upheld the legality of LTP clauses in Drexel Burnham Lambert Products v. Midland Bank PLC.

Under the Second Method of calculating net payments following a default-based termination, the net value of all transactions between the parties is exchanged. So, under this method—sometimes referred to as full two-way payments (FTP)—if the defaulting party owes a positive lump-sum termination net payment, then that party must pay it to the non defaulting party. Conversely—and unlike the First Method—if the close-out lump-sum payment is owed to the defaulting party, then the defaulting party is entitled to payment by the non defaulting party.

The 1987 ISDA Master Agreements specified the First Method, or limited two-way payments, as the contractual default, thereby requiring an addendum to the contract for full two-way payments. As such, a number of outstanding swap transactions, especially long-term transactions entered into prior to 1992 that were not renegotiated after the introduction of the revised 1992 agreements, still contain LTP clauses.

The presence of LTP clauses does not always lead to problems, but it can. Consider, for example, the insolvency of the Development Finance Corporation (DFC) of New Zealand. At the time of its failure, the DFC derivatives portfolio consisted primarily of swaps and had approximately NZ$4 billion in notional value. It consisted of 108 swap transactions with over 60 counterparties, most of which were foreign and most of which had relatively high credit quality. Though most of the DFC portfolio had not been negotiated under ISDA Master Agreements, many of the contracts included a form of LTP provision.

Most of the counterparties which chose to avail themselves of LTP provisions after DFC's failure did so immediately. Within the first few days after DFC went into statutory management, several counterparties gave notice of early swap termination—despite claims by the statutory managers that DFC could meet its off-balance sheet obligations. A few more counterparties followed suit within the next several weeks.

Largely to preserve the value of the combined DFC portfolio for sale en masse, DFC strongly resisted overtures by counterparties to terminate their contracts and enforce their rights to limited two-way payments. Indeed, DFC continued to make payments on all its interest rate swaps and foreign exchange agreements. Many counterparties that acted on the LTP provision were persuaded either to reinstate some type of relationship with DFC or to settle with DFC for some cash payment. In a few cases, the contracts were not reinstated due to impending maturity. In only one case did the counterparty insist on full application of the LTP.

LIABILITY FOR STRATEGIC RISK MANAGEMENT FAILURES

Another type of legal risk can arise when inadequate attention is paid to the liability implications of the risk management strategy adopted by the firm. A firm runs the risk of lawsuit, for example, whenever it measures market risk reasonably accurately, concludes that its exposures are above its tolerances, and takes no corrective action.

At a more subtle level, U.S. case law provides some reasons to believe that broader strategic risk management decisions can also expose the firm to legal risk. Specifically, if directors err in their articulation of the firm's risk tolerances, liability can result.

The Indiana Court of Appeals ruled in 1992 that the failure of a grain elevator to hedge its exposure to declining grain prices constituted a breach of the fiduciary duty of the elevator's directors to the cooperative shareholders. The grain elevator received 90% of its operating income from the sale of grain. Typically, a corporate director can avoid such liability in acting as a fiduciary to shareholders by exercising good faith and honest judgment. But in this case, the court argued that the directors had no such protection because they did not take reasonable steps to identify hedging opportunities that could have mitigated their losses.

A similar case arose a year earlier when the shareholders of Compaq Computer Corporation filed suit against the company's chief executive officer and chairman of the Board of Directors for alleged violations of securities laws concerning representations about future company performance. The plaintiffs alleged that the president's comments about the firm's growth prospects were materially misleading because he omitted to disclose a lack of hedging against foreign exchange risk, despite the fact that Compaq then derived 54% of its revenues from foreign markets.

REGULATORY RISK

Regulatory risk can take three forms. First, procedural regulatory risk is the risk that legal uncertainties and financial losses will result from ill conceived and costly changes to statutory or administrative regulations. Congressional actions precipitate the first, and unilateral regulatory actions the latter.

The second type of regulatory risk is judgmental regulatory risk. This risk stems from inadequately informed examiners and regulatory auditors who attempt to review the risk management activities of a firm based on incomplete information. Very complex, dynamic trading strategies can be difficult to explain to examiners in a short period of time. Examiners may be likely to draw conclusions based on conservatism, thereby resulting in actions taken to discourage the use of such complex programmes. Similarly, examiners and regulatory auditors may not possess the quantitative skills necessary to evaluate the mathematical models used by firms for risk management.

Third, unexpected changes in regulation also may account for legal risk if such regulatory changes affect the legality of certain transactions. This can arise in part because no single corpus of law defines the regulation of financial products and their users. Instead, financial product regulation in most countries—especially the United States—is comprised of a mixture of other legal fields, including banking, securities, commodities, and bankruptcy law. And any time multiple areas of law and regulation come together, complexities arise.

The regulation of risk transformation products is also troublesome because significant jurisdictional ambiguities arise on a very regular basis both regarding financial products and the users of financial products. Certain types of financial products are subject to stringent regulations, whereas others fall outside the jurisdiction of any regulatory agency. Similarly, some participants in financial markets are subject to duplicative and costly supervision by three or four different agencies, while others are not regulated at all. Infighting between agencies vying for ill-defined and constantly changing regulatory turf further exacerbates these jurisdictional uncertainties.

Further adding to complexity and reinforcing the need for sound counsel—especially for suppliers of risk transformation products—some financial products such as derivatives are not specifically regulated per se— no Federal Derivatives Commission or comparable body is charged with the supervision and regulation of derivatives. That does not mean that derivatives and their users are unregulated.

On the contrary, derivatives are regulated in essentially two distinct ways. First, certain institutions that are already subject to government regulation (e.g., banks and thrifts) may have their derivatives activities scrutinized by their institutional supervisors as part of the broader institution-specific regulations. Second, specific types of derivatives—namely, futures and certain options—are federally regulated as financial products.

The model for the regulation of derivatives as a hodgepodge of financial instrument regulation and financial market participant regulation serves as a useful framework for the prospective regulation of all risk management and risk transformation financial products. Some regulation is based on who the user or supplier is, and other regulations are contract or instrument specific. To develop a better understanding of the role of the legal counsel in the risk management process, a deeper look at this regulatory distinction is warranted with an admittedly U.S. bias.

Institutional Regulation of Risk Management Activities

Certain institutions are regulated because they are perceived as special. Banks, for example, are regulated because they take deposits that are federally insured and because they often are perceived as being systemically important. The risk management activities of such special firms may be subject to specific regulations promulgated by their institutional supervisors. Institutions that are regulated in this manner include nationally chartered and state-chartered commercial banks, bank holding companies, thrifts, insurance companies, and some pension plans.

Because institutions are regulated—or not, as the case may be—based on their type of corporate charter or firm classification, a user or supplier of risk transformation products can be subject to multiple institutional regulators, most of which oversee derivatives activities in slightly different ways. Regulators that have issued supervisory guidance on derivatives usage by their constituent firms include the Federal

Reserve, the Office of the Comptroller of the Currency (OCC), the Federal Deposit Insurance Corporation (FDIC), and the Office of Thrift Supervision (OTS). So, a national bank affiliate of a bank holding company, for example, might have to comply with both OCC and Federal Reserve regulatory guidance on derivatives activities.

Risk management activities that are scrutinized by institutional regulators typically are subject to three types of supervision. First, regulators of these institutions often specify permissible activities for the institution. This allows some firms to engage in derivatives while prohibiting others from doing so. In addition, some agencies allow risk management products to be used only in certain circumstances. Thrifts, for example, may engage in interest rate swaps, but only for the purpose of hedging or reducing their overall interest rate risk.

Second, risk management activities are subject to prudential oversight. This oversight usually includes examinations of derivatives portfolios, risk management policies and procedures, risk limits administration and compliance, derivatives position and risk reporting, and related back-office activities. Institutional regulators typically give their constituents a significant degree of autonomy in whatever transactions they are permitted to engage—institutional regulators tend to monitor more than regulate once an activity has been deemed permissible.

Finally, institutional regulators may adopt special provisions for financial instruments in any capital adequacy requirements imposed on their constituent institutions. Specifically, to the extent that the use or supply of risk transformation products are deemed to expose an institution to additional credit or market risk, the institution's regulator likely will demand additional capital to cover those risks.

Product-Based Regulation

Unlike the regulation of risk management activities at firms already subject to institutional government regulation, product-based financial instrument regulations are targeted at the financial products themselves and, hence, any institution that uses them. Three types of financial products are separately regulated in the United States, for example, as distinct financial products— futures, options, and securities.

Futures In 1936, Congress amended the Grain Futures Act of 1922 and adopted the Commodity Exchange Act (CEA), which remains the primary statute underlying U.S. futures regulation today. The legislators' primary objective was protecting the integrity of markets whose main perceived functions were risk shifting and price discovery.

The initial focus of futures regulation thus was on deterring fraud and market manipulation. Congress created the Commodity Exchange Commission to fulfill this legislative mandate. That commission delegated day-to-day regulatory authority to the Secretary of Agriculture who, in turn, formed the Commodity Exchange Administration (later renamed the Commodity Exchange Authority).

To promote the integrity of futures markets in practice, Congress relied heavily on a provision of the CEA known as the "exchange trading requirement." This clause of the CEA provides that unless specifically exempted by the CFTC, a futures contract is illegal unless it is traded on a board of trade. The term futures contract, however, is never explicitly defined by the CEA. Instead, futures contracts are implicitly defined as "any transaction in, or in connection with, a contract for the purchase or sale of a commodity for future delivery." The statute thus rests heavily on terms like commodity and future delivery, but those definitions, too, are far from straightforward in the CEA.

In 1974, Congress significantly revised the CEA in the Commodity Futures Trading Commission Act (CFTC Act). Among other things, the Act moved responsibility for futures regulation from the Secretary of Agriculture to the Commodity Futures Trading Commission (CFTC), which was created in the 1974 act. The CFTC Act also expanded the definition of the term commodity. Previously, commodities were limited to specific agricultural products, but the CFTC Act broadened the list to include a variety of unspecified financial assets. The resulting definitional ambiguity simultaneously broadened the jurisdiction of the CFTC and muddied the water concerning exactly what products fall under the purview of the CFTC.

CFTC regulations now include significantly more than the antifraud and antimanipulation rules Congress originally envisioned. Today, the CFTC regulates almost everything having to do with futures and options on futures. CFTC regulations now cover a wide spectrum, ranging from delivery requirements for commodity futures to audit trail requirements on trading. One of the most notorious regulations obligates futures exchanges to obtain the approval of the CFTC in advance of listing a new futures contract. The approval process can take as long as two years, during which time privately negotiated derivatives dealers may offer a nearly identical product subject to no approval process.

Although CFTC regulations are all based on products, those productbased regulations also affect institutions. Unlike institutional regulation, which targets only those institutions deemed "special, " CFTC product based regulations affect all institutions using "futures contracts" and options on "futures contracts." Product-based regulations aimed at institutions include registration and capital requirements for futures commission merchants, registration and permissible activity requirements on Commodity Trading Advisors (CTAs), and risk management standards for exchange members.

Because all CFTC regulations ultimately trace to the definition of a futures contract and because that definition is itself ambiguous in the CEA, numerous institutions that are not actually CFTC-regulated live with the threat of possible CFTC regulation.

A nonfinancial corporation that renders advisory services to its customers about privately negotiated derivatives along the lines of either the efficiency enhancement or risk transformation risk management business models, for example, may be called a CTA if the CFTC subsequently determines that the products in question actually were futures contracts. And sometimes it is not at all obvious just when the CFTC will make such a determination. So, ambiguity about the legal status of a particular financial product also translates into ambiguity about the regulatory status of certain institutions.

Securities Various laws establish the regulatory framework for securities. The Securities Act of 1933 (33 Act) regulates the public offering of securities, ostensibly because Congress deemed necessary the protection of capital formation in public markets. Unlike the CEA which never explicitly defines futures, however, the 33 Act does explicitly define securities, including those securities exempt from the Act. The 33 Act also prohibits fraud in the public sale of securities and requires that any public offering of a nonexempt security be conducted through a firm registered with and regulated by the appropriate federal agency.

The Securities Exchange Act of 1934 (34 Act) elabourated on and broadened much of what was behind the 33 Act. The 34 Act accomplished three primary objectives in securities regulation. First, it established the Securities and Exchange Commission (SEC) as a formal regulator of securities, securities markets, and security market participants. Second, the 34 Act established new regulations on the trading of securities in secondary markets.

Third, the 34 Act expanded on the 33 Act by promulgating such regulations as prohibitions on market manipulation and fraud, registration requirements for broker/dealers, and permissible activities for broker/dealers. The 34 Act also established registration requirements and regulations for securities exchanges, clearing associations, and transfer agents.

Apart from regulating securities, the SEC also regulates certain types of derivatives—listed options on nonexempt securities, to be precise. This jurisdictional oddity traces to a long-standing dispute between the SEC and CFTC over financial products that have attributes of both a security and a futures contract.

An "exclusivity clause" granting the CFTC exclusive jurisdiction over futures was adopted in the CFTC Act of 1974. Because the 1974 Act also widened and muddied CFTC jurisdiction by broadening the definition of commodities, the SEC demanded that Congress preserve its jurisdiction over securities that might also be deemed futures contracts or options on futures contracts. Accordingly, a SEC "savings clause" was included in the CFTC Act providing that among other things, the inclusion of the savings clause was intended to secure the SEC's jurisdiction over options on securities, such as options on common stock.

A year after the CFTC Act was adopted; the scope of the SEC savings clause was tested. Based on a CFTC determination that Government National Mortgage Association (GNMA) certificates were "commodities" under the amended CEA, that agency approved the listing of futures on GNMAs for trading at the Chicago Board of Trade. The SEC, however, argued that "GNMA certificates are securities, as that term is defined in the federal securities laws. The SEC also believe[s] it to be quite clear that contracts for future delivery of those securities are also 'securities.'" The CFTC rejected the SEC's argument, and GNMA futures continued to trade on the CBOT.

The SEC took its jurisdictional grievance to Congress in hearings regarding the Futures Trading Act of 1978. The agency argued that futures contracts on securities and options on securities were functionally indistinguishable. The SEC further maintained that because the SEC savings clause gave it jurisdiction over securities options, it should also have jurisdiction over futures on securities. Congress disagreed and left the CFTC's exclusive jurisdiction intact over all types of futures.

The burgeoning jurisdictional dispute was finally litigated in Board of Trade of the City of Chicago v. SEC (hereinafter GNMA Options). This case arose after the SEC approved, in February 1981, a proposal by the CBOE to trade options on GNMA certificates. The SEC claimed that the products were options on securities and hence were securities, protected under the SEC savings clause.

The CFTC and the CBOT, on the other hand, claimed that because GNMA futures had already been deemed futures by the CFTC, GNMA certificates had implicitly been deemed commodities, which made GNMA options equivalent to futures options under the CEA. In November 1981, the Seventh Circuit Court of Appeals agreed with the line of reasoning presented by the CFTC and CBOT and granted a motion by the CBOT for a stay pending review, thereby blocking the CBOE from listing GNMA options on the grounds that GNMA options were futures options under the CEA.

Still unhappy with the jurisdictional uncertainty surrounding products with attributes of both futures and securities, the SEC and CFTC took matters in their own hands in December 1981 while GNMA Options was still pending.

They reached an agreement called the "Shad-Johnson Accord" that provided four basic ground rules:

1. The CFTC would regulate all futures and options on futures, even if the futures are based on securities;
2. The SEC would regulate all options on securities;
3. Futures on individual securities, such as stocks, were prohibited; and
4. The SEC would play a formal role in the CFTC's approval of then-evolving stock index futures contracts.

Shortly after the Shad-Johnson Accord, the GNMA Options decision called the Accord into question, specifically noting that "the CFTC and SEC [cannot be allowed] to reapportion their jurisdictions in the face of a clear, contrary statutory mandate." Congress subsequently decided to give force to the Accord, however, and enacted it into law almost verbatim in 1982.

Chapter 8

Staffing for Housekeeping Operations

Prelude to Staffing Staffing is the third sequential function of management. Up until now the executive housekeeper has been concerned with planning and organizing the housekeeping department for the impending opening and operations. Now the executive housekeeper must think about hiring employees within sufficient time to ensure that three of the activities of staffing—selection (including interviewing), orientation, and training—may be completed before opening. Staffing will be a major task of the last two weeks before opening. The development of the Area Responsibility Plan and the House Breakout Plan before opening led to preparation of the Department Staffing Guide, which will be a major tool in determining the need for employees in various categories. The housekeeping manager and laundry manager should now be on board and assisting in the development of various job descriptions.

The hotel human resources department would also have been preparing for the hiring event. They would have advertised a mass hiring for all categories of personnel to begin on a certain date about two weeks before opening. Even though this chapter reflects a continuation of the executive housekeeper's planning for opening operations, the techniques described apply to any ongoing operation, except that the magnitude of selection, orientation, and training activities will not be as intense. Also, the fourth activity—development of existing employees— is normally missing in opening operations but is highly visible in ongoing operations.

Job Specifications Job specifications should be written as job descriptions are prepared. Job specifications are simple statements of what the various incumbents to positions will be expected to do. An example of a job specification for a housekeeper is as follows: Job Specification—Example Housekeeper (hotels). The incumbent will work as a member of a housekeeping team, cleaning and servicing for occupancy of approximately 18 hotel guestrooms each day. Work will generally include the tasks of bed making, vacuuming, dusting, and bathroom cleaning. Incumbent will also be expected to maintain equipment provided for work and load housekeeper's cart before the end of each day's operation. Housekeepers must be willing to work their share of weekends and be dependable in coming to work each day scheduled.

EMPLOYEE REQUISITION

Once job specifications have been developed for every position, employee requisitions are prepared for first hirings (and for any follow-up needs for the human resources department). Note the designation as to whether the requisition is for a new or a replacement position and the number of employees required for a specific requisition number. The human resources department will advertise, take applications, and screen to fill each requisition by number until all positions are filled. For example, the first requisition for GRAs may be for 20 Staffing Housekeeping Positions. The human resources department will continue to advertise for, take applications, and screen employees for the housekeeping department and will provide candidates for interview by department managers until 20 GRAs are hired. Should any be hired and require replacing, a new employee requisition will be required.

Staffing Housekeeping Positions

There are several activities involved in staffing a housekeeping operation. Executive housekeepers must select and interview employees, participate in an orientation programme, train newly hired employees, and develop employees for future growth. Each of these activities will now be discussed.

Selecting Employees Sources of Employees

Each area of the United States has its own demographic situations that affect the availability of suitable employees for involvement in housekeeping or environmental service operations. For example, in one area, an exceptionally high response rate from people seeking food service work may occur and a low response rate from people seeking housekeeping positions may occur. In another area, the reverse may be true, and people interested in housekeeping work may far outnumber those interested in food service. Surveys among hotels or hospitals in your area will indicate the best source for various classifications of employees. Advertising campaigns that will reach these employees are the best method of locating suitable people. Major classified ads associated with mass hirings will specify the need for food service personnel, front desk clerks, food servers, housekeeping personnel, and maintenance people. Such ads may yield surprising results.

If these sources do not produce the volume of applicants necessary to develop a staff, it may become necessary to search for employees in distant areas and to provide regular transportation for them to and from work. If aliens are hired, the department manager must take great care to ensure that they are legal residents of this country and that their green cards are valid. More than one hotel department manager has had an entire staff swept away by the Department of Immigration after hiring people who were illegal aliens. Such unfortunate action has required the immediate assistance of all available employees (including management) to fill in.

Processing Applicants

Whether you are involved in a mass hiring or in the recruiting of a single employee, a systematic and courteous procedure for processing applicants is essential. For example, in the opening of the Los Angeles Airport Marriott, 11,000 applicants were processed to fill approximately 850 positions in a period of about two weeks. The magnitude of such an operation required a near assembly-line technique, but a personable and positive experience for the applicants still had to be maintained.

Employee requisition, used to ask for one or more employees for a specific job. The efficient handling of lines of employees, courteous attendance, personal concern for employee desires, and reference to suitable departments for those unfamiliar with what the hotel or hospital has to offer all become earmarks for how the company will treat its employees.

The key to proper handling of applicants is the use of a control system whereby employees are conducted through the steps of application, prescreening, and if qualified, reference to a department for interview. Note the opportunity for employees to express their desires for a specific type of employment. Even though an employee may desire involvement in one classification of work, he or she may be hired for employment in a different department. Also, employees might not be aware of the possibilities available in a particular department at the time of application or may be unable to locate in desired departments at the time of mass hirings.

Employees who perform well should therefore be given the opportunity to transfer to other departments when the opportunities arise. According to laws regulated by federal and state Fair Employment Practices Agencies (FEPA), no person may be denied the opportunity to submit application for employment for a position of his or her choosing. Not only is the law strict on this point, but companies in any way benefiting from interstate commerce (such as hotels and hospitals) may not discriminate in the hiring of people based on race, colour, national origin, or religious preference. Although specific hours and days of the week may be specified, it is a generally accepted fact that hotels and hospitals must maintain personnel operations that provide the opportunity for people to submit applications without prejudice.

Prescreening Applicants

The prescreening interview is a staff function normally provided to all hotel or hospital departments by the human resources of the organization. Prescreening is a preliminary interview process in which unqualified applicants—those applicants who do not meet the criteria for a job as specified in the job specification–special qualifications—are selected (or screened) out. For example, an applicant for a secretarial job that requires the incumbent to take shorthand and be able to type 60 words a minute may be screened out if the applicant is not able to pass a relevant typing and shorthand test. The results of prescreening are usually coded for internal use and are indicated on the Applicant Processing Record. If a candidate is screened out by the personnel, he or she should be told the reason immediately and thanked for applying for employment.

The Interview

An interview should be conducted by a manager of the department to which the applicant has been referred. In ongoing operations, it is often wise to also allow the supervisor for whom the new employee will work to visit with the candidate in order that the supervisor may gain a feel for how it would be to work together. The supervisor's view should be considered, since a harmonious relationship at the working level is important. Although the acceptance of an employee remains a prerogative of management, it would be unwise to accept an employee into a position when the supervisor has reservations about the applicant.

Certain personal characteristics should be explored when interviewing an employee. Some of these characteristics are native skills, stability, reliability, experience, attitude toward employment, personality, physical traits, stamina, age, sex, education, previous training, initiative, alertness, appearance, and personal cleanliness. Although employers may not discriminate against race, sex, age, religion, and nationality, overall considerations may involve the capability to lift heavy objects, enter men's or women's restrooms, and so on.

In a housekeeping (or environmental services) department, people should be employed who find enjoyment in housework at home. Remember that character and personality cannot be completely judged from a person's appearance. Also, it should be expected that a person's appearance will never be better than when that person is applying for a job. Letters of recommendation and references should be carefully considered. Seldom will a letter of recommendation be adverse, whereas a telephone call might be most revealing.

If it were necessary to select the most important step in the selection process, interviewing would be it. Interviewing is the step that separates those who will be employed from those who will not produce a result that can be both frustrating and damaging for both parties. In addition, inadequate interviewing will result in gaining incorrect information, being confused about what has been said, suppression of information, and, in some circumstances, complete withdrawal from the process by the candidate.

The following is a well-accepted list of the steps for a successful interview process.

1. *Be prepared:* Have a checklist of significant questions ready to ask the candidate. Such questions may be prepared from the body of the job description. This preparation will allow the interviewer to assume the initiative in the interview.
2. *Find a proper place to conduct the interview:* The applicant should be made to feel comfortable. The interview should be conducted in a quiet, relaxing atmosphere where there is privacy that will bring about a confidential conversation.
3. *Practice:* People who conduct interviews should practice interviewing skills periodically. Several

managers may get together and discuss interviewing techniques that are to be used.

4. *Be tactful and courteous:* Put the applicant at ease, but also control the discussion and lead to important questions.
5. *Be knowledgeable:* Be thoroughly familiar with the position for which the applicant is interviewing in order that all of the applicant's questions may be answered. Also, have a significant background knowledge in order that general information about the company may be given.
6. *Listen:* Encourage the applicant to talk. This may be done by asking questions that are not likely to be answered by a yes or no. If people are comfortable and are asked questions about themselves, they will usually speak freely and give information that specific questions will not always bring out. Applicants will usually talk if there is a feeling that they are not being misunderstood.
7. *Observe:* Much can be learned about an applicant just by observing reactions to questions, attitudes about work, and, specifically, attitudes about providing service to others. Observation is a vital step in the interviewing process.

Interview Pitfills

Perhaps of equal importance to the interviewing technique are the following pitfalls, which should be avoided while interviewing.

1. Having a feeling that the employee will be just right based on a few outstanding characteristics rather than on the sum of all characteristics noted.
2. Being influenced by neatness, grooming, expensive clothes, and an extroverted personality—none of which has much to do with housekeeping competency.
3. Over generalizing, whereby interviewers assume too much from a single remark (for instance, an

applicant's assurance that he or she "really wants to work").

4. Hiring the "boomer," that is, the person who always wants to work in a new property; unfortunately, this type of person changes jobs whenever a new property opens.
5. Projecting your own background and social status into the job requirement. Which school the applicant attended or whether the applicant has the "proper look" is beside the point. It is job performance that is going to count.
6. Confusing strengths with weaknesses, and vice versa. What is construed by one person to be over aggressiveness might be interpreted by another as confidence, ambition, and potential for leadership, the last two traits being in chronic short supply in most housekeeping departments. These are the very characteristics that make it possible for management to promote from within and develop new supervisors and managers.
7. Being impressed by a smooth talker—or the reverse: assuming that silence reflects strength and wisdom. The interviewer should concentrate on what the applicant is saying rather than on how it is being said, then decide whether his or her personality will fit into the organization.
8. Being tempted by overqualified applicants. People with experience and education that far exceed the job requirements may be unable for some reason to get jobs commensurate with their backgrounds.

Even if such applicants are not concealing skeletons in the closet, they still tend to become frustrated and dissatisfied with jobs far their level of abilities. The application of the techniques and avoidance of the pitfalls will be valuable tools in the selection of competent personnel for the housekeeping and environmental service departments. For many years, the approach of many managers was to write a job description and then fill it by attempting to find the perfect person. This approach may overlook many qualified people, such as disadvantaged people or slow learners. Job descriptions may be analyzed in two ways when filling positions:

1. What is actually required to do the work, and
2. What is desirable. Is the ability to read or write really necessary for the job? Is the ability to learn quickly really necessary?

A person who does not read or write or who is a slow learner can be trained and can make an excellent employee. True, it may take additional time, but the reward will be a loyal employee as well as less turnover. It has been proven many times that those who are disadvantaged or slightly retarded, once trained, will perform consistently well for longer periods. There are agencies who seek out companies that will try to hire such people.

Results of the Interview

If the results of an interview are negative and rejection is indicated, the candidate should be informed as soon as possible. A pleasant statement, such as "Others interviewed appear to be more qualified," is usually sufficient. This information can be handled in a straightforward and courteous manner and in such a way that the candidate will appreciate the time that has been taken during the interview. When the results of the interview are positive, a statement indicating a favorable impression is most encouraging. However, no commitment should be made until a reference check has been conducted.

Reference Checks

In many cases, reference checks are made only to verify that what has been said in the application and interview is in fact true. Many times applicants are reluctant to explain in detail why previous employment situations have come to an end. It is more important to hear the actual truth about a prior termination from the applicant than it is to hear that they simply have been terminated. Reference checks, in order of desirability, are as follows:

1. Personal (face-to-face) meetings with previous employers are the least available but provide the most accurate information when they can be arranged.
2. Telephone discussions are the next best and most often used approach. For all positions, an in-depth conversation by telephone between the potential new manager and the prior manager is most desirable; otherwise a simple verification of data is sufficient to ensure honesty.
3. The least desirable reference is the written recommendation, because managers are extremely reluctant to state a frank and honest opinion that may later be used against them in court.

Applicants who are rated successful at an interview should be told that a check of their references will be conducted, and, pending favorable responses, they will be contacted by the personnel department within two days. Applicants who are currently employed normally ask that their current employer not be contacted for a reference check. This request should be honored at all times. Applicants who are currently working usually want to give proper notice to their current employers. If the applicant chooses not to give notice, chances are no notice will be given at the time he or she leaves your hotel. In some cases, the applicant gives notice and, upon doing so, is "cut loose" immediately. If such is the case, the applicant should be told to contact the department manager immediately in order that the employee may be put to work as soon as possible.

Interview Skills versus Turnover

There is no perfect interviewer, interviewee, or resultant hiring or rejection decision in regard to an applicant. We can only hope to improve our interviewing skills in order that the greatest degree of success in employee retention can be obtained. The executive housekeeper should expect that 25 percent of initial hires into a housekeeping department will not be employed for more than three months. (This is primarily because the housekeeping skills are easily learned and the position is paid at or near minimum wage.) Some new housekeeping departments have as much as a 75 percent turnover rate in the first three months of operation. Certainly this figure can be improved upon with adequate attention to the interviewing and selection processes. However, regardless of the outcome of the interview, the processing record should be properly endorsed and returned to the personnel department for processing.

Orientation

A carefully planned, concerned, and informational orientation programme is significant to the first impressions that a new employee will have about the hospital or hotel in general and the housekeeping department in particular. Too often, a new employee is told where the work area and restroom are, given a cursory explanation of the job, then put to work. It is not uncommon to find managers putting employees to work who have not even been processed into the organization, an unfortunate situation that is usually discovered on payday when there is no paycheck for the new employee. Such blatant disregard for the concerns of the employee can only lead to a poor perception of the company.

A planned orientation programme will eliminate this type of activity and will bring the employee into the company with personal concern and with a greater possibility for a successful relationship. A good orientation programme is usually made up of four phases: employee acquisition, receipt of an employee's handbook, tour of the facility, and an orientation meeting.

Employee Acquisition

Once a person is accepted for employment, the applicant is told to report for work at a given time and place, and that place should be the personnel department. Pre-employment procedures can take as much as one-half day, and department managers eager to start new employees to work should allow time for a proper employee acquisition into the organization.

At this time it should be ensured that the application is complete and any additional information pertaining to employment history that may be necessary to obtain the necessary work permits and credentials is on hand.

Usually the security department records the entry of a new employee into the staff and provides instructions regarding use of employee entrances, removing parcels from the premises, and employee parking areas. Application for work permits, and drug testing, will be scheduled where applicable. All documents required by the hotel's health and welfare insurer should be completed, and instructions should be given about immediately reporting accidents, no matter how slight, to supervisors.

The federal government requires that every employer submit a W-4 (withholding statement) for each employee on the payroll. The employee must complete this document and give it to the company. Mandatory deductions from pay should be explained (federal and state income tax and Social Security FICA), as should other deductions that may be required or desired. Note the permanent information that will be carried on file.

The PAF is serially numbered, is created from data stored on magnetic discs, and is maintained in the employee's personnel file. When a change has to be made, such as job title, marital status, or rate of pay, the PAF is retrieved from the employee's record, changes are made under the item to be changed, and the corrected PAF is used to change the data in the computer storage. Once new information is stored, a new PAF is created and placed in the employee's record to await the next need for processing. A long-time employee might have many PAFs stored in the personnel file.

Once an applicant has been prescreened and interviewed, has had references checked, and has received an offer of employment, the checklist is used to ensure completion of data required to place the employee on the payroll. When either regular or special performance appraisals are given, the last (most current) PAF will be used to record the appraisal. These forms are usually found on the reverse side of the PAF. Since performance appraisals may signify a raise in pay, the appropriate pay increase information would be indicated on the front side of the PAF. All recordings on PAFs, whether on one side or both, require the submission of data, storage of information, and creation of a new PAF to be stored in the employee's record.

The PAF and performance appraisal system should be thoroughly explained to the new employee, along with assignment of a payroll number. The employer should also explain how and when the staff is paid and when the first paycheck may be expected.

The Employee Handbook

The new employee should be provided with a copy of the hotel or hospital employee's handbook and should be told to read it thoroughly. Since the new housekeeping employee is not working just for the housekeeping department but is to become integrated as a member of the entire staff, reading this handbook is extremely important to ensure that proper instructions in the rules and regulations of the hotel are presented. The handbook should be developed in such a way as to inspire the new employee to become a fully participating member of the organization.

Note the tone of the welcoming letter and the manner in which the rules and regulations are presented. Upon completion of the acquisition phase, a facility tour should be conducted for one or all new employees. For new facilities, access to the property should be gained within about one week before opening, and many new employees can be taken on a tour simultaneously. It is possible for employees to work in the hotel housekeeping department for years and never to have visited the showroom, dining rooms, ballrooms, or even the executive office areas. A tour of the complete facility melds employees into the total organization, and a complete informative tour should never be neglected.

The reverse side of the PAF may be used to record performance appraisals, written warnings, or matters involving terminations. For ongoing operations, after acquisition, the new employee may be turned over to a department supervisor, who becomes the tour director. An appreciation of the total involvement of each employee is strengthened when a facilities tour is complete and thorough. If necessary, the property tour might be postponed until after the orientation meeting; however, the orientation activity of staffing is not complete until a property tour is conducted.

Orientation Meeting

The orientation meeting should not be conducted until the employee has had an opportunity to become at least partially familiar with the surroundings. After approximately two weeks, the employee will have many questions about experiences, the new job, training, and the rules and regulations listed in the Property and Department Handbooks. Employee orientation meetings that are scheduled too soon fail to answer many questions that will develop within the first two weeks of employment. The meeting should be held in a comfortable setting, with refreshments provided. It is usually conducted by the director of human resources and is attended by as many of the facility managers as possible.

Most certainly, the general manager or hospital administration members of the executive committee, the security director, and the new employees' department heads should attend. Each of these managers should have an opportunity to welcome the new employees and give them a chance to associate names with faces. All managers and new employees should wear name tags. In orientation meetings, a brief history of the company and company goals should be presented. A planned orientation meeting should not be concluded without someone stressing the importance of each position. Every position must have a purpose behind it and is therefore important to the overall functioning of the facility.

An excellent statement of this philosophy was once offered by a general manager who said, "The person mopping a floor in the kitchen at 3:00 A.M. is just as valuable to this operation as I am—we just do different things." The orientation meeting should be scheduled to allow for many questions. And there should be someone in attendance who can answer all of them. Although the new employee will be gaining confidence and security in the position as training ends and work is actually performed, informal orientation may continue for quite some time. The formal orientation, however, ends with the orientation meeting (although the facility tour may be conducted after the meeting). Finally, it should be remembered that good orientation procedures lead to worker satisfaction and help quiet the anxieties and fears that a new employee may have. When a good orientation is neglected, the seeds of dissatisfaction are planted.

The efficiency and economy with which any department will operate will depend on the ability of each member of the organization to do his or her job. Such ability will depend in part on past experiences, but more commonly it can be credited to the type and quality of training offered. Employees, regardless of past experiences, always need some degree of training before starting a new job. Small institutions may try to avoid training by hiring people who are already trained in the general functions with which they will be involved. However, most institutions recognize the need for training that is specifically oriented toward the new experience, and will have a documented training programme. Some employers of housekeeping personnel find it easier to train completely unskilled and untrained personnel.

In such cases, bad or undesirable practices do not have to be trained out of an employee. Previous experience and education should, however, be analyzed and considered in the training of each new employee in order that efficiencies in training can be recognized. If an understanding of department standards and policies can be demonstrated by a new employee, that portion of training may be shortened or modified. However, skill and ability must be demonstrated before training can be altered. Finally, training is the best method to communicate the company's way of doing things, without which the new employee may do work contrary to company policy.

First Training

First training of a new employee actually starts with a continuation of department orientation. When a new employee is turned over to the housekeeping or environmental services department, orientation usually continues by familiarizing the employee with department rules and regulations. Many housekeeping departments have their own department employee handbooks. For an example, which contains the housekeeping department rules and regulations for Bally's Casino Resort in Las Vegas, Nevada. Compare this handbook with that of the generic handbook. Although these handbooks are for completely different types of organizations, the substance of their publications is essentially the same; both are designed to familiarize each new employee with his or her surroundings. Handbooks should be written in such a way as to inspire employees to become team members, committed to company objectives.

A Systematic Approach to Training

Training may be defined as those activities that are designed to help an employee begin performing tasks for which he or she is hired or to help the employee improve performance in a job already assigned. The purpose of training is to enable an employee to begin an assigned job or to improve upon techniques already in use. In hotel or hospital housekeeping operations, there are three basic areas in which training activity should take place: skills, attitudes, and knowledge.

SKILLS TRAINING

A sample list of skills in which a basic housekeeping employee must be trained follows: 1. Bed making: Specific techniques; company policy 2. Vacuuming: Techniques; use and care of equipment 3. Dusting: Techniques; use of products 4. Window and mirror cleaning: Techniques and products 5.

Setup awareness: Room setups; what a properly serviced room should look like 6. Bathroom cleaning: Tub and toilet sanitation; appearance; methods of cleaning and results desired 7. Daily routine: An orderly procedure for the conduct of the day's work; daily communications 8. Caring for and using equipment: Housekeeper cart; loading 9. Industrial safety: Product use; guest safety; fire and other emergencies The best reference for the skills that require training is the job description for which the person is being trained.

ATTITUDE GUIDANCE

Employees need guidance in their attitudes about the work that must be done. They need to be guided in their thinking about rooms that may present a unique problem in cleaning. Attitudes among housekeepers need to be such that, occasionally, when rooms require extra effort to be brought back to standard, it is viewed as being a part of rendering service to the guest who paid to enjoy the room. Carol Mondesir,1 director of housekeeping, Sheraton Centre, Toronto, states that: A hotel is meant to be enjoyed and, occasionally, the rooms are left quite messed up. However, as long as they're not vandalized, it's part of the territory. The whole idea of being in the hospitality business is to make the guest's stay as pleasant as possible. The rooms are there to be enjoyed. Positive relationships with various agencies and people also need to be developed.

The following is a list of areas in which attitude guidance is important:

1. The guest/patient
2. The department manager and immediate supervisor
3. A guestroom that is in a state of great disarray
4. The hotel and company
5. The uniform
6. Appearance
7. Personal hygiene Staffing Housekeeping Positions.

The most important task of the trainer is to prepare new employees to meet standards. With this aim in mind, sequence of performance in cleaning a guestroom is most important in order that efficiency in accomplishing day-to-day tasks may be developed. In addition, the best method of accomplishing a task should be presented to the new trainee. Once the task has been learned, the next thing is to meet standards, which may not necessarily mean doing the job the way the person has been trained.

KNOWLEDGE TRAINING

Areas of knowledge in which the employee needs to be trained are as follows:

1. Thorough knowledge of the hotel layout; employee must be able to give directions and to tell the guest about the hotel, restaurants, and other facilities
2. Knowledge of employee rights and benefits
3. Understanding of grievance procedure
4. Knowing top managers by sight and by name for all employees, regardless of how long they have been members of the department.

There are two instances when additional training is needed:

(1) The purchase of new equipment, and

(2) Change in or unusual employee behaviour while on the job. When new equipment is purchased, employees need to know how the new equipment differs from present equipment, what new skills or knowledge are required to operate the equipment, who will need this knowledge, and when. New equipment may also require new attitudes about work habits. Employee behaviour while on the job that is seen as an indicator for additional training may be divided into two categories: events that the manager witnesses and events that the manager is told about by the employees. Events that the manager witnesses that indicate a need for training are frequent employee absence, considerable spoilage of products, carelessness, a high rate of accidents, and

resisting direction by supervisors. Events that the manager might be told about that indicate a need for training are that something doesn't work right (product isn't any good), something is dangerous to work with, something is making work harder. Although training is vital for any organization to function at top efficiency, it is expensive.

The money and man-hours expended must therefore be worth the investment. There must be a balance between the dollars spent training employees and the benefits of productivity and high-efficiency performance. A simple method of determining the need for training is to measure performance of workers: Find out what is going on at present on the job, and match this performance with what should be happening. The difference, if any, describes how much training is needed. In conducting performance analysis, the following question should be asked: Could the employee do the job or task if his or her life depended on the result? If the employee could not do the job even if his or her life depended on the outcome, there is a deficiency of knowledge (DK).

If the employee could have done the job if his or her life depended on the outcome, but did not, there is a deficiency of execution (DE). Some of the causes of deficiencies of execution include task interference, lack of feedback (employee doesn't know when the job is being performed correctly or incorrectly), and the balance of consequences (some employees like doing certain tasks better than others). If either deficiency of knowledge or deficiency of execution exists, training must be conducted. The approach or the method of training may differ, however. Deficiencies of knowledge can be corrected by training the employee to do the job, then observing and correcting as necessary until the task is proficiently performed. Deficiency of execution is usually corrected by searching for the underlying cause of lack of performance, not by teaching the actual task.

Training Methods

There are numerous methods or ways to conduct training. Each method has its own advantages and disadvantages, which must be weighed in the light of benefits to be gained. Some methods are more expensive than others but are also more effective in terms of time required for comprehension and proficiency that must be developed. Several useful methods of training housekeeping personnel are listed and discussed.

ON-THE-JOB TRAINING

Using on-the-job training (OJT), a technique in which "learning by doing" is the advantage, the instructor demonstrates the procedure and then watches the students perform it. With this technique, one instructor can handle several students. In housekeeping operations, the instructor is usually a GRA who is doing the instructing in the rooms that have been assigned for cleaning that day. The OJT method is not operationally productive until the student is proficient enough in the training tasks to absorb part of the operational load.

SIMULATION TRAINING

With simulation training, a model room (unrented) is set up and used to train several employees. Whereas OJT requires progress toward daily production of ready rooms, simulation requires that the model room not be rented. In addition, the trainer is not productive in cleaning ready rooms. The advantages of simulation training are that it allows the training process to be stopped, discussed, and repeated if necessary. Simulation is an excellent method, provided the trainer's time is paid for out of training funds, and clean room production is not necessary during the workday.

Coach-Pupil Method

The coach-pupil method is similar to OJT except that each instructor has only one student (a one-to-one relationship). This method is desired, provided that there are enough qualified instructors to have several training units in progress at the same time.

Lectures

The lecture method reaches the largest number of students per instructor. Practically all training programmes use this type of instruction for certain segments. Unfortunately, the lecture method can be the dullest training technique, and therefore requires instructors who are gifted in presentation capabilities. In addition, space for lectures may be difficult to obtain and may require special facilities.

Conferences

The conference method of instruction is often referred to as workshop training. This technique involves a group of students who formulate ideas, do problem solving, and report on projects. The conference or workshop technique is excellent for supervisory training.

Demonstrations

When new products or equipment are being introduced, demonstrations are excellent. Many demonstrations may be conducted by vendors and purveyors as a part of the sale of equipment and products. Difficulties may arise when language barriers exist. It is also important that no more information be presented than can be absorbed in a reasonable period of time; otherwise misunderstandings may arise.

Training Aids

Many hotels use training aids in a conference room, or post messages on an employee bulletin board. Aside from the usual training aids such as chalkboards, bulletin boards, charts, graphs, and diagrams, photographs can supply clear and accurate references for how rooms should be set up, maids' carts loaded, and routines accomplished. Most housekeeping operations have films on guest contact and courtesy that may also be used in training. Motion pictures speak directly to many people who may not understand proper procedures from reading about them. Many training techniques may be combined to develop a well-rounded training plan.

Development

It is possible to have two students sitting side by side in a classroom, with one being trained and the other being developed. Recall that the definition of training is preparing a person to do a job for which he or she is hired or to improve upon performance of a current job. Development is preparing a person for advancement or to assume greater responsibility. The techniques are the same, but the end result is quite different. Whereas training begins after orientation of an employee who is hired to do a specific job, upon introduction of new equipment, or upon observation and communication with employees indicating a need for training, development begins with the identification of a specific employee who has shown potential for advancement. Training for promotion or to improve potential is in fact development and must always include a much neglected type of training— supervisory training.

Many forms of developmental training may be given on the property; other forms might include sending candidates to schools and seminars. Developmental training is associated primarily with supervisors and managerial development and may encompass many types of experiences. Note the various developmental tasks that the trainee must perform over a period of 12 months. Development of individuals within the organization looks to future potential and promotion of employees. Specifically, those employees who demonstrate leadership potential should be developed through supervisory training for advancement to positions of greater responsibility.

Unfortunately, many outstanding workers have their performance rewarded by promotion but are given no development training. The excellent housekeeper who is advanced to the position of senior housekeeper without the benefit of supervisory training is quickly seen to be unhappy and frustrated and may possibly become a loss to the department. It is therefore most essential that individual potential be developed in an orderly and systematic manner, or else this potential may never be recognized. While undergoing managerial development, student and management alike should not lose sight of the primary aim of the programme, which is the learning and potential development of the trainee, not departmental production.

Even though there will be times that the trainee may be given specific responsibilities to oversee operations, clean guestrooms, or service public areas, advantage should not be taken of the trainee or the situation to the detriment of the development function. Development of new growth in the trainee becomes difficult when the training instructor or coordinator is not only developing a new manager but is also being held responsible for the production of some aspect of housekeeping operations.

Records and Reports

Whether you are conducting training or a development programme, suitable records of training progress should be maintained both by the training supervisor and the student. Periodic evaluations of the student's progress should be conducted, and successful completion of the programme should be recognized. Public recognition of achievement will inspire the newly trained or developed employee to achieve standards of performance and to strive for advancement. Once an employee is trained or developed and his or her satisfactory performance has been recognized and recorded, the person should perform satisfactorily to standards. Future performance may be based on beginning performance after training. If an employee's performance begins to fall short of standards and expectations, there has to be a reason other than lack of skills. The reason for unsatisfactory performance must then be sought out and addressed. This type of follow-up is not possible unless suitable records of training and development are maintained and used for comparison.

Evaluation and Performance Appraisal

Although evaluation and performance appraisal for employees will occur as work progresses, it is not uncommon to find the design of systems for appraisal as part of organization and staffing functions. This is true because first appraisal and evaluation occurs during training, which is an activity of staffing. Once trainees begin to have their performance appraised, the methods used will continue throughout employment. As a part of training, new employees should be told how, when, and by whom their performances will be evaluated, and should be advised that questions regarding their performance will be regularly answered.

Probationary Period

Initial employment should be probationary in nature, allowing the new employee to improve efficiency to where the designated number of rooms cleaned per day can be achieved in a probationary period (about three months). Should a large number of employees be unable to achieve the standard within that time, the standard should be investigated. Should only one or two employees be unable to meet the standard of rooms cleaned per day, an evaluation of the employee in training should either reveal the reason why or indicate the employee as unsuitable for further retention.

An employee who, after suitable training, cannot meet a reasonable performance standard should not be allowed to continue employment. Similarly, an employee who has met required performance standards in the specified probationary period should be continued into regular employment status and thus achieve a reasonable degree of security in employment.

Evaluation

Evaluation of personnel is an attempt to measure selected traits, characteristics, and productivity. Unfortunately, evaluations are generally objective in nature, and raters are seldom trained in the art of subjective evaluation. Initiative, self-control, and leadership ability do not used to cycle the trainee through the various functions involved in a hotel housekeeping department. Note the position of the person who will coach the development in the various skills, and the time expected to be spent in each area lend themselves to measurement; therefore such characteristics are estimated. How well they are estimated depends to a great extent on the person doing the estimating. Two raters using the same form and rating the same person will probably arrive at different conclusions.

Certain policies on the use of evaluations should be established so that they are understood by both the person doing the evaluating and the person being evaluated. These policies must be established and disseminated by management. In order to establish such policies, the following questions, among others, must be answered and communicated to all those involved in the evaluation: What will evaluations be used for? Will evaluations influence promotions, become a part of the employee's record, be used as periodic checks, or be used for counseling and guidance? What qualities are going to be evaluated? Who is going to be evaluated? Who will do the evaluating? Reliable evaluations require careful planning and take considerable time, skill, and work. An evaluation must be understood by the employee.

Evaluation should be used at the end of a probationary period, and the employee must understand at the Staffing Housekeeping Positions beginning of the period that he or she will be observed and evaluated. Each item, as well as what impact the evaluation will have on future employment, should be explained to the employee. People undergoing periodic evaluations, such as at the end of one year's employment, should also know why evaluations are being conducted and what may result from the evaluation. In both situations, the evaluation should be used for counseling and guidance so that performance may be improved.

Evaluations should be made for a purpose and not for the sake of an exercise. They should ultimately be used as management tools. Evaluations should be developed to fit the policies of the particular institution using it and the particular position being evaluated. The same evaluation may not be suitable for every position.

Outsourcing

In certain locales, such as isolated resorts, hotels are tempted to use contract labour because the local market does not support the necessary number of workers, particularly in housekeeping. Advocates of outsourcing are quick to point out the advantages of the practice. Scarce workers are provided to the property, and there is no need to provide expensive employee benefits. The entire staffing function is assumed by the contractor. There are no worries regarding recruiting, selecting, hiring, orienting, or even training the employees. Merely issue them uniforms and send them off to clean rooms. Some employers may even be willing to relax their responsibilities regarding employment law such as immigration and naturalization requirements.

Management should never forget that once a contracted employee dons a company uniform, the guest believes (and has no reason not to) that person is an employee of the hotel. The guest also believes the hotel has made every reasonable effort to screen that person in the hiring process to ensure that he or she is of good moral character, who has the best interest of the guest at heart. Unfortunately, there have been several incidents in which the outsourced employees did not quite have the best interest of the guest in their hearts.

There have been more than a few cases in which outsourced workers were wanted felons who inflicted considerable bodily harm on guests during the performance of their duties. A number of these incidents have resulted in lawsuits, with awards against the hotel in the millions of dollars. This author does not recommend outsourcing in housekeeping, and cautions operators who ignore this advice to keep their guard up and continue to meet their legal and ethical responsibilities regarding employees and employment law.

Staffing for both hospital and hotel housekeeping operations involves the activities of selecting, interviewing, orienting, training, and developing personnel to carry out specific functions in the organization for which they are hired. Each activity should be performed with consistency, dispatch, and individual concern for each employee brought into the organization. Whereas the major presentation of staffing in this text has been developed for the model hotel where a mass hiring has been performed, each and every aspect of selecting, orienting, and training new employees applies equally to situations in which replacement employees (perhaps only one) are brought into the organization. Job specifications are the documents that indicate qualifications, characteristics, and abilities inherently needed in applicants.

The Employee Requisition is the instrument by which specific numbers and types of candidates for employment are sought by the personnel department for each of the operating departments. The next step is interviewing, which should be done by people from various departments. Actual selection, however, should only be performed by the department manager for whom the employee will work. The employee acquisition phase is vital to the successful orientation of a new employee and should not be omitted.

Upon acquisition of the new employee, presentation of an Employee's Handbook is appropriate. This handbook should contain major company rules, procedures, and regulations, along with relevant facts for the employee. Orientation is the basis for allowing the new employee to become accustomed to new surroundings. The quality of orientation will determine whether the new employee will feel secure in a new setting, and it will set the stage for the relationship that is to follow. As training begins, orientation continues but is now conducted by the specific department in which the new employee will work.

There are several methods of training, each of which should be used so as to gain the best effect for the least cost. Employee performance in training should be evaluated by methods similar to those used in evaluating operational performance that will follow. After new employees receive approximately 24 hours of on-the-job training in the cleaning of rooms, they should become productive and be able to clean a reasonable number of rooms (about 60 percent efficient). Continued application of skills will develop greater productivity as the new employee spends each day working at the new skills. As preliminary training ends, orientation should be completed by ensuring that an employee orientation meeting and a tour of the entire facility has taken place.

Failure to complete an orientation or to provide sufficient training can plant the seeds of employee unrest, discontent, and possible failure of the employee's relationship with the company that might well have been prevented. Whether conducting training or development, adequate records of employee progress should be maintained. Records of training that have been successfully completed establish a base for future performance appraisal. Employees have a right to expect evaluations, and usually consider objectively prepared statements about their performance a mark of management's caring about employees.

Chapter 9

Prospects for Development via International Business

The fundamental focus of this book has been the relationship between international business and development. This focus reflects the concern with development that permeates all aspects of the environment of the world's developing countries. The theme that permeates the book is that a principal, if not the principal, contributor to development is the international business activities of firms and individuals within the society.

This is not by any means to suggest that development relates only to international business activities. Clearly, the social, political, and economic characteristics of a country provide an important foundation upon which international business activities can build; and managers in developing countries need also to assist in the building of this foundation. Indeed, one might argue that while social, political, and economic stability are necessary conditions for competitive success and development, the development of a range of internationally competitive industries is a sufficient condition for national competitiveness. Clearly, no country will find that all of its industries are competitive by international standards; but the more of such industries a country can boast, the more competitive the entire country is and the higher the level of development.

Yet managers in many developing countries have fundamental concerns, many of which have been identified throughout the book, about their ability to spawn internationally competitive industries. In examining the prospects for development via international business, it is useful to revisit some of these concerns, particularly in the context of an examination of factors that lead to the creation of internationally competitive industries and firms.

CREATING COMPETITIVE INDUSTRIES

The traditional perspective on the factors that spawned competitive industries within countries placed the primary focus on a country's endowments of resources in the form of the factors of production of labour, land, and capital. The Heckscher—Ohlin extension to the Ricardian theory of comparative advantage focused on these resources as the critical components that identified the industries in which countries would have a comparative advantage; that is, these were the industries in which a country would be internationally competitive.

The discussion however, also pointed out that, increasingly, efforts to understand the industries in which a country would be competitive have meant adding to a natural resource explanation for the creation and expansion of competitive industries a broader group of variables. These variables have an important impact on the determination of which industries are likely to be competitive and over what period.

To a large extent, studies that found a role for factors other than a country's resource endowments in explaining the set of competitive industries in a country trace their intellectual origin to Vernon's product cycle study of 1966. That study found a role for home-country demand patterns in determining the industries in which a country would be competitive. It also introduced the notion of dynamism to studies of industry competitiveness; that is, a country does not inherit a set of competitive industries based on its resource endowments and then relax with the knowledge that it will always host these industries. Rather, competitive industries could be and often were created through timely innovations.

These creations, however, can prove fickle; and these same industries are likely, at some point, to migrate to other countries.

Porter's study on the competitiveness of nations continued this tradition by indicating the factors likely to be important in determining the international competitiveness of a nation's industries and thus, by extension, the competitiveness of the nation. He identified a set of principal variables—factor conditions, demand conditions, firm strategy, structure and rivalry, and related and supporting industries—and a set of secondary variables—the role of government and the role of chance.

In developing the variables that appeared to have the most significant impact on whether a country was able to spawn competitive industries and identifying which particular industries might be generated in particular countries, Porter identified the critical role of resource endowments (factor conditions) as embodied in classical trade theories. He also focused on the importance of home-country demand patterns as outlined in the work of Vernon (demand conditions).

To these two sets of characteristics, Porter added another two primary determinants of national competitiveness. In the tradition of classical economists with their emphasis on the importance of competition in generating efficient economic activity, Porter emphasized the importance of rivalry among firms. He posited that a country was likely to be host to a competitive industry where competitive rivalry among the domestic participants in that industry was particularly intense. He suggested further that where an industry could draw upon the resources of other competitive industries that together formed a cluster, the industry and other related industries in that cluster of industries would be better able to compete internationally.

In addition to these four primary determinants of national competitiveness, Porter added two secondary determinants. He suggested that there was an important role for government but that this role was to influence the four primary determinants and that the role of government should not, of itself, be considered a determinant. Last, for completeness, Porter suggested that some countries were simply lucky in their development of competitive industries. Thus, he suggested a role for chance in determining national competitiveness.

Competitiveness in Developing Countries

These studies that place significant emphasis on the nature of the home market and industry structure in creating competitive industries might be viewed, from the perspective of the world's developing countries, as providing hope while creating despair. They provide hope in the sense that they emphasize the notion that a country born with few competitive industries, which is the case in most developing countries, has the possibility of adding to its portfolio of such industries over time. At the same time, they exude despair because the conditions they delineate as important to the creation of competitive industries do not, in large part, exist in many developing countries.

These conditions typically involve firms honing their skills while they produce products particularly oriented to the needs of a home market comprised of sophisticated consumers. Once they have been able to satisfy these consumers, they are well positioned to extend their operations to segments of consumers with similar needs in other countries. A related condition is that firms are able to hone their skills while producing products for large domestic markets. In producing for these large domestic markets, their expertise expands over time and with increases in the volume of goods produced. This gradually evolving expertise provides these first-mover firms with a competitive advantage over follower companies, including those from other countries.

For most developing countries, the notion of large markets comprised of sophisticated consumers demanding and willing to buy state-of-the-art or innovative products is a very alien condition. The markets of these countries tend to be small in terms of the number of consumers that can effectively demand products, that is, can add to an interest in a good the wherewithal to purchase that good. This is clearly true of small developing countries, but it is also true of some of the relatively large countries.

This is not to suggest that there are no exceptions to this general observation. The Brazilian company, Embraer, for example, was able to spearhead the development of a small-aircraft industry in Brazil in part because of the demand characteristics of the Brazilian environment. As a physically large country with a very rugged terrain that had led to an underdeveloped surface transportation network, Brazil placed significant emphasis on the use of small aircraft. Early in Embraer's history, guaranteed purchases from the Brazilian military provided a market that allowed the company to hone its expertise in its home environment. Embraer went on to develop models that were successfully sold in the United States, but Embraer's experience was an exception rather than the rule. The Embraer route is not the route most developing countries have traveled in creating competitive industries.

For the majority of developing countries, competitive industries have arisen almost exclusively from the natural endowments of those countries, whether in terms of climatic conditions in industries such as agriculture or tourism, or low-cost factors of production, primarily labour, in industries such as textiles, footwear, electronic assembly, and data conversion. Indeed, the developing countries have developed competitive industries in a manner very much in keeping with the implications of the Heckscher-Ohlin extension of comparative advantage trade theory and the industry migration effects of Vernon's product cycle theory. Even India's booming software industry fits a resourcebased, rather than a home-market based, notion of industry competitiveness with that country's plentiful supply of trained but low-cost software programers.

Indeed, the developing countries are not concerned so much about how they develop competitive industries as long as they are, in fact, able to develop these industries. The history of national competitiveness has demonstrated quite clearly that countries can improve their competitiveness over time (and also that countries can lose their competitiveness over time as the example of Argentina, among others, demonstrates quite clearly). The task then is for these countries to advance over time, adding additional competitive industries to their arsenals of competitive industries and upgrading the sources of competitive advantage upon which these industries rely.

In so doing, developing countries will be likely to go through stages. These stages take their starting point, however, with the development of competitive industries based upon the country's resource base, including the important resource of skilled labour. Porter's work addresses this issue of the stages countries are likely to go through in pursuit of the widest array of competitive industries based on increasingly more sustainable forms of competitive advantage.

As indicated Porter identifies four stages of national development through which countries may pass: factor driven, investment driven, innovation driven, and wealth driven.

The factor-driven stage is one in which competitive firms and industries derive their competitive advantage from the country's endowments of resources. Firms operating in such countries export primarily standardized products. This stage of national development corresponds to the initial stages of export marketing, the investment-driven stage have established a set of firms that are willing and able to invest aggressively in the development of modern, efficient facilities with the best available process technology. Firms in the innovation-driven stage compete by creating new products and processes based on their resources of highly skilled and creative workers but also in response to the demands of highly sophisticated consumers.

Competitive industries in this stage would draw their competitive advantage from all the sources of competitive advantage identified by Porter and other analysts. Last, in the wealth-driven stage, a country's competitive industries draw their competitiveness from prior investments and innovation. Firms in such countries rest upon their first-mover advantages but have lost the urge or ability to innovate in new areas. This stage has the potential of leading countries to ultimate decline unless the movement in this direction is arrested and countries are able to return to the innovation-driven stage of national development.

Most developing countries operate at varying points in the factor-driven stage. A few have moved from the factor-driven stage to the investment-driven stage. Those countries that have moved (e.g., Korea) gained the momentum for moving from their success in the factor-driven stage.

Korean companies, like the large conglomerate Daewoo, provide a firmbased example of how the entire Korean economy has moved from factordriven to investment-driven sources of competitive advantage, with a corresponding expansion in the types of activities in which the company en gages. Daewoo began its international life as an exporter of textiles and garments. In 1967, 100 percent of the company's exports comprised textile and garment exporters. By 1985, however, textile and garment exports constituted about 16 percent of total exports. By that time, Daewoo had become a well known producer of ships, automobiles, rolling stock, and machinery—and even an installer of telephone lines. In the early 1990s, Daewoo's car imports were not at the level of its local competitor, Hyundai; but the company was exporting cars, primarily to developing countries around the world.

The immediate task for most developing countries, then, is to become internationally competitive, based on the country's resources, including skilled labour, in an array of industries. Once that goal has been achieved, these countries can seek to move to more advanced stages, where competitiveness is based on more durable advantages than low-cost factors of production. These countries, particularly the smaller ones, might also be able to move immediately to niche markets in which they can produce specialty products that have a competitive position built not on low costs but on the existence of unique, differentiated products.

IMPEDIMENTS TO THE CREATION OF COMPETITIVE INDUSTRIES

In moving in the direction of expanding their portfolio of competitive industries, and indeed in preserving the competitiveness of existing industries that have done well internationally, developing countries contend that they face many impediments and that these impediments retard their development prospects.

Access to Intemational Markets

In order for firms in developing countries to take advantage of their competitive abilities, they need to have unimpeded access to the markets of other countries. In today's world, companies will receive no such guarantees.

Here, it is important to note that developed countries have been largely unwilling to engage in the transition from one set of industries to another as the competitive imperatives within that industry change. Thus, an industry such as textiles in which firms in developing countries have a significant cost advantage relative to their counterparts in developed countries has seen the institutionalization of protection in order to shield producers in developed countries from their more cost-efficient counterparts elsewhere. Protectionism has been similarly rampant in agriculture sectors in the developed countries of North America, Europe, and Japan.

Developed countries have not been the only countries engaged in protectionist policies. Developing countries have also been extremely resistant to providing other developing countries with unimpeded access to their markets. The discussions have focused on the developed countries because of the significance of the developed country market.

For developing countries that are poised to become a part of one of the major trading blocs that are being spawned in different parts of the world, the problem of markets made inaccessible by government policy should largely disappear. Very few developing countries, however, are thus poised.

Mexico is the first developing country to have obtained a secure position in a trading bloc. There may soon be similar opportunities for Chile and possibly Turkey prior to the end of the century. Other countries in Latin America and the Caribbean have indicated a desire for membership in NAFTA; and many Eastern European, Middle Eastern, and North African countries have been knocking on the door of the EU. It is hard to be as sanguine about the prospects for inclusion of these other countries, based on the dilemma of difference discussed.

Beyond awaiting a more liberal trade climate in which trade barriers are eliminated, developing countries can only find relief in the fact that the protectionism of most developed countries did not stall the export thrust of the NICs in the 1970s and 1980s. These countries found innovative solutions to the problems of protectionism.

There are, of course, significant implications to developing countries of the movement to a more liberal trade climate and to accession to major trading blocs. A more liberal trading climate and entry into major trading blocs that involve developed and developing countries is increasingly going to occur only on the basis of reciprocal trade concessions. Thus, developing countries will also be unable to protect their own industries, increasingly including their service industries.

Trends in Foreign Direct Investment

Even where countries do not impose barriers to imports from developing countries, there is still a concern that firms from developing countries will find it difficult to gain access to the markets of developed countries because they lack institutional linkages with those markets. One of the institutions that has been viewed as valuable in creating those linkages is the multinational firm. These firms, so the argument goes, can help the exports of developing countries gain access to distribution channels in developed countries. In light of this benefit, there are those in developing countries who express concern at the reduction in the flows of foreign direct investment destined for developing countries.

It is indeed true that, apart from a blip in the late 1980s and early 1990s associated with privatization, the trend shows declining flows of foreign direct investment to developing countries. This does not, however, represent as strong an impediment to the creation of competitive firms as it might appear at first glance. Clearly, more foreign direct investment designed to use developing countries as an export platform would assist these countries in their bid to develop international competitive industries, particularly if the skills of the foreign investor can be captured throughout the wider economy.

The reality, however, is that the bulk of foreign direct investment in past years was not of that form. Rather, it was investment to serve domestic markets. In engaging in such investments, particularly where they were established behind high tariff walls, foreign investors were never major contributors to the international competitiveness of the countries that were their hosts. The loss of such investment does not, therefore, necessarily have a detrimental impact on national competitiveness.

What is true, on the other hand, is that developing countries in this new investment climate cannot look to foreign investors to provide the engine of growth for their economies. Virtually every developing country is wooing foreign investors. Thus, the demand for export-oriented foreign direct investment far exceeds the supply of this investment. Singapore, in particular, gained first-mover advantages by being the first developing country to attract export-oriented foreign investment. This country has reaped significant fruits from its boldness. A boldness that, among other things, involved guaranteeing a return for investors on their commercial operations. Other developing countries will find it difficult to replicate that strategy.

The Nonresponsiveness of the World Financial Community

Many in developing countries have bemoaned the lack of understanding of the world's financial community and its monetary systems. The lack of responsiveness of these institutions is viewed by many in the South to be an impediment to the development of the developing countries. The efforts at creating a new international economic order came directly out of the view that the current world financial order was stacked against the developing countries. The criticisms of the IMF, and increasingly of the WB with its structural adjustment policies, is another manifestation of the view that the world's major multilateral institutions are unconcerned about the plight of the developing countries.

The response of the multilateral institutions would be that they have actually assisted countries in embarking down the path of enhanced competitiveness with the structural reforms they have insisted upon as a condition of their loans and that, although these prescriptions may have had a bitter taste, their medicinal effects are now working, as evidenced by the extent to which many countries are now prescribing the same medicine for themselves outside of the context of loan programmes. The experience of several Latin American countries, most notably Mexico, and even some countries in sub-Saharan Africa would be presented as evidence of the wisdom of eliminating budget defi cits, reducing inflation, privatizing inefficient state industries, allowing local farmers to get market prices for their produce, and so forth.

Ultimately, however, the multilateral agencies and the bilateral aid organizations also must be accountable to the countries that provide the funding or that own their shares. In a competitive arena in which developing countries are pitted against developed countries, the developing countries can expect a degree of non responsiveness at times. This was aptly demonstrated in the significant reductions in the U.S. Agency for International Development (AID) financing of investment-promotion activities in Central American countries after a television programme in the United States suggested that the agency was assisting developing countries in their efforts to lure U.S. investors to their countries. The U.S. population asked why U.S. taxpayers should contribute to what may eventually be job losses within the United States. Developing countries might respond by saying that such an activity could well lead to enhanced productivity within the United States as U.S. workers make a transition toward jobs requiring greater skills. They would be likely, however, to encounter a non responsive organization.

The Limitations of South-South Economic Integration

As the efforts to create an NIEO floundered, developing countries placed much hope on the possibilities of development via South—South economic integration. The individual markets of developing countries might be too small for efforts at self-sufficiency or the scale required for production for export markets, but the combined markets of several countries might allow for efficient production.

The limitations of these efforts became readily apparent, however, since neighbouring developing country economies basing their competitive activities on resource endowments have found that they have similar economies, whose products substitute for each other—this in contrast to the more appropriate base for economic integration efforts, that is, economies that produce a broad range of dissimilar products and are complementary to each other. Thus, the integration efforts of developing countries are unlikely to allow for self-sufficiency with any more effectiveness than the efforts of an individual economy to seek such self-sufficiency. This is especially true of the groupings of particularly small countries such as that of the Caribbean countries of CARICOM.

The Limitations of National Government Policy

Managers of private firms in many developing countries would regard the most significant impediment to the country's attempts at national competitiveness to be inept government policy. There is, to begin with, a major controversy on the appropriate role for government in developing competitive industries within a country. Porter argues for a supportive but unobtrusive role for government that involves creating the requisite infrastructure and enforcing competition while avoiding the temptation to engage in intrusive efforts at subsidizing particular industries. The work of strategic trade theorists, albeit in a limited number of special cases, sees the possibility of governments influencing which industries the country gains a competitive position in through subsidy and incentive policies that help firms gain a first-mover advantage relative to their rivals elsewhere.

For developing countries, there are two general areas of potential government involvement. The first involves creating a climate that is conducive to productive economic activity. This is largely ignored in studies of developed countries or of the more successful developing countries because this role is taken for granted. In concluding, for example, that the role of government was secondary, Porter based this conclusion on the situation that prevailed in the countries that he studied; but he studied the following ten countries: Denmark, Germany, Italy, Japan, Korea, Singapore, Sweden, Switzerland, the United Kingdom, and the United States.

For countries that have not reached the level of development of these ten countries, the role of government is likely to be much more fundamental. It seems reasonable, for example, to expect that a government will not allow inflation rates of 2,000 percent per annum. These expectations are not always met. Inflation rates at that level were seen in several Latin American countries during the 1980s. In such a situation, the role of government in solving the inflation problem is the most important factor in putting the country on a path that may lead to development. Many governments in developing countries enact policies that lend no economic, social, or political stability to the country. Stability of this type is a necessary prerequisite to the vibrant economic activity that is associated with the development of internationally competitive industries.

Once such stability is achieved, there still remain other roles for government. In pursuing these roles, governments should focus on activities that are socially beneficial but in which profits are not easily captured by a private firm. There are many critical areas of a society, from infrastructure to primary education, which are critical to a society's well-being but in which there would be underinvestment in the absence of collective investments managed by a central government. Several of the export management-assistance programmes provide more specific examples of the types of assistance that a government might usefully provide in an effort to develop competitive industries.

The more controversial role for government surrounds its discriminating in favour of one industry over another in an effort to pick the industry that is most likely to be internationally competitive and provide support for that industry. Here, the evidence is mixed. The Asian success stories as vindications of the appropriateness of an activist government policy. Others argue that there was less intervention in these cases than is generally believed and that many of the examples of intervention failed.

THE PROSPECTS FOR DEVELOPMENT

The prospects for development of the world's developing countries lie as much in the ability of public- and private-sector managers in these countries as they do anywhere else. This is not to say that the external environment is unimportant, but it is to say that the managerial challenge is to make the best use of one's resources given a particular set of environmental conditions. Developing countries could bemoan the unattractiveness of the external environment unceasingly; but these moans will not change the environment, as the experiment with the NIEO demonstrated. In fact, they might not even be heard. A recurring theme of this book is that the development of developing countries is in the hands of the individuals that manage institutions in those countries.

Developing countries do, of course, have a fundamental choice. A developing country might suggest that it is too difficult to compete on international markets or that it does not believe that it is possible to develop a sufficiently wide array of internationally competitive firms to support the expectations of its population. The option such a country has is to retreat from the international marketplace and seek self-sufficiency or autarky.

Such a country would endeavor to satisfy the expectations of its population in that manner. To a large extent, this is a less risky strategy for a country to pursue. The country will remove itself from the vagaries of the international marketplace and from the "clutches" of the international monetary system. The larger the country, the more desirable such a strategy might become. In many respects, it is a strategy that India pursued for many years.

There are, however, obvious problems associated with this "low-risk" strategy. It is more viable for larger developing countries than for smaller developing countries. Such a strategy is also more viable for large countries that are already developed, but it is not a viable strategy for smaller developing countries. Even India, the second largest developing country in terms of population, has moved away from this approach beginning in 1991 with the liberalization programme of the Rao regime. India's change in approach was as a result of the "low returns" associated with its "low-risk" strategy. India was simply developing far too slowly to accommodate the legitimate expectations of its citizenry.

The options for most developing countries, therefore, are few. Their success in creating competitive industries will rest on two interrelated managerial phenomena. The public-sector managers will have to manage the economy and society well, creating an economic and social environment that is stable and conducive and engaging in the provision of socially useful services that would be underprovided were the state not so engaged. The provision of these services and political, social, and economic stability should make the national environment conducive to the pursuit of international business opportunities.

Thereafter, the international competitiveness of the country will rest on the shoulders of entrepreneurs within these countries who are prepared to find opportunities and to pursue these opportunities relentlessly. These are not individuals who become complacent once they can provide an adequate standard of living for themselves. Rather, these entrepreneurs are desirous of doing as well as their counterparts in other countries of the world and are creative in their pursuit of opportunities.

This is a creativity that will increasingly have to be imbued to citizens of developing countries through educational systems, training programmes, and a general societal orientation. Some developing countries have gone far down the road to development through the pursuit of international business activities. Others can continue that trend but not by replication; rather, by innovation and creative application. Indeed, in today's competitive world, there may be no other route to development.

Chapter 10

Operation of Pricing Decisions and Strategies

INTRODUCTION

The pricing process is a central mechanism of a private enterprise or market system. Price adjustments facilitate the logical allocation of resources; both buyers and sellers use them to clear markets of gluts and to stimulate production when supply is short. A competitive price system features such adjustments to achieve maximum economic efficiency. From an industry's perspective, pricing can extend or limit markets; from a company's perspective, it can increase or reduce its share of the market.

Price is the ingredient of the marketing mix that has been subjected to the most intensive analysis — particularly by economists. But as an aspect of the mix, it cannot be divorced from other ingredients. It must incorporate and reflect them. Optimal prices cannot be established, and pricing remains an art with a host of factors to be evaluated for which there are no precise measures and weights.

Although theoretical models exist for establishing optimal prices, in practice, theory does not enable managers to determine the correct price. Marketing management is guided by personal assessments of market conditions, costs, and competitive situations. The actual price established is usually the result of executive value judgments.

Pricing Factors

Marketing managers may not share the economists' concern with price as the primary marketing factor. In a survey of 200 businesses, it was found that "business management did not agree with the economic views of the importance of pricing — one-half of the respondents did not select pricing as one of the five most important policy areas in their firm's marketing success." Consumers do not respond to price alone; they respond to value. A lower price does not necessarily mean expanded sales. Moreover, marketing activities influence price. For example, governmental agencies have investigated advertising as a cause of higher prices.

What is price? It is the amount paid to purchase something, or a monetary summation of the conditions that give value to a product or service. How important is the pricing decision? In microeconomic theory it has received great attention; in marketing, the significance of price varies among industries, competitive situations, and products. Pricing is significant where the market impact, profit results, or both, of price variations is great, and where firms have considerable discretion over the prices charged.

In many instances pricing decisions are severely constrained and are sometimes relatively unimportant. Large purchasers of industrial goods, for instance, may specify prices at which they will buy, determine product specifications, and send specifications to suppliers for competitive bids. For other products price may not be a relevant factor. In some technical areas where products require much research and development and involve much uncertainty, a cost-plus scheme may be used. In other situations, sellers may be almost completely free to set prices, while in still others, they may only be able to decide whether or not to sell at a price.

Where industries are dominated by relatively few large firms, price is not usually the critical competitive variable. Each firm recognizes that price reductions will be met by the other large firms and the profits of all will suffer. Greater attention may then be given to non price factors.

In an economy of scarcity, price is accorded more attention than any other marketing factor. In an economy of abundance, non price factors assume increasing marketing importance and products are differentiated on other bases than price. Style, colour, symbols, and brands become more significant and higher rather than lower prices may actually increase sales. For abundance brings widespread discretionary income, and price becomes a less significant component of the marketing mix than the economic literature might lead one to believe.

Non price competition and price confusion, rather than price clarity, now seem to be the rule. Buyers are concerned not only with price, in their purchases, but also with service, status, and image. Low price alone does not result in a transaction. Consumers are not mechanical price calculators and price reactors, as so much theory leads one to believe. They do not know all the prices, for in reality, discounts, trade-ins, special deals, and premiums cloud the actual price. Prices are limited by direct and indirect competition, costs, and consumer reaction.

Several disciplines help in improving pricing decisions. Economic theory affords guidelines and concepts of demand and elasticity. Accounting furnishes considerations of costs, break-even, and rate of return on investment. Marketing adds to this a consideration and understanding of market behaviour particularly the role of consumers and intermediaries.

Pricing is a sensitive and complex decision area affecting sales, costs, and profits for both industrial and consumer goods. For consumers, price reductions and increases have symbolic meanings. A customer may associate a price reduction with a reduction in quality, the anticipation of new models, or even lower prices or poor market acceptance. Higher prices may indicate better quality, a good image, and good value. Customer perceptions of price are important.

Whereas pricing is usually perceived as a short-run action, its implications can be long-run, even to the point of shaping industry structures. Markets that may be viewed as systems of information on cost and demand determine the appropriateness of prices. They contain signals that businessmen must decode. But market information is ambiguous, fragmentary, and imperfect; it contains much uncertainty and is interpreted differently by various executives. To those who can read the signals properly, increased profits are the results. But invariably, pricing decisions are wrong and must be altered, as is evidenced by changing list prices. Thus, pricing is a process of adjustment in which incomplete data are used for important decisions. As new information is gathered, the offering can be adjusted in two ways: alteration of the price, or alteration of the product to meet the price.

The Pricing Decisions

No single pricing programme is suitable for all firms, since the complexity of pricing situations varies by product, cost, demand, and industry structure, and prices must relate to objectives, information, knowledge of alternative policies, and strategies and adjustments.

The business executive is faced with the problem of establishing the best price under assumed cost-and-demand conditions. The lack of information, the dynamics of the market, and the problems of measuring both costs and demand make it a difficult task. Yet, estimates must be made of what management expects demand, cost, and competition to be under various conditions. Then it can develop pricing programmes that affect survival, profits, growth, volume, market share, R & D, and image.

A distinction is often made between price determination and price administration. The activities and focus of each are different. Price determination refers to the processes and activities employed to arrive at a price for a product. It includes consideration of relative prices of products within the same line, and differences in price for similar products of differing grades and qualities. Price administration refers to the activities involved in fitting basic prices to particular sales situations. For example, prices may be administered to bring them into line with such factors as geographic locale, functions performed by customers, position of distribution channel members, or special sales situations. Included in price administration is the determination of discount structures. Thus, price determination refers to the establishment of a "base price" that is adjusted through price administration to reflect varying sales and competitive situations.

Six concepts and considerations useful in establishing prices are as follows:

1. Pricing decisions should adopt a systems perspective. Executives must consider the whole marketing system — manufacturers, wholesalers, retailers, and consumers — and the impact at each stage.
2. Prices must be related to market segments. The kind and strength of customer attitudes and the purchase desires of various market segments affect the prices that can be charged, and customer acceptance of prices by a sufficient market sector is essential.
3. The determination of the best price is usually impossible, and executives must often settle for satisfactory prices in view of profit and market-share objectives.
4. Price is not to be considered merely as the result of costs; it is also a method of stimulating sales.
5. Since they have both economic and political dimensions, pricing policies are more likely to be governed by tradition than by innovation. They are concerned not only with competition, elasticity of demand, marginal and average costs, industry structure, substitutability of products, and product and market characteristics, but also with numerous governmental constraints.
6. Pricing policies must be reviewed and changed as basic conditions shift. This means that good pricing practices are research based.

What are the major pricing decisions to be made? They include determination of:

1. Prices for each product or service.
2. Discount structures.
3. Price relationships among products.
4. Price maintenance level.

These decisions should be based on information from market research, sales analysis, distribution cost accounting, standard costs, surveys, experiments, sales forecasts, simulations, and statistical techniques. The information required concerns competitive prices, cost data, demand estimates, product profitability, salesmen and customer reactions, and middlemen needs. But information about future demand schedules, future competitive reactions, and future costs is incomplete at best. Thus prices must be based on guesses and assumptions, yet they should be determined logically.

USEFUL CONSTRUCTS AND GUIDES

Although each pricing decision is unique, some constructs and concepts are useful in analyzing pricing situations. The models of market structure (oligopoly, monopoly, and monopolistic competition), concepts of costs (variable, fixed, marginal, and sunk), demand concepts (elasticity and demand schedules), and the company philosophy of followership or leadership, are very helpful. With full knowledge of them, a "right price" can be established. But decision makers are confronted with incomplete or outdated information. The reasoning process they employ considers answers to two kinds of questions.

First is "what if" or conditional reasoning. They assess possible courses of action, and the probable consequences of each. For example, if I change prices to A, what is the probability that competitors will meet the change, will not meet it, or will meet it partially, and what will be the consequences of each competitive reaction? Second, there is a consideration of the relationship of price changes to changes in the other aspects of the marketing programme, advertising, distribution channels, product packaging, and personal selling.

Prices may also be established through research. Various prices may be tested in limited areas and the "best" price selected. Research of customers' opinions and reactions to products is often sought as a basis for price. Sometimes products are tailored to meet predetermined price points, and product quality is changed so that prices can be maintained and product-line requirements and distributors' price points met.

Although price is not merely the result of costs, price-cost factors are accorded major consideration. Moreover, since price affects volume, volume affects costs, and costs affect prices, the pricing decision is a circular one. Also, a variety of cost concepts may be applied. Prices can be based on total costs, average, or variable costs. The last basis leads to a marginal approach to costs. The major contribution of economic reasoning to the consideration of costs is the idea of marginal cost.

Businessmen tend to rely more on an average cost approach to pricing than on a marginal approach. Average costs, which are rarely pertinent to an optimal decision, satisfy the desire to "cover our costs and make a profit." In reality, this reliance on average costs can lead to a decision that can actually reduce sales, increase costs, and reduce profits. However, some executives advocate that sunk costs (costs that cannot be revoked and that are not part of the current pricing decision) should be ignored. They are not affected by current decisions — nothing can be done about them. Yet it is also recognized that over the long run, they must be covered.

A consideration of the impact of sales volume on costs provides a useful train of thought. For instance, price theory suggests a U shape for average costs — they decline to a point with increasing volume, reach their minimum, and then increase as volume increases. This seems to make sense, since the concept introduces the notion of economies of scale and the impact of capacity on costs, indicating that volume beyond a certain point may increase costs.

In addition to cost factors, pricing decisions in basic industries are greatly influenced by governmental considerations. Some industries such as steel are treated like public utilities and, sensitive to governmental reaction, must justify price increases. Although no laws exist that require governmental approval of price increases in these industries, such increases are judged as to their being warranted.

A variety of pricing practices are of particular concern to certain industries. For example, bidding is significant in defence marketing, hedging in commodity marketing, markdown in fashion merchandise, dumping in international marketing, price deals in food marketing, and loss leaders and discounting in retailing.

In formulating marketing strategy, we have dealt with only the broader relationships of pricing to selected elements in the marketing mix. Price decisions in specific situations require both experience and practical knowledge. Theory alone will not suffice. In fact, where pricing is of critical concern, pricing specialists become necessary.

Pricing Influences

Since prices have great impact on both revenue and competitive reactions, pricing policies are usually determined at a high executive level. The pricing task involves not only a maze of variables but also conflicting situations. Conflicts exist among manufacturers and distributors, retailers and wholesalers, and consumers and retailers. For example, intermediate and ultimate customers weigh the prices they pay, competitors are influenced and react, suppliers watch margins carefully, financial institutions consider the impact on stock, and the government assesses competitive implications.

Among the present and future external factors that influence pricing policy are number and concentration of competitors, the degree of competition, profitability, ease of entry, product heterogeneity, size, legal aspects, channels of distribution, elasticity of demand, total industry demand, kind and size of buyers, and spatial forces. But basically these are handled through consideration of anticipated cost-revenue relationships.

For in the long run, prices are constrained at their upper bound by market reaction and competition (since firms cannot charge substantially more than immediate competitors) and at their lower bound by costs full or incremental. The latter are most significant in the immediate term, whereas total costs reflect a long-run situation. Prices may also be the result of competitive conditions such as total collusion or "cutthroat" competition. Either is unlikely for any protracted period of time, however — the former for legal reasons and the latter for economic considerations.

Although precise cost information cannot be obtained, it is even more difficult to gain information about consumer reactions to prices. The latter is obtained from surveys, experiments, and observation. For example, consider the cost-price relationships of an automobile with its thousands of parts. What are the actual materials and labour costs of each? What is the overhead burden and how should it be spread? How are joint costs to be allocated? How many autos can be sold at each price? What are the price interrelationships among items of a product line? These are difficult problems to face. But such costs, particularly increased costs, are price factors and the cost-price spiral is widely recognized. Also, as prices increase, sales may decline, which often results in increasing costs, since fixed costs are spread over fewer units.

In reality, cost accounting of the marginal variety, which is advocated as a basis for pricing, is not often used. Both the ambiguity of costs and the difficulty of deriving the data make this impractical. In practice, the relationship of actual costs to prices may be rather loose, and in fact the prices of finished goods and raw materials or components can move in different directions.

Prices should be based on both costs and market influences. In essence, maximum prices are governed by market factors and minimum prices by costs, and as they change, so should prices. The tendency exists, however, to maintain prices once they have been established. It should be noted that it is not the actual price or price change that is so significant, but rather the customer's perception and interpretation of these changes.

Problems in Setting Prices

What are the major problems in establishing prices? First, costs cannot be determined precisely. Second, management must deal with expectations-expected demand, expected costs, and the maximization of expected profits. This is particularly true of new products. Although cost estimates are more reliable than demand estimates, both are subject to wide error. They are based on the patterns of past data, which may deviate widely in the future, especially demand data, which incorporate a host of unpredictable market forces.

Pricing must also be viewed from the perspective of a company's total product line, since products have complementary and competitive demands, joint and common costs, and by-products. Sometimes the demand for product A influences the demand for product B. This relationship is termed the cross elasticity of demand, with a negative cross elasticity referring to products that are complementary, a positive cross elasticity to substitutable products, and a zero cross elasticity to unrelated products. For example, an increase in the demand for pizza will increase the consumption of certain cheeses, while a large increase in the use of a company's brand R detergent may decrease the use of its brand S detergent.

Since market situations confronting products within a line differ, sellers have varying degrees of discretion in setting prices for particular items in a line, and should consider products both as separate entities and as members of a product set. Cost-plus pricing or uniform markups ignore individual product acceptance, market demands, and competitive conditions.

In reacting to competitors' price changes, a company can sit tight, meet the change, or modify its own price or other elements of its marketing mix. Where customers consider not only price, but also availability, delivery, quality, service, and reliability, sensitivity to price diminishes. When products are not homogeneous, companies have wider latitude in pricing situations. But when products are homogeneous and a price is cut, competitors may have to meet the reduction. Companies have the choice of following a price rise or not. Executives should study the reasons for price changes, their temporary and permanent effects, the impact on profits and. market share, likely industry response, and the alternatives available, before making decisions.

Both purchasing situations and the decentralization of authority affect pricing policies. Prices may vary by the quantity purchased, and the purchaser's geographic area, trade position, and the functions he performs, as well as by the method and timing of purchases. In large, decentralized companies featuring profit-centre accounting, intra company pricing and transfer pricing, (prices charged by one company unit to another) can influence product prices and raise significant conflicting problems.

In some industries price changes in basic commodities occur frequently. Can computer programmes be developed to spell out the decision maker's thought processes in reacting to price changes? After studying a pricing executive in action over a period of time, one researcher developed a flow-chart programme that quite accurately predicted price reactions. The programme included such information as personal biases and organizational influences in price reactions as well as market shares, anticipation of competitors' reactions, and intentions of the district office. The computer programme provided a simulation of the price-reaction process.

Pricing policies are sometimes charged with emotion. Monopoly prices, price determination, and administered pricing are among the terms evoking emotional reaction. Also, the practice of price-cutting is often viewed with disdain or as an unethical practice by others in an industry, even to the point of indicating shoddy merchandise and service.

Typically, new products have a monopoly position for a period a degenerative monopoly position. Eventually competitors will develop competing and even improved products. The pricing executive must decide whether to charge relatively high or low initial prices, and the marketing consequences and related strategies are quite different in each situation.

Obviously, regardless of economic models, it is difficult to establish an optimum price because demand and costs change over time. The attention usually settles on current profit maximization rather than on the long-run maximization; the whole life cycle of a product and the total product line, rather than a single item, must be considered in pricing; and price must be considered from the perspective of the total marketing mix.

Where products are relatively homogeneous; several large firms constitute a significant part of the market; and buyers are well informed, then estimates of buyer reaction become a significant aspect of the pricing picture. So do competitive reactions that may be ferreted out by the use of marketing intelligence. Studies of what competitors have done in the past, coupled with detailed analyses of the current competitive situation, may furnish guides on what they are likely to do. This reasoning process, utilizing subjective probability estimates, can provide decision makers with good guides for contemplated price changes. A specific illustration is seen in the following example:

Since early 1955, the Everclear Plastics Company had been producing a resin called Kromel, basically designed for certain industrial markets. In addition to Everclear, three other firms were producing Kromel resin. Prices among all four suppliers (called here the Kromel industry) were identical; and product quality and service among producers were comparable. Everclear's current share of Kromel industry sales amounted to 40%.

Four industrial end uses comprised the principal marketing area for the Kromel industry. These market segments will be labeled A, B, C, and D. Three of the four segments (B, C, and D) were functionally dependent in segment A in the sense that Kromel's ultimate market position and rate of approach to this level in each of these three segments was predicated on the resin's making substantial inroads in segment A.

The Kromel industry's only competition in these four segments consisted of another resin called Verlon, which was produced by six other firms. Shares of the total Verlon-Kromel market (weighted sums over all four segments) currently stood at 70% Verlon industry, and 30% Kromel industry. Since its introduction in 1955, the superior functional characteristics per dollar cost of Kromel had enabled this newer product to displace fairly large poundages of Verlon in market segments B, C, and D.

On the other hand, the functional superiority per dollar cost of Kromel had not been sufficiently high to interest segment A consumers. While past price decreases in Kromel had been made, the cumulative effect of these reductions had still been insufficient to accomplish Kromel sales penetration in segment A. (Sales penetration is defined as a market share exceeding zero.)

In the early fall of 1960, it appeared to Everclear's management that future weakness in Kromel price might be in the offing. The anticipated capacity increases on the part of the firm's Kromel competitors suggested that in the next year or two potential industry supply of this resin might significantly exceed demand, if no substantial market participation for a Kromel industry were established in segment A. In addition, it appeared likely that potential Kromel competitors might enter the business, thus adding to the threat of oversupply in litter years.

Segment A, of course, constituted the key factor. If substantial inroads could be made in this segment, it appeared likely that Kromel industrial sales growth in the other segments not only could be speeded up, but that ultimate market share levels for this resin could be markedly increased from those anticipated in the absence of segment A penetration. To Everclear's sales management, a price reduction in Kromel still appeared to represent a feasible means to achieve this objective, and (even assuming similar price reductions on the part of Kromel competitors) perhaps it could still be profitable to Everclear.

However, a large degree of uncertainty surrounded both the overall attractiveness of this alternative, and under this alternative the amount of the price reduction which would enable Kromel to penetrate market segment A.

PROBLEM STRUCTURING AND DEVELOPMENT OF THE MODEL

Formulation of the problem required a certain amount of artistry and compromise toward achieving a reasonably adequate description of the problem. But it was also necessary to keep the structure simple enough so that the nature of each input would be comprehensible to the personnel responsible for supplying data for the study. Problem components had to be formulated, such as: (a) length and planning period; (b) number and nature of courses of action; (c) payroll functions; and (d) states of nature covering future growth of the Verlon-Kromel market, interindustry (Kromel vs. Verlon) and inter-Kromel industry effects of a Kromel price change, implications on Everclear's share of the total Kromel industry, and Everclear's production costs.Initial discussions with sales management indicated that a planning period of five years should be considered in the study. While the selection of five years was somewhat arbitrary, sales personnel believed that some repercussions of a current price reduction might well extend over seven years into the future.A search for possible courses of action indicated that four pricing alternatives covered the range of actions under consideration:

1. Maintenance of status quo on Kromel price, which was $1.00/1b.
2. A price reduction to $.93/1b. within the next three months.

3. A price reduction to $.85 1b. within the next three months.
4. A price reduction to $.80/1b. within the next three months.

Inasmuch as each price action would be expected to produce a different time pattern in the flow of revenues and costs, and since no added investment in production facilities was contemplated, it was agreed that cumulative, compounded net profits over the 5-year planning period would constitute a relevant payoff function. In the absence of any unanimity as to the "correct" opportunity cost of capital, it was decided to use two interest rates of 6 and 10% annually in order to test the sensitivity of outcomes to the cost of capital variable. Another consideration came to light during initial problem discussions.

Total market growth (for the Kromel or Verlon industry) over the next five years in each market segment constituted a "state of nature" which could impinge on the Everclear's profit position. Accordingly, it was agreed to consider three separate forecasts of total market growth, a "most probable, optimistic, and pessimistic" forecast. From these assumptions a base case was then formulated. This main case would first consider the pricing problem under the most probable forecast of total Verlon-Kromel year-by-year sales potential in each segment, using an opportunity cost of capital of 6% annually. The two other total market forecasts and the other cost of capital were then to be treated as sub-cases, in order to test the sensitivity of the base case outcomes to variations in these particular states of nature. However, inter- and intra-industry alternative states of nature literally abounded in the Kromel resin problem. Sales management at Everclear had to consider such factors as:

1. The possibility that Kromel resin could effect penetration of market segment A if no price decrease were made.
2. If a price decrease were made, the extent of Verlon retaliation to be anticipated.

3. Given a particular type of Verlon price retaliation, its possible impact on Kromel's penetration of segment A.
4. If segment A were penetrated, the possible market share which the Kromel industry could gain in segment A.
5. If segment A were penetrated, the possible side effects of this event on speeding up Kromel's participation in market segments B, C, and D.
6. If segment A were not penetrated, the impact which the price reduction could still have oil speeding up Kromel's participation in segments B, C, and D.
7. If segment A were not penetrated, the possibility that existing Kromel competitors would initiate price reductions a year hence.
8. The possible impact of a current Kromel price reduction on the decisions of existing or potential Kromel producers to increase capacity or enter the industry.

While courses of action, length of planning period, and the payoff measure (cumulative, compounded net profits) for the base case had been fairly quickly agreed upon, the large number of inter- and intra-Kromel industry states of nature deemed relevant to the problem would require rather lengthy discussion with Everclear's sales personnel.

Accordingly, introductory sessions were held with Everclear's sales management, in order to develop a set of states of nature large enough to represent an adequate description of the real problem, yet small enough to be comprehended by the participating sales personnel. Next, separate interview sessions were held with two groups of Everclear's sales personnel; subjective probabilities regarding the occurrence of alternative states of nature under each course of action were developed in these sessions. A final session was held with all contributing personnel in attendance; each projection and/or subjective probability was gone over in detail, and a final set of ground rules for the study was agreed upon. A description of these ground rules appears.

Nonprice Competition

Given acceptable levels of prices, non price factors can become most important. Yet, adequate economic theories of non price competition are lacking. In marketing, great attention is given to such non price aspects as product- differentiation, branding, imagery, packaging, service, buyer behaviour, and styling. The most important factor in modern competition is not price, but product research and development, according to a survey of more than 200 successful firms. Then come (in order) sales research and planning, management of sales personnel, advertising and sales promotion, product service, and finally, pricing. These non price factors, which are ignored in economic theory, must be considered in establishing pricing policies.

Economic Analysis and Pricing Decisions

Although each pricing decision represents a different situation, and hypothetical models do not correspond exactly with real-world situations, knowledge of market structures and economic pricing models is helpful in developing logical approaches. Consideration of product characteristics (branded or homogeneous), substitutability, number, size, and market share of competition, as well as the competitive situation (oligopoly, monopolistic competition, or monopoly) is useful.

To help determine the "best" price, economic analysis suggests that management apply the marginal principle, namely, set the price at the point where the marginal revenue of a sale is equated with the marginal cost. Thus, management estimates the quantity likely to be sold and the costs at various price points. An extension of this is the Bayesian approach, which recognizes the uncertainty in estimating both quantities sold at various prices and costs, and introduces probabilistic reasoning.

Marginal cost refers to the addition to total cost of a unit increase in output. Marginal revenue refers to the addition to total revenue of the sale of an additional unit. The marginal model assumes that costs and revenues can be estimated accurately, that price is the significant marketing variable, and that immediate profits are to be maximized on each product. Given such theoretical conditions, an optimal price may be established. But such assumptions do not correspond to reality.

Essentially, marketing executives are concerned with three sets of relationships in setting prices: the demand function, the cost function, and the revenue function. Their relationship can be presented as follows:

Let Q = quantity demanded = f(P), where P = price
C = total cost = f(Q)
R = total revenue = PQ
Z = R — C where Z = profit

The basic model may be stated simply, but the actual mathematical functions may not. Functions can be linear, curvilinear, or much more complex. However, given such functions, a price that maximizes profits can be determined through elementary calculus. For instance, let us assume that we have functions for R and C and hence can calculate Z = R — C, and that $Z = 100{,}000 + 100P - 30P^2$. We calculate the first derivative of Z with respect to P:

$$\frac{dz}{dp} = 100 - 60P$$

To maximize, we set dZ/dP = 0 and solve for P:
100 - 60P = 0
P = $1.67

Readers will recognize that marginals refer to nothing more than the first derivatives. Therefore, in the approach of marginal economics, the technique is to find the first derivative of both revenue and cost with respect to quantity, to equate them, and to solve the equation to determine the optimal output.

For instance, let us assume the following:
Q = 500 - 2P
C = 300 + 100Q

Then

$$R = PQ$$

$$P = 250 - \tfrac{1}{2}Q$$

$$R = 250Q - \tfrac{1}{2}Q^2$$

$$\frac{dR}{dQ} = 250 - Q$$

$$\frac{dC}{dQ} = 100$$

Now we set

$$\frac{dR}{dQ} = \frac{dC}{dQ}. \quad \text{or} \quad 250 - Q = 100$$

$$Q = 150 = \text{the optimum output}$$

By and large, economic models treat demands as the relationship between price and the quantity demanded, and skirt the problem of determining the optimal marketing mix. For pricing, as we have emphasized, is only one factor that must be considered in conjunction with such factors as quality, style, colour, advertising, and selling, and it may not even be the most significant one. Moreover, these theoretical approaches to pricing contain much mythology and are often impotent in practice. For example, in economic theory, pricing is set by supply and demand, and businessmen reflect continuously over marginal revenue and marginal cost curves, disregarding non-price competition.

But this does not mean that economic analysis is of no use. It provides us with conceptual market models useful for understanding pricing situations: the models of oligopoly — both differentiated and undifferentiated — and monopolistic competition. They underscore interdependent pricing situations, where company A's decisions can affect B. But they recognize that all often have considerable price discretion because of product, brand, and spatial differences, as monopolistic competition explains. In certain instances, as with an innovation, companies can even be in a monopoly position — be it a temporary or a deteriorating monopoly.

In oligopoly situations, where few large firms are significant, companies are always cognizant of competitors' potential retaliatory reaction to price cutting. Executives are concerned with adjusting prices without generating chaotic price competition. Sometimes price leaders emerge and set the price trend for an industry. Economic models ot oligopoly are useful for analyzing possible reactions.

Elasticities

In addition to understanding the nature of demand (market and company; actual and potential), the measurement of various aspects of demand is basic to good pricing strategy. In particular, the measurement of price elasticities and buyer price expectations are significant. Elasticities vary with the substitutability and characteristics of products.

The concepts of price or demand elasticity refers to the sensitivity of buyers to price changes. When small variations in price bring about relatively large variations in buyer reaction, the price elasticity is high. The situation is reversed for low elasticity. Since various customers react differently to price changes, knowledge of demand elasticities helps to set prices. But the major problem is that detailed data are not available. Yet, several techniques can be used to approximate elasticities, including market tests, statistical techniques of historical or cross-sectional analysis, and surveys. Management need not determine precise elasticities; rather it needs reliable estimates and guides as to the break-even levels and likely profitability of price changes.

There are two basic ways of measuring elasticities — cross-cut analysis and historical data. Cross-cut analysis pertains to a point in time. Examples are interviewing buyers, using panels, simulating price situations, and conducting pricing experiments. Often, companies conduct experiments by increasing or decreasing prices in test cities and analyze the impact on sales, market share, and profits. The problems of statistical interpretation are many, however. Historical data are analyzed by time series analyses that portray the association between prices and sales over time; this method is widely used in estimating elasticities. Regression and correlation analysis are its major tools, and the analysis ignores factors other than price that affect demand.

Pricing Strategies and Techniques

Pricing strategies depend on a point in time. Are markets rising or falling? What are competitors' reactions? What is happening to costs? Strategies can be adopted that tend to discourage or invite competitors, that relate to the payout in research and development, or that generate images of qualities or bargains. Companies can decide to have high, low, or competitive prices.

They can be price followers or leaders and can use several bases for price variations: geographical price discrimination (single and multiple basing points, f.o.b. factory, freight allowance and equalization, and zone pricing), discounts and allowances (quantity, seasonal, cash, trade, and promotional discounts), channel and service discounts, guarantees against price declines, and firm prices over time. Regardless, pricing strategies must be reviewed and realistically overhauled, for they tend to become "baked in" and to reflect traditional approaches, especially in retailing.

Prices are often set mechanistically by following formulas or rules. This procedure, although easy to follow, does not lead to "good pricing." Yet the most common technique of pricing is a mechanistic one – cost plus pricing, the addition of a margin to a cost base.

Prices are often built up from an estimate of average cost and are not necessarily related to market opportunity. Total unit costs are determined and a percentage markup is added that ignores cost-price sales relationships and market factors. In reality, however, pricing is not so rigidly determined, and market factors force modification of prices specified by formula. Often, variations of this average-cost method are used in which different markups are added to various products, based on what each product can bear in the marketplace.

New-product pricing presents different problems from those of pricing mature products. New products place the manufacturer more or less in a monopoly position, but one that will erode. They also create situations in which price reactions are largely guesswork. Two general pricing strategies are used here — skimming or penetration pricing.

The former refers to "skimming the cream" from a number of market segments in succession by means of a relatively high price, thus recouping investments quickly. It encourages new competitors to enter the market because of attractive margins. The philosophy is one of segmenting markets by time, getting a premium price from those segments that will pay it; and then gradually reducing prices. Thus, the core markets are cultivated first, and then attention is directed to the fringes.

Penetration pricing refers to the establishment of price levels low enough to penetrate markets deeply, and to discourage potential competitors from entry. Although prices are set relatively low, expanding markets arc recognized. Pursuit of this policy slows down the recouping of investments and expenses. Which policy to use depends on the total marketing plan and an assessment of cost-revenue market factors.

A skimming policy is effective where demand is relatively inelastic. It pays with new products, where smaller volumes can be produced economically and a high price does not attract heavy competition. Penetration pricing is suited to markets that are price sensitive. Its value is greatest in situations where production or distribution costs, or both, decrease with volume and low prices discourage competition.

In addition to penetration and skimming, pricing objectives may be stated in terms of realizing a satisfactory rate of return on investment, such as 18 percent. Or they may be expressed in terms of satisfactory profit objectives or sales volume goals at any rate of return.

Pricing strategies must be perceived in terms of the whole product line rather than in terms of each individual product.

For instance, some products are priced to engender prestige for the rest of the line rather than to gain their own sale, as is the case with fine china and silverware. Other prices are set to permit "trading up," to establish images, or to meet price lines and price points.

Government Influences on Pricing

Price differentials are competitive weapons. To implement them, markets must be segmented and the bases for differentials established. The former requires consideration of demand elasticities; the latter has legal dimensions.

Government involvement in pricing decisions takes a number of legal forms. Others include governmental pressure to prevent price rises, or even to roll them back in basic industries such as steel. Governmental involvement seems to relate price increases to the impact on inflation and increased productivity. Such actions as withholding governmental orders or dumping metals from stockpiles back up such informal price control. Government has the influence to block or roll back price increases.

Price differentials are subject to government scrutiny and regulation. They are established on the basis of quantity, distribution level, geo graphic area, and cash payment. Distribution discounts may be instituted on a net or list basis according to distribution levels. Quantity discounts may be cumulative or non cumulative, and may apply to part of a line or a whole line. Basing points, f.o.b. factory, and uniform delivered pricing are examples of geographic differentials. Discounts for cash are very common.

Legally, price discrimination can be defended on the bases of meeting competition in good faith, of cost savings in dealing with different customers, and of promoting and not injuring competition. It is the effect of price discrimination, and not the act itself, that determines legality. The legal aspects of price discrimination and government involvement in pricing, particularly the provisions of the Robinson-Patman Act, arc. Although these legal constraints are significant in establishing price differentials, the practical guidelines are confusing and the economic consequences are mixed, since price discrimination can actually benefit society.

Both the Federal Trade Commission and the Justice Department are interested in pricing practices, particularly in the administration of prices. In the administration of price differentials, marketing managers must be concerned with legal problems of collusion and price discrimination as well as the impact on sales, profits, and competition. Undoubtedly more government involvement in pricing practice is the wave of the future.

Price is the ingredient of the marketing mix that has enjoyed the most extensive economic analysis. In deciding marketing strategies, however, it cannot be separated from the other components. The importance of price as a marketing factor varies with kinds of products and market situations. Sometimes non price factors become more significant than price ingredients.

Pricing programmes of firms, even within the same industry, vary greatly. Pricing strategies should consider both cost and demand conditions, and the dynamics of markets, thereby accounting for both internal and external variables. Although the determination of an optimal price is usually impossible, a satisfactory one can be developed by analysis.

The major pricing decisions include determining prices for each product or service, discount structures, price relationships among product lines, and price maintenance levels. Problems encountered in establishing prices relate to the inability to determine costs precisely, the difficulties of dealing with expectations, and the variations in impact of policies on different products in a company's product line. Marketing intelligence is a critical component of effective price determination.

Index

D

E

F

G